Guillermo Calles

ALSO BY ROGELIO AGRASÁNCHEZ, JR.

*Mexican Movies in the United States:
A History of the Films, Theaters and
Audiences, 1920–1960* (McFarland, 2006)

Guillermo Calles

A Biography of the Actor and Mexican Cinema Pioneer

Rogelio Agrasánchez, Jr.

McFarland & Company, Inc., Publishers
Jefferson, North Carolina, and London

The images in this book have been
scanned and digitally restored
at the Agrasánchez Film Archive.

LIBRARY OF CONGRESS CATALOGUING-IN-PUBLICATION DATA

Agrasánchez, Rogelio.
Guillermo Calles : a biography of the actor and
Mexican cinema pioneer / by Rogelio Agrasánchez, Jr.
p.   cm.
Includes bibliographical references and index.
Includes filmography.

ISBN 978-0-7864-4945-3
softcover : 50# alkaline paper ∞

1. Calles, Guillermo. 2. Motion picture actors
and actresses — Mexico — Biography.   3. Motion picture
actors and actresses — United States — Biography.   4. Motion
picture producers and directors — Mexico — Biography.
5. Screenwriters — Mexico — Biography.   I. Title.
PN2318.C255A37   2010
791.430′28092 — dc22   [B]   2010011994

British Library cataloguing data are available

©2010 Rogelio Agrasánchez, Jr. All rights reserved

*No part of this book may be reproduced or transmitted in any form
or by any means, electronic or mechanical, including photocopying
or recording, or by any information storage and retrieval system,
without permission in writing from the publisher.*

Front cover: Guillermo Calles donning an Indian costume for a film
he made at Vitagraph Studios (Agrasánchez Film Archive)

Manufactured in the United States of America

*McFarland & Company, Inc., Publishers
Box 611, Jefferson, North Carolina 28640
www.mcfarlandpub.com*

To my wife, Xóchitl Fernández,
whose enthusiasm for
Willie Calles is contagious.

Acknowledgments

I would like to thank the following people who assisted me in preparing this book. Manuel G. Gonzales, author and professor of History at Diablo Valley College, eagerly read my manuscript and made appropriate stylistic corrections. I value his generosity, dedication and professionalism. Historians Esperanza Vázquez Bernal and Federico Dávalos offered their commentaries and also supplied me with copies of documents found in their archives. Ángel Miquel put at my disposal newspaper articles that he had collected for his own research on the silent cinema. Eduardo de la Vega gave me access to important reviews of *El indio yaqui* and showed interest in my research. Viviana García Besné and Alistair Tremps readily shared information on the production of *Pescadores de perlas*. Volunteers at the Harlingen Family History Center, Ofelia Olson, Santos Canales and Mina Zapata, guided me to population censuses and other helpful genealogical tools. Filmmaker Héctor Galán sent me a copy of his enlightening documentary *Los Mineros*.

Many of the photographs appearing in this book come from the family albums of Rudy Calles and Dick and Ernie Domínguez. I am indebted to Gloria Ortega, who donated Rudy's memorabilia collection to the Agrasánchez Archive. I must also acknowledge Dick and Ernie Domínguez. My conversations with Dick were very stimulating, particularly because we always spoke in Spanish. Similarly, I had the privilege of speaking with Beatrice Calles de Roiz, who holds a wealth of family anecdotes. *La Opinión*'s current archivist, Miss Georgina González, courteously granted me permission to reproduce material from this newspaper. Francisco Peredo Castro gave me a pleasant surprise; he shared with me *El vuelo de la muerte*, a film recently found and shown on cable TV. Roberto Fiesco put at my disposal his excellent collection of movie stills. Carlos Hinojosa, a friend and a passionate cinema collector, gave me copies of movies that are hard to find. Not to forget, I was fortunate to have access to the Mexican movie library formed by my father, Rogelio Agrasánchez, Sr. Finally, I am grateful to my wife, Xóchitl Fernández, who supported me at every stage of this project.

Table of Contents

Acknowledgments	vi
Preface	1
1. From Chihuahua to Arizona	7
2. Becoming an Actor in Hollywood	18
3. Riding the Wave of Nationalism	33
4. "The Vindication of Our Race on the Celluloid"	47
5. The Popular Appeal of Guillermo Calles's Films	65
6. On the Road: From Los Angeles to Mexico City	86
7. A Pioneer of Mexican Talkies	102
8. Last Films as a Director	120
9. Confrontation with Labor Unions and Hunger Strike	132
Epilogue: The Calles Family	146
Appendix 1: Filmography	155
Appendix 2: Exhibition of Films	162
Appendix 3: Pro-Patria	165
Appendix 4: Recovering a Film Script of El indio yaqui	179
Chapter Notes	181
Bibliography	187
Index	191

Preface

Leading his countrymen, Guillermo Calles became the first Mexican artist to appear in films made in California in the 1910s. Drawing on limited resources, he turned to producing and directing his own movies, which gained recognition among the Spanish-speaking public. In 1929, Calles completed one of the earliest Spanish-language movies with synchronized sound, beating other Mexican filmmakers in this endeavor. His work as an actor in more than a hundred pictures rounds out an amazing career that spanned half a century. In spite of all this, contemporary cinema historians are largely unaware of Calles's achievements. Part of the reason is the unavailability of his silent productions. Missing from film archives are *El indio yaqui*, *Raza de bronce*, *Sol de gloria*, and *Dios y ley*, which represent his undying efforts to restore the image of Indians and Mexicans. In an age dominated by Hollywood stereotypes, this vision is quite exceptional. Also responsible for the scant interest in the work of Calles is a general tendency among scholars to focus on the so-called "celebrities" of Mexican cinema. This perception, regrettably, leaves out other less stylish but equally important contributors to the medium.

The critical body of work in English on the history of Mexican cinema has failed to mention the significance of Guillermo Calles. In reviewing some of the most important titles available, I have confirmed this opinion. For example, Paulo A. Paranaguá's collection of essays for the general reader, *Mexican Cinema* (1996), cites the name of Calles in passing. Andrea Noble's *Mexican National Cinema* (2005) dedicates just one paragraph to silent movies. *Mexico's Cinema: A Century of Films and Filmmakers* (1999), a collection of essays edited by Joanne Hershfield and David Maciel, contains chapters on the silent and early sound eras but, unfortunately, the information on the work of Calles is inaccurate and sometimes misleading. Another English-language source is Carl Mora's *Mexican Cinema: Reflections of a Society, 1896–2004* (2005). I included this title in my bibliography because it offers a good summary of Mexico's silent and sound movies, but yet again, this impressive study does not acquaint readers with Calles's films.

Bringing back a pioneer actor and director whose work stirred the curiosity and esteem of his contemporaries is the goal of this book. I became aware of the importance of Guillermo Calles while researching the history of Mexican film exhibition in the United States. His name appeared frequently in the Spanish-language newspapers of Los Angeles, *La Opinión* and *El Heraldo de México*. It surprised me that so much printer's ink went into discussing his career as an actor in Hollywood as well as the films he directed in the 1920s and 1930s. The profusion of ads and commentaries dedicated to his productions seemed to imply that he once held a central place in the cultural life of Mexicanos. Films with emblematic titles—

Preface

Raza de bronce, *Sol de gloria*, *Dios y ley*— were once the staple of Spanish-language theaters in Los Angeles and the rest of the U.S. Southwest. One could immediately sense the strong nationalist appeal by glancing at these ads and learning of crowded openings at the Teatro México and Teatro Hidalgo, two popular entertainment spots in L.A. Captivated by the newspapers' suggestive publicity and rousing accounts, I determined to find out more about this filmmaker of Tarahumara origin.

The life and career of Guillermo Calles is an example of the rising consciousness of a Mexican in the United States. The distinct Indian traits that he inherited from his mother at once set him apart. Dark skin, abundant black hair, and a small and lean but muscular stature were some of his physical attributes. After crossing the border into Arizona at the beginning of the 1900s, the young Calles experienced the hardships of immigrants working in remote mining towns. Growing up surrounded by Mexicans, Mexican Americans, Anglos, and Indians gave Calles a unique opportunity for self-discovery. At age twenty-one, he settled in Los Angeles and got a job performing in movies. His appearance in the popular serials starring William Duncan established him as a character player. In 1926, Calles surprised everyone when he decided to produce a film, *El indio yaqui*. The simplicity of this story struck a chord with viewers, the majority of whom were working-class Mexican immigrants who applauded the movie's Indian hero and his resolve to fight injustice. More than anyone in cinema, the name of Guillermo Calles became associated with patriotic feelings and the defense of Mexicans.

Calles lived in the U.S. Southwest for thirty years, but he always reserved a deep admiration for his country of origin. As he became an adult, he developed into a man of innate modesty and habitual silence, two qualities that complemented his fiercely independent character. People meeting him for the first time were struck by his straightforward manner. María Luisa Garza ("Loreley"), a writer for the magazine *Ilustrado*, hailed the "naturalness of a border Mexican" found in Calles; she also commended "his valor and his enormous affection toward the mother country that he adamantly wants to exalt." The artist made a strong impression on Loreley, who observed keenly: "Possessed by a youthful ardor and a creative impulse that ripples like a three-colored flag, Guillermo Calles ... proudly makes known the brave heritage of [his] race."[1]

By the late 1920s, Calles had become a noted Mexican filmmaker known for his passion in exalting the homeland. Such fervor only proves that he was a man of his time. In a post-revolutionary age, Mexicans sought to redefine their racial and cultural heritage. Taking the banner of *Indigenismo*, nationalist advocates turned away from European influences, giving preeminence to the legacy of Native American civilizations. One of the most influential scholars in this movement was Manuel Gamio, an anthropologist and novelist in charge of excavating the Quetzalcóatl pyramid of Teotihuacán. Gamio's achievements included the first comprehensive study of Mexican immigration to the United States, an investigation that soon involved American society's racial prejudices. He not only filmed the excavations at Teotihuacán but also documented the daily life and traditional rites of indigenous people. Gamio commissioned the artist Franz Bom to film the Mayan ruins at Palenque, Chichén-Itzá and Uxmal. These documentaries were shown in the United States and Europe in an effort to promote the knowledge of pre–Columbian cultures.

Preface

Images of daunting ruins, ancient civilizations and exotic scenery, together with the portrayal of present-day Indians, came to California by way of newspapers, books and magazines. But the movies had the most far-reaching influence. Theaters exhibited travelogues depicting archaeological sites as well as modern life and society. In San Francisco, painter Pancho Cornejo established his "Estudio Azteca" in an effort to cultivate an appreciation of Mexican art. In addition to displaying original works, the studio screened motion pictures like *Confesión trágica* and the documentary *México antiguo y moderno*. Professor José Amable's orchestra provided accompaniment to the moving images and delighted the guests with typical songs.[2]

Just as the old cultures of Mexico were being revisited, a new trend in movie theater architecture developed in the Southwest. The luxurious Aztec Theater of San Antonio, Texas, opened in the spring of 1926 and became known as "the only one of its kind in the U.S." The publicity emphasized that the building "follows the lines of Ancient Temples" and boasted that "the seating capacity including the balcony will be nearly 3,000." In addition to the offering of a Hollywood movie, the opening program included a live performance of "The Court of Montezuma," presenting a troupe of "16 Aztec girls and beautiful stage settings."[3] In Los Angeles, the Mexican community of Belvedere had their own Teatro Azteca, a "small but clean theater" that began to operate in November 1926. Its façade imitated Aztec architecture and the walls of its 350-seat auditorium featured evocative Indian paintings. This trend reached a high point in Los Angeles the following year with the inauguration of the splendid Mayan Theater. The building's exterior and interior decorative details were the work of Pancho Cornejo, who ingeniously mixed Zapotec, Aztec and Mayan motifs to striking effect.

South of the border, the cultural nationalism that exploded in the 1920s permeated all aspects of Mexican life. Murals on public buildings depicted the glorious emancipation of the country from Colonial rule and extolled the virtues of the Reform and the Revolution. Diego Rivera, José Clemente Orozco, and David Alfaro Siqueiros were the most conspicuous muralists of the era. In the realm of music, Carlos Chávez and Silvestre Revueltas created compositions inspired by Mexico's aboriginal heritage. Gregorio López y Fuentes illustrated the harsh reality of Indians and their distrust of whites in his perceptive *El indio*, a novel that later was adapted to the screen. Many people, including filmmakers, contributed to Mexico's artistic renaissance under the influence of *Indigenismo*.

Guillermo Calles was not an intellectual nor did he have encyclopedic knowledge of his culture, but surely various contemporary ideas and attitudes influenced his outlook. Habitually, when presenting his movies to an audience, Calles donned elaborate Indian costumes related to his ancestral past. His enthusiasm for the motherland was contagious. He once told a reporter: "I am going to make movies that will amaze the world. When? I don't know but I have to make them; Mexico has something unspeakable in the ruins of Mitla and in the Cruz de Palenque; nothing can compare to its majesty and I cannot let foreigners go in there and exploit these archaeological treasures."[4] He partially fulfilled his ideal in 1932, making a travelogue of the towns and scenery along the Mexican Pacific Coast. With his own resources, Calles traveled by car from Los Angeles to Mexico City filming *Pro-Patria*.

One of the climactic moments of the documentary showed director Calles meeting with Mexican president Pascual Ortiz Rubio.

Ironically, while the enthusiasm for *Indigenismo* reached a high point in Mexico in the 1930s and 1940s, the actual condition of the Indians changed very little. The Mexican upper and middle classes continued to look upon members of these ethnic groups as second-class citizens. This explains in part why Calles met with opposition to his comeback as a film director in the 1950s. At that time, the entrenched interests of those at the top of Mexican bureaucratic institutions (the elite of film directors) segregated him. Feeling discriminated against and having no alternative, Calles went on a hunger strike, which led to his official acceptance into the Director's Union. Yet this was a merely symbolic concession that did not guarantee him a job. Gone were the days when the press and the public enthusiastically supported him.

Many times, I found myself in virgin territory regarding the facts of Guillermo Calles's life and work. Unearthing forgotten films or discovering new sources of information only fueled my interest. Tracking his appearances in Hollywood silent pictures became quite an adventure, especially since the Vitagraph serials in which he acted no longer exist. In general, after the initial exploitation of a movie, production companies disposed of the prints, extracting any silver content from their emulsion. Destroying the films helped protect the studios against widespread piracy practices. In the 1920s, the Vitagraph Company turned over its remaining catalog to Warner Bros., which unfortunately made little effort to preserve it. The inventories of smaller companies ended up in the hands of individual collectors after the distribution exchanges closed. In recent years, enthusiasm for the silent era has grown and movie fans are finding many "lost" treasures thanks to the Internet. That is how I discovered several oldies with samples of Calles's early performances, among them *Joan the Woman* (1917), *The Fighting Strain* (1923), *Behind Two Guns* (1924), and *Daniel Boone Thru the Wilderness* (1926). I was also thrilled to find on the Internet a few original publicity stills showing the Mexican actor in such obscure titles as *The Silent Vow* (1922) and *The Dirty Little Half-Breed* (1924).

There were more than a few fortunate discoveries during the course of this research. I came across unexpected sources that revealed information on the plots of many lost Hollywood silent films. For example, pulp magazines such as *Boys' Cinema Weekly* (London) and *La Novela Film* (Barcelona) contained engaging accounts of Vitagraph's popular serials in which Calles took part. More interesting is that these magazines included photographs depicting sensational action scenes. The New York State Archives happened to be another revelation, containing original dialogue transcripts of *Regeneración* (1930), *El vuelo de la muerte* (1934), and *La virgen de la sierra* (1938). These transcripts were used for censorship purposes at the time of the films' release; they have come to be a primary source for the reconstruction of movies' plots. It is through the surviving film censorship records, pulp magazines, original stills and periodicals that a study of these forgotten movies is now feasible.

Tracing the life and cinematic career of Guillermo Calles has been a lengthy and complex endeavor. A few facts guided me at the start of this research; one of them was a sketchy

Preface

autobiography of the artist that appeared in the newspaper *La Opinión* in 1933. In order to be more precise about Calles's origins, I refurbished my aptitude for amateur genealogy and went on a hunt for his vital records. Gradually, I learned of the existence of other members of the Calles family, most of whom had immigrated to the United States at the beginning of the 20th century. After consulting several U.S. population censuses and immigration records, I was able to outline the whereabouts of the family in Arizona and California. In an effort to recreate the spirit of the era and learn about geographical locations, I turned to a number of published sources. Among them was Linda Gordon's *The Great Arizona Orphan Abduction*, which I found particularly useful and inspiring.

One of the most rewarding moments in my investigation was coming across several members of the Calles family who live in California. Even though Guillermo Calles did not have children, I was able to find Mrs. Beatrice Calles de Roiz, an eighty-eight-year-old niece of the filmmaker. Telephone conversations with her made me aware of the family's close ties and their high regard for "Uncle Willie," as his folks affectionately called him. Beatrice and her daughter Marianne still remember when they visited the actor in Mexico City in the 1950s. Showing a characteristic affability, he invited them to taste the local food at a friend's restaurant, where they had a lively conversation.

The Internet turned out to be a very useful tool in locating several relatives of the filmmaker. I was thrilled when I got in touch with Gloria Ortega, another member of the Calles family. By chance, Ms. Ortega noticed one of my search ads and immediately responded from California. She generously offered to send a package with old photographs and newspapers that belonged to her stepfather, the late Rodolfo "Rudy" Calles, a nephew of the Tarahumaran artist. This treasure chest of memorabilia included fascinating portraits of the 1920s showing Calles dressed in Indian costume. The inscriptions on some of them gave me a hint of Guillermo's affection for his family. Rudy's collection also included a movie still that corroborated the existence of *El charro*. Ms. Ortega not only gave me these photographs but also helped me to make contact with Richard "Dick" Domínguez.

Dick is one of the sons of José Domínguez, who was a bit player in Hollywood films and Guillermo's closest nephew. Dick and his brother Ernest gave me access to photo albums and family documents that rounded out my research. They had kept a page from an unidentified Mexico City newspaper with wonderful stories about Guillermo Calles. Interviewed by Raúl Talán in the mid–1950s, Calles remembered many details of his career in Hollywood and Mexico. Reading this interview gave me insight into the artist's relaxed attitude and excellent sense of humor.

With so many facts in hand, I put together a last chapter dedicated to the Calles and Domínguez families. The epilogue's purpose is to look at Guillermo Calles's intimate circle of relatives, putting emphasis on their common interests as well as their differences. I hope to offer in the final pages a view of a close-knit group of Mexican immigrants and their assimilation into mainstream Anglo American culture. As Mexican Americans, the members of the Calles and Domínguez families are proud of their roots and have become an asset to their community.

It is my hope that the "lost" films directed by Guillermo Calles will be recovered. At the time of this investigation I received news that Calles's only documentary, *Pro-Patria*, had been found in a private film collection. By chance, the reels had been kept in a vault since the movie's last public exhibition in 1933. The recovery of *Pro-Patria* is important because it will allow for a better appraisal of Calles's nationalistic outlook. Moreover, a review of this travelogue filmed on the road from Los Angeles to Mexico City will enrich the study of Mexico's economic and cultural history. In advance of its eventual overhaul, this book offers a detailed account of *Pro-Patria*. In the appendix, the reader will find the letters written by Guillermo Calles while on the road, which Gabriel Navarro edited and published in Los Angeles's *La Opinión*.

1

From Chihuahua to Arizona

From the time he started acting in the movies, Guillermo Calles took pride in being "a pure Indian," a fact that stood out in his physical makeup and personality. Although he rarely elaborated on his Indian background, he once mentioned that his mother was a Tarahumara from Chihuahua.[1] But for some reason, almost everybody considered him of Yaqui extraction. In fact, these ethnic groups that populate the northern part of Mexico were hard to differentiate even by a seasoned journalist like Esteban V. Escalante, who once confessed to being unsure of the precise origin of his filmmaker friend.[2] The confusion probably stemmed from Calles's first independent production, *El indio yaqui*. In this 1926 silent picture, he played a besieged Yaqui Indian who crosses the Mexican border into Arizona and ends up sacrificing his life for a romantic ideal. Naturally, the movie's popularity forged the myth that Calles had Yaqui ancestors. This perception only encouraged his deep nationalism, making him feel flattered whenever someone called him *El Indio*.[3]

Guillermo Calles was born in Chihuahua City on June 25, 1891, the youngest son of Juan Nepomuceno Calles Parra and Anatolia Guerrero Reyes.[4] His father's birthplace was also the city capital of Chihuahua, while his mother was a native of Ciudad Guerrero, Chihuahua. In all probability, Juan Nepomuceno was not an Indian but had mixed blood. His parents were Mariano Calles and Apolonia Parra. On the other hand, Anatolia descended from Tarahumara Indians, her parents being Francisco Guerrero and Jesús Reyes. Born on July 3, 1853, Anatolia married Nepomuceno when she was 16 years old. She bore ten children, of which seven reached adult age: Juan (born 1874); Rosendo (born 1876); María de Jesús (born 1878); Pascual (born 1880); José de la Luz (born 1882); María (born 1884); and Guillermo (born 1891). All of the children were natives of Ciudad Guerrero, Chihuahua, except Guillermo, whose birth took place in the state's capital.

The head of the family, Juan Nepomuceno Calles, was born in 1828 and married three times; first to Francisca González, with whom he had three sons and one daughter: Mariano (born 1854), Encarnación, Ramón, and Antonia. After Francisca's death, Nepomuceno married Dolores Tena, with whom he had one daughter. After becoming a widower again, Nepomuceno married Anatolia Guerrero on November 22, 1869. When Nepomuceno died on July 22, 1893, seven children of this union survived him. His death certificate indicates that he lived on Ojinaga Street in Chihuahua and worked as a musician ("filarmónico"). The record states that the cause of his death was an acute stomach infection ("entero colitis"). We also know from this source that Nepomuceno's mother, Apolonia Parra, was "about ninety years of age and a widow." The elder son of the deceased, also called Juan Nepomuceno, testified at the Civil Registry Office regarding the passing of his father. However, he did not sign the death certificate because he was illiterate. Many years later, Guillermo Calles gave a more dramatic explanation for the loss of the head of the family, claiming that partisans of the Porfirio Díaz government had killed Nepomuceno. Today, senior members of the family only remember that Guillermo's older brother, Rosendo, was fatally shot in 1911 during the Mexican Revolution.

Living conditions for the Calles family changed quickly following the death of Nepomuceno. To their dire economic straits was added a host of other problems. Even before Nepomuceno's death, the hostility of the government toward certain Indian groups in Ciudad Guerrero and the surrounding area threatened the security of the family. Throughout the last decade of the nineteenth century, the Mexican armed forces engaged in a continuous war against rebel tribes, targeting mainly those spread out in the states of Chihuahua and Sonora. Yaquis were particularly persecuted as they represented an obstacle to the thrust of the regime's "Order and Progress" ideology. Besides killing them, the army pushed Indians off of their lands and forced the younger males into military service. In 1891, inhabitants of the town of Tomochic rose up against the government, which failed to subdue them on two different occasions. The locals held their town for several months, being wiped out in the end. In April 1893, another uprising took place near Tomochic, in Ciudad Guerrero. Not until the following year was this upheaval put down, together with one more revolt that had developed in the village of Palomas. In all probability, the unstable circumstances of the day aggravated the dilemma of the Calles family.

Economic factors no doubt had a bearing on the decision of the Calles family to abandon Chihuahua. At the beginning of the twentieth century, the demand for workers in the U.S. Southwest attracted people from all over. As *The Bisbee Daily Review* made manifest, the number of Mexicans moving into Arizona was staggering. The editor of this newspaper witnessed the "thousands of Mexicans [who] were brought into Arizona during 1901 to work on the railroads and in the mines." According to an estimate, "between 60,000 and 100,000 Mexicans crossed the border annually" seeking jobs in the area.[5] Even before this year, some members of the Calles family had been moving back and forth as migrant workers. People could enter the United States with almost no restrictions in those days.

Guillermo left his birthplace in Chihuahua and came with his family to Arizona in 1901. They first lived in the mining towns of Clifton-Morenci and Metcalf, which were located high in the mountains of Eastern Arizona, near the New Mexico border. Guillermo's half-brother, the fifty-year-old Mariano Calles, was already living in the region when the others arrived. Judging from an outdoor family photograph taken in Morenci around 1902, the members of this kin were numerous. Appearing in this picture are the young Guillermo, his mother, three brothers, two sisters, and his nephew José Domínguez, in addition to other relatives. This crowd of seventeen people showed up in their best attire,

Opposite: **The family of Guillermo Calles migrated from Chihuahua to Arizona in 1901 (Agrasánchez Film Archive).**

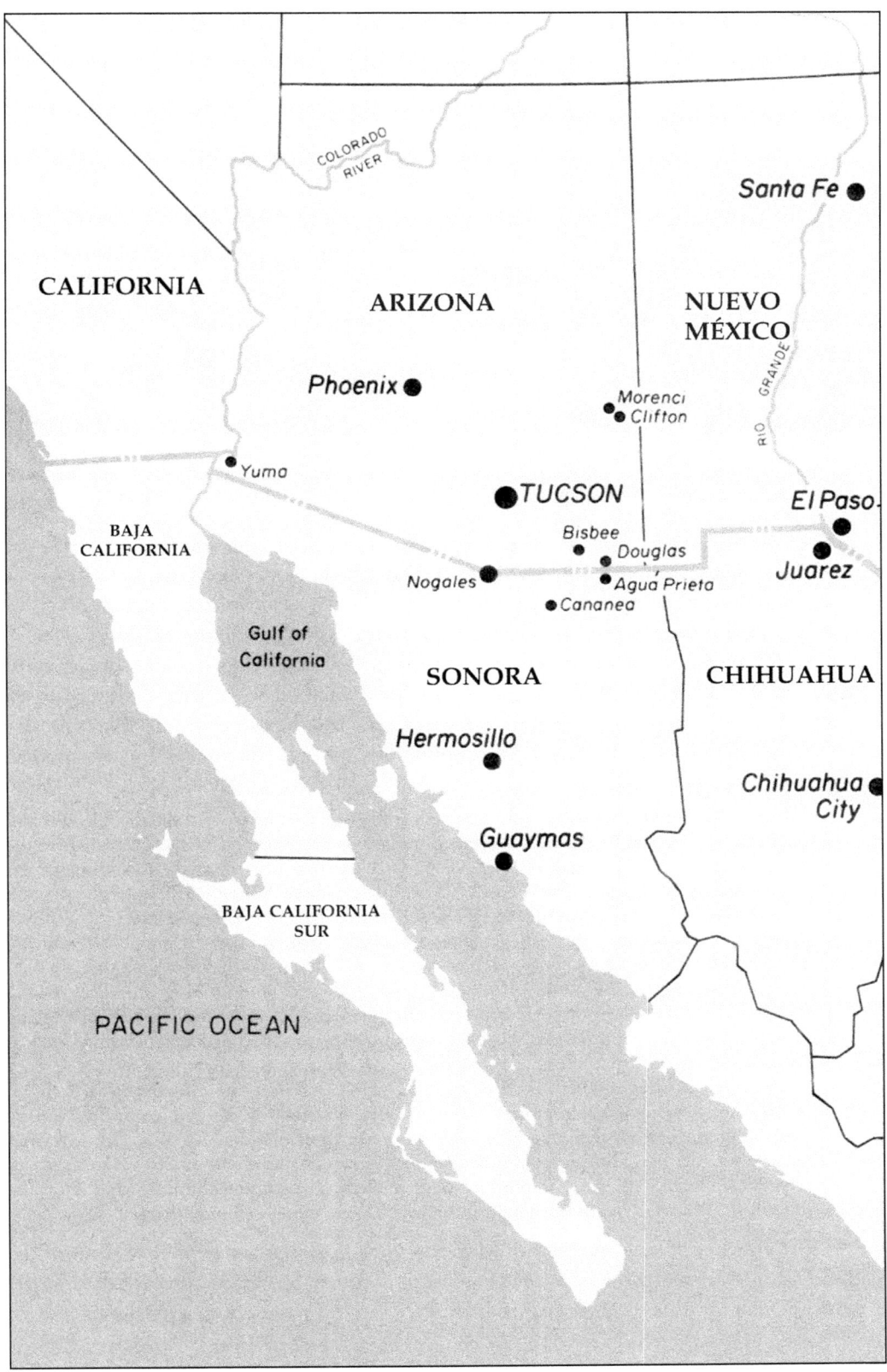

The mining town of Clifton-Morenci, located high in the mountains of Eastern Arizona, attracted many Mexican workers. Photograph ca. 1909 (Library of Congress, LC-USZ62–128065).

some of them wearing formal clothes. The occasion was most likely the baptism of Belén, a daughter of Pascual Calles who was born in May of that year. One thing that stands out in the picture is the rocky landscape. Morenci was known as one of the toughest places in Arizona; the mining camp stood 1,500 feet up from the nearby village of Clifton.

Surrounded on all sides by cliffs, Clifton seemed more developed than Morenci, with its commercial buildings lined along its single main street. The settlement seemed to be squeezed in the narrow valleys created by Chase Creek and the San Francisco River. Author Linda Gordon offers an enlightening description of Clifton in her book *The Great Arizona Orphan Abduction*:

> [There was] the oldest district, where miners and smelter workers lived on the hillsides and drank in the saloons; North Clifton, a strip upriver on the west side of the Frisco, where the better-off workers and managers lived; Chase Creek, a narrow strip along a tributary of the Frisco, mainly Mexican, where a rapidly expanding, raucous business district vied for space with the houses that climbed up the hillsides; South Clifton ... the flattest and broadest residential area, the home of the "best" Anglos; and a new neighborhood for the poorer workers, Shannon Hill. Chase Creek consisted of a creek, usually dry, paralleled by a dirt road — which meant, depending on the season, either dust, mud, or flood — with building entrances usually four to six feet above street level to protect them from floods.... For some short distances there were plank or concrete sidewalks, but they were discontinuous and pedestrians had to walk in the street along with the horses, burros, and occasional buggies — there was no way to keep clean while venturing into Chase Creek and you had to be always watching for holes, garbage, and the horse and donkey droppings.... If you could momentarily look up, you would see the electric lines overhead, the steep hills, and the smoke from the smelters. When an inversion held the air still, the sulfur fumes drizzled painfully into one's nose and throat; the sulfur dioxide gas combined with water to produce sulfurous acid and it stung and burned.... Everyone in Clifton then tried to stay inside until the winds came up and cleaned the air.[6]

The presence of large numbers of Mexican immigrants was apparent at the time of the 1903 Clifton-Morenci workers strike. Following an order by the Arizona legislature, the mine operators in this territory reduced the ten-hour daily routine to eight hours, but in the process they also cut down the pay to only nine hours. This measure slashed the workers' salaries by one-tenth. Consequently, about 3,500 men walked out on strike. Of this number, eighty to ninety percent were Mexican. Led by a man called Abram Salcido, president of a Mexican mutual aid society, the immigrant workers "prevented the loading of any ore in the cars which haul it to the Arizona [Copper Company] reduction works at Clifton." A newspaper reported that one or two prominent leaders were speaking to the Mexican workers. These leaders "are very industrious [and] have used harsh language concerning the gringos.... This morning at 5 o'clock, more than two hundred Mexicans were already gathered at the mouth of the Humboldt tunnel, listening to the harangues by the leaders and music by the band," *The Bisbee Daily Review* added.[7]

What started as a small strike gradually turned into an organized uprising of Mexican workers. Two thousand strikers hung around, making it appear as a massive threat to the established order. The local sheriff asked that the U.S. Army protect the town, resulting in one of the biggest deployments since the Indian wars. In spite of all the agitation, there was no violence on the part of the strikers. Still, Anglos seemed to be frightened and the mining companies became increasingly worried in the face of the movement and its demands. The workers requested a wage of $2.50 for eight hours of work, plus other services sorely needed, like locker and shower rooms. They also asked that the companies provide medical and death insurance. Above all, however, was the issue of discrimination: Mexicans felt that Anglos should not exploit them simply because of race, religion, or nationality differences.

When the Arizona Rangers arrived in the streets of Morenci to protect the interests of the mining company, the demonstrators marched in defiance of the mounted police. The Mexican consul, Arturo Elías, had come in hopes of negotiating a deal with the strikers. Coinciding with the strike, on June 9, a huge downpour washed away many houses in the Clifton area. Thunderstorms and a wild flood destroyed $100,000 in property, killing nearly

In 1903, Mexicans in Clifton-Morenci went on strike. Arizona Rangers moved in to protect the interests of mining companies (Agrasánchez Film Archive).

fifty persons. Most of the damage affected the area settled by Mexican laborers and their families. Gordon describes what happened next:

> The flood did not completely quell the strike, which continued on, fragmented, for a few days; but the anguish, demoralization, and distraction created by the flood allowed the soldiers to take control. As mineworkers searched for bodies, attempted to salvage belongings, and mourned, the army was establishing martial law. Commanding Colonel McClintock prohibited all assemblies, used his bayonets to round up "unruly subjects," and began searching Mexican homes.... The 1903 strike altered racial meanings.... The walls between whites and Mexicans rose higher. Mexicans gained a new reputation among whites: dangerous, radical, and capable of violent surprises, qualities in some tension with earlier stereotypes of them as placid, lethargic, unambitious.... Whites strengthened their reputation among Mexicans as ruthless, money-grubbing, only out for themselves.[8]

Once the rebellion was put down, their leaders were tried and then jailed in the Territorial prison at Yuma. Nevertheless, the Mexican workers' movement in Morenci did not end entirely. Three years later, in 1906, the recently arrived political activist Praxedis G. Guerrero founded the group "Obreros Libres." This union had links with the Partido Liberal Mexicano, an anarchist movement organized in St. Louis, Missouri, by the exiled journalist Ricardo Flores Magón to combat the government of Porfirio Díaz. As pointed out by Gordon: "Mexicans were at this time easily as militant, solidaristic, and committed to unionism as any other group in the United States, and in Arizona they were the leaders." Gordon also acknowledged that Mexican workers led four of the five strikes in Arizona between 1896 and 1915.[9]

The Clifton-Morenci workers' movement and its aftermath occurred when Guillermo Calles was only twelve years old. Seeing hundreds of people united and standing up to the army was surely an episode that made a deep impression. The incident set in motion a growing awareness of the dignity of Mexicans. Although the powerful mining companies rejected their demands, the strikers' bold stance created a feeling of solidarity among the local community of Mexican immigrants. While a young and intuitive Calles absorbed the lessons of this confrontation, he might have also wondered in amazement at the undeserved catastrophe caused by the flood. He later turned this sort of experience into anecdotal material for his films, usually praising the moral fiber of the Indian when confronting adverse circumstances.

The following year, another episode highlighted even more dramatically the racial conflicts in the Clifton-Morenci district. A group of nuns from New York arrived in the area bringing forty orphaned and abandoned Irish children who were to be adopted immediately by Catholic Mexican families. When local Anglos noticed what was going on, they became infuriated. Resentful of the Mexicans and worried that white children would end up in the Mexican homes, they recruited the sheriff, grabbed nineteen orphans from the nuns, and distributed them to people of their own race. Next, they ordered all religious women to get out of town as soon as possible. One account stated that "the Morenci crowd turned its fury on the Sisters," and that "men with guns invaded the nuns' hotel rooms, trailed by [local] women calling them slave traders and worse." The next morning, the embattled Sisters of Charity left the town on the 7 A.M. train. Nineteen children stayed behind.[10]

1. From Chihuahua to Arizona

Morenci, shown here ca. 1909, had a reputation of being one of the toughest places in Arizona. Life for the Calles family was anything but easy (Library of Congress, LC-USZ62–138580).

Although Mexicans and Mexican Americans were a majority in Clifton-Morenci, their Anglo bosses regarded them as second-class workers. Like in any other town, white people "got the best jobs and the best pay." According to author Margaret Regan, the racial category of whites "took in Americans of English descent, Scotsmen and, a notch down, Irish, Italians and Spaniards: anyone, in short, who wasn't Mexican or Chinese."[11] The daily life of the Calles family was anything but easy, and they tried to make the best of it. At least their economic situation had improved, assuring their most basic needs. Moreover, they could even use part of the money earned to move to another area. An advantage of living near the international boundary was that anyone could come and go at any time. This proximity guaranteed a constant flow of people, goods, and information from Mexico.

Mexicans in Clifton-Morenci, Metcalf, and other Arizona mining regions kept abreast of events in the mother country. One notable occurrence was the railroad tragedy of Nacozari, Sonora. In November 1907, a train loaded with dynamite exploded near the mining town of Nacozari, causing enormous damage to property and killing several men. Among the dead was Jesús García Corona, a locomotive engineer whose final deed was to run the burning train away from the main part of town. His bold action made him a hero and the local people erected a monument to his memory. Because García Corona worked for a foreign railroad company, his survivors received the Royal Cross of Honor. This incident was etched indelibly on the mind of Guillermo Calles. Many years later, when he became a filmmaker, such tragedy inspired him to direct *El héroe de Nacozari*.

Another famous occurrence in Clifton-Morenci at this time involved young Teresita Urrea, a half–Indian woman who "miraculously" healed the sick and had the ability to foresee coming events. Since the day she started curing people in Cabora, Mexico, Teresita was known as "La Santa de Cabora." In 1896, she left the country because the Mexican government accused her of standing behind the rebellious acts of the Yaqui and Mayo Indians. While living in Clifton, she continued to restore people's health. In some instances, Teresita was even asked to baptize ailing infants and adults before they died. Her followers included the poor as well as the rich, and she made no distinction among racial groups. One of her biographers, William Curry Holden, stated, "The Indians of Clifton are devoted to her, as are the Indians wherever she has been." Holden explained Teresita's personality in detail: "The glance of her beautiful brown eyes is half sad and wholly intelligent, without any of the cunning or the sleepiness or the furtive watchfulness of the ordinary Mexican or Indian, and she has in her modest, fragile person and her quiet manner such a dignity, such earnestness and sincerity and gentleness and serenity that one cannot deny her respect, even when faith is unconvinced."[12] Teresita Urrea died at age 33. During the January 13, 1906, memorial service, Holden reported, almost everyone in Clifton filed by to pay their last respects. Musicians played the Mexican farewell song "La Golondrina." The funeral procession was "the longest in the history of Clifton; hundreds of mourners stood with bowed, bared heads as Teresita's body was buried."[13]

In 1909 Guillermo and other members of his family moved from Clifton-Morenci and Metcalf to the Arizona mining town of Silverbell. Located to the west of Tucson, in Pima County, Silverbell had a population of approximately one thousand. There were numerous ore mines controlled by the Imperial Copper and the Oxide Copper Companies. The small community consisted of several ethnic groups: Anglos, Mexicans, Indians, and a few Asians. Each of these groups lived in separate quarters. Silverbell had a school, hospital, post office, grocery and dry goods stores, and a Chinese bakery. In addition, there were two firehouses and a movie house. In spite of its mining wealth, the town did not have enough drinking water; the only water available was saturated with minerals and its use was restricted to laundry and other chores. Thus, the precious liquid had to be brought in first by mule and wagon, and eventually by rail. In addition, potable water was piped twice a day through two taps and sold to local residents.[14]

The 1910 population census of Silverbell confirms that Anatolia Guerrero de Calles rented a house in town. She was a widow who presided as the head of the family. According to this record, Anatolia was 54 years old and had given birth to ten children, of whom seven still lived. She shared the same dwelling with her sons Rosendo, José, and Guillermo. Also belonging to the household were José's wife Josefina and their two small children. Rosendo and José declared that they made a living working in the copper mines, while Guillermo said he did not have a profession. This census indicated that Anatolia and José were illiterate, though Rosendo, Josefina, and Guillermo could read and write in Spanish only.

1. From Chihuahua to Arizona

Mexicans in Arizona mining towns, like Metcalf shown here ca. 1904, kept up with what was happening in Mexico thanks to a constant flow of people, goods and information from Mexico (Agrasánchez Film Archive).

Next to Anatolia's house lived her daughter María de Jesús Calles with husband Juan Calvillo, who also worked at the copper mines. María de Jesús had a 16-year-old son from a previous marriage, José "Pepe" Domínguez, who was living with her and helped do chores for the family. Every day, Pepe would bring buckets of water to the miners. In their spare time, Pepe and Guillermo played at being stage performers. Guillermo had a passion for organizing stage plays, posing as the director and instructing other boys how to play their roles.

Silverbell experienced a gradual depopulation after 1910, as the fortunes of the Imperial Company declined. Not only was clean water scarce but also profits were down, putting many commercial establishments out of business. Following a fire in the mine a year later, the Imperial declared bankruptcy and the post office closed, forcing most of the inhabitants to leave town. Already in 1909, unemployment was rampant in Silverbell. Rosendo had been out of work for a full month in that year, José remained inactive 20 weeks and Guillermo spent 32 weeks looking for a job. In all probability, they had saved enough money

Guillermo had a large family. In this 1902 photograph taken in Morenci, he is sitting next to his mother, Anatolia Guerrero, who holds a newborn granddaughter in her arms (Rudy Calles Collection).

for such a contingency. Very soon, though, the family abandoned Silverbell and moved somewhere else.

By 1911, Guillermo and several members of his family were living in Ciudad Juárez, Chihuahua. Pascual Calles made his residence here in the company of his wife Justina Hernández and five children. He got a job as a mechanic and labored at the mines. Before marrying, he had been an "amateur of drama and comedy" touring various Mexican states as an actor. He was greatly impressed by the magnificent theater companies that visited the border towns of Ciudad Juárez and El Paso. On one occasion, accompanied by his brother Guillermo, he attended a performance of the eminent Mexican actress Virginia Fábregas. One of the most charismatic stage personalities in the country, Fábregas was mentioned in the same breath with Eleonora Duse and Sarah Bernhardt.

Following in his brother's footsteps, the enthusiastic Guillermo started to take the performing arts seriously. But being unable to make a living as a stage actor, he accepted odd jobs wherever he could find them. The Revolution had just begun in Mexico, with the northern states leading the rebellion against the Porfirio Díaz regime. Thousands of refugees

1. From Chihuahua to Arizona

made their way to El Paso, San Antonio, Laredo, and other Texas cities. For many of them, finding work was essential. One of the places that offered plenty of jobs for Mexicans was California. Around 1912, Guillermo Calles set off for Los Angeles, where the newly founded movie studios caught his attention. A way to get into them was by sweeping floors. Yet, being an actor was his dream and he did not rest until he found a place among the performers. Thus, he began a career that would last a lifetime.

2

Becoming an Actor in Hollywood

Being an Indian guided Guillermo Calles's life in unexpected ways. His admission in 1912 to the nascent California movie industry is an example of this. A newcomer in Los Angeles, strolling along Pasadena Avenue, he peeked in at the studios of the Lubin Manufacturing Company. By sheer coincidence, the producers were preparing to shoot a feature called *A Mexican Tragedy* and still needed to complete the roster of secondary players and extras when the young Calles showed up. "I came in there as if fallen from heaven," he recounted, "because they were looking for Indian-like types and I happen to be a pure-blooded Indian." After taking a standard acting test, he signed a contract to join the cast. Thereafter, his noticeable ethnic traits and performing abilities put him in the stock of numerous motion picture companies, usually executing dangerous stunts but also portraying Indians and other types.[1]

During the heyday of the one-reel production, filmmaking in California was a casual affair. Lubin, Essanay, Selig, Kalem, and Vitagraph were among the first movie companies that built studios in and around Los Angeles. As J. Stuart Blackton of the Vitagraph studios put it: "Everything was so absolutely new that the first producers had to evolve their own standards." Most of the time, making a picture called for improvisation in an effort to remedy any unexpected turn of events. One of the era's actors, James Morrison, recalled, "If they needed extras in a scene, they would use their stock company, anyone who was there. A director could walk through and see you, probably walking out to the gate, going home, and he would nab you for a scene."[2] When production budgets were too tight, there was always the option of hiring the "chronically unemployed." Many of those seeking work could be found "at the studio door each morning, begging to be given a crack at greasepaint and glory."[3]

The New York–based Lubin Company started business in 1902. Ten years later, it established its Los Angeles branch at 4550 Pasadena Avenue. The studios were located "upon a beautiful, well-kept plot of ground, 150 by 450 feet." Around an 80-foot-square stage were grouped commodious property room, wardrobe room, scene dock, paint bridge, etc. Besides the stables and corrals for the horses, there was a building of the colonial type, containing offices, dressing rooms, and green rooms. The tracks of the Salt Lake train route were in the rear of the studio. A private station could be used "for the arrival and departure of characters by train in the photoplays."[4] The Lubin Company had already released more than one thousand short features by 1913. Many of the two-reelers centered on events taking place in Mexico in the recent past. Besides the trendy border adventures, the company released documentaries in the style of *Mexican War Pictures* (1913). According to the publicity, this movie showed the "fighting between the Federals and the Constitutionalists during the Mexican War, and the guarding of the United States border by American troops." Other Lubin features put out this year were *The Mexican Spy, An Adventure on the Mexican Border, A Girl Spy in Mexico,* and *Love and War in Mexico*.

A Mexican Tragedy belonged in the category of films that had the Mexican Revolution as a backdrop. Its cast included Ray Gallagher, Henry King, William Ryno, Velma Whitman, and Calles. Henry King played the revolutionary General Laredo, while Calles interpreted a young rebel soldier called Miguel. Although the movie has long disappeared, its plot can be recovered from the era's newspaper publicity. Thanks to a review published by a Utah paper, we are now better acquainted with the story:

> Manuel Terrizar, innkeeper in a small Mexican town, professes to be in sympathy with the revolution: his son, Miguel, joins the insurrectos. Teresa, Terrizar's daughter, and Gen. Laredo, leader of the revolutionists, are sweethearts. The federal government sends an agent, Sancho, to Terrizar, offering a large reward if he will accomplish the secret assassination of Laredo. Terrizar's greed for gold triumphs and he agrees to try the scheme. Terrizar invites Gen. Laredo to the inn that night for Teresa's betrothal feast. Laredo, accompanied only by Miguel as a guard, arrives for the feast. Miguel is plied with wine to get him out of the way. Then the boy is carried upstairs and dumped into the room at the right of the landing. Miguel, aroused, later staggers into the hallway as if to go downstairs, then changes his mind and, entering the room at the left of the landing, falls across the bed in a stupor. The feast is over. Terrizar persuades Laredo to spend the rest of the night at the inn and conducts him to and sees him enter the room at the left of the landing. In the left room Laredo finds Miguel, tries in vain to arouse him, then decides to find another bed. He goes into the hallway, finds the opposite door open and retires in the empty room at the right of the landing. The plot to kill Laredo falls on Terrizar. He draws his knife, ascends the stairs, and, blowing out the hall lamp, enters the room at the left of the landing. A moment later he returns to the drinking room, announcing that he has killed Laredo. In the morning, Laredo, ignorant of events, descends the stairs to the room where the conspirators are sleeping at the tables. The conspirators are terrified, believing that Laredo's ghost is walking. When he speaks to them they realize there has been a slip. Wildly, Terrizar rushes upstairs and into the left room, where he finds that he has killed his son.[5]

All of a sudden, the Mexican Revolution had become top news and Hollywood took advantage by churning out a string of melodramas connected with the civil war. Theater managers knew that the images of combat and the tales of the Revolution could be a magnet for audiences. While the printed media carried appalling news of the revolt, the cinema made this reality quite fascinating. *A Mexican Tragedy* was chosen for the inauguration of the Lyric Theater in Lima, Ohio, in September 1913. Confident of the appeal of the spectacle, a newspaper ad simply mentioned, "Dealing with the Present Mexican Revolution."[6]

Being part of the cast of the Lubin production established Calles as a forerunner among his countrymen. In this early period he was being paid three dollars a day. "I was the first Mexican working in the movies in the United States; following me came the late Beatrice Domínguez, José de la Cruz and others that I convinced gradually, because in those days nobody wanted to be a film actor."[7] The young dancer Beatrice Domínguez started in the

Being a film actor was Guillermo Calles' dream. Since 1912, his noticeable ethnic traits and performing abilities put him in the stock of motion picture companies. Photograph ca. 1917 (Rudy Calles Collection).

movies in 1914; she appeared briefly in *The Four Horsemen of the Apocalypse*, performing a tango with Rudolph Valentino. Domínguez completed one last film before her premature death in 1921. José "Joe" de la Cruz participated in many pictures since the late teens, posing as henchmen, Indians and half-breeds, but never received on-screen credit. Other Mexicans working in Hollywood at this time were Valerio Olivo, Carlos Esteves and Manuel R. Ojeda. Olivo later became an assistant director in Mexico, while Ojeda directed a series of films starting in the 1920s.

Due to his initial contacts at the Lubin Company, Calles was able to enter the cluster of actors and extras working for Cecil B. DeMille. In 1913, he played one of the Indians appearing briefly in *The Squaw Man*, DeMille's directorial debut. He also performed in *The Virginian* (1914), which DeMille partially shot at Monte Palomar, near San Diego, California. Regarded as the first feature-length Western, *The Squaw Man* quickly became a success. A theater in Fort Wayne, Indiana, called it "one of the best visualizations of a stage play ever shown on a screen. It was a source of delight and surprise from end to end.... The audience leans forward involuntarily to catch every move of the personages on the screen.... *The Squaw Man* represents the triumph of the pictures over stage productions."[8]

Other DeMille movies in which Calles took part were *The Girl of the Golden West* (1914), *The Arab* (1915), and *Joan the Woman* (1917). This last epic, starring Geraldine Farrar as Joan of Arc, utilized hundreds of extras as soldiers. Calles played one of these fearless fighters; in a climactic moment, he is seen among a yelling crowd celebrating a battle victory. A pivotal film for DeMille, *Joan the Woman* illustrates the efforts by Hollywood producers in promoting the cause of the Allies during World War I.

Willie Calles — as people began to call him — participated in an action picture that almost cost him his life. He recalled that it was called *La Marie*. The story required that he perform a couple of hazardous stunts. A leap from a seaplane flying at high altitude already was a feat for the actor. When the director asked him to jump off from a moving ship, the situation got more frightening. Suddenly, the strong current formed by the propeller violently suctioned him; it was only by "a true miracle" that he lived to tell the tale.

After filming *The Captain of the Grey Horse Troop* (1917) with Antonio Moreno, Calles was hired by the Vitagraph Company to work as a stuntman and occasional actor. The contract specified that he let his hair grow in order to portray Indians. During the next five years he was frequently seen in the studios, not only perform-

Portrait of Guillermo Calles done by Nelson H. Evans around 1917. Anyone aspiring to fame hired the services of Evans's exclusive photography studio (Rudy Calles Collection).

ing Indian roles but taking other parts as well. Willie's image was publicized through scene stills and studio photographs. He posed for numerous glamour shots. It was customary for the stars of the era, or for anyone aspiring to fame, to visit Nelson H. Evans's exclusive photography studio on Hollywood Boulevard. In private life, however, the Tarahumaran artist was very modest. Frequently while everybody in the studios ate sandwiches for lunch, the unadorned Calles brought "tacos y tortas" made at home.

Very soon, the Vitagraph Company turned into one of the most prosperous film enterprises. Its owners were proud of the quality of their movies, which they regarded as "clean, wholesome action pictures with a real entertainment punch."[9] Located in Santa Monica, the studios were bursting with activity in the late teens as many talents came to join the crowd. Among them was actor William Duncan. This popular action hero not only starred in but also directed seven serials for Vitagraph: *The Fighting Trail, Vengeance and the Woman, A Fight for Millions, Man of Might, Smashing Barriers, The Silent Avenger,* and *Fighting Fate.* All of them included appearances by Calles, who sometimes got billing after the stars' names.

Duncan's first hit at the company was *The Fighting Trail* (1917), a fifteen-chapter serial whose cast included Carol Holloway, George Holt, Joe Ryan, Fred Burns, Walter Rodgers, H. Ducrow and, without getting a credit, Willie Calles. A typical action picture, its plot revolved around a secret mine containing strategic war material. The arrival of some German spies gave ample pretext for lots of fighting and suspense. Ducrow played a Yaqui Indian in the first three chapters; he was a "faithful Indian servitor of Western mine owner." Like most serials produced by the studio, *The Fighting Trail* was made rapidly, the company churning out a chapter every week. Work at the Vitagraph required everyone to move fast. Production increased to two five-reel features per week. In his dual role as actor-director, William Duncan used little time for resting during the shooting. People said he worked "like a Trojan." The five-foot-ten-inch Irish-Scotsman was an athletic person of jovial character who enjoyed working outdoors. He made friends with Calles easily. According to journalist Gabriel Navarro, "His Indian type, his athletic body and riding abilities, in spite of his short stature, won him the sympathy of William Duncan." An occurrence at the moment of filming *The Fighting Trail* demonstrates the connection between the two actors. Calles recounted:

> In one of its episodes shot at Santa Cruz Island, I had to plunge into the sea from an altitude of 134 feet while riding a vigorous horse. But the animal did not want to make the leap in all eight times that I had tried; until Duncan, who was the director, took notice of my predicament and ordered me to dismount from the horse and take a dive, which I did. Because of the air pressure during the fall, I hit the water unconscious. Fortunately, three days after the accident I was completely recovered. On another occasion, it so happened that the person that was doubling for Duncan, had to jump to the water from the same altitude that I had done before, but he got scared and did not want to do it. For that reason, I had to substitute him. Even though my clothes were very sturdy, they were torn to pieces when hitting the sea and I ended up in such a bad shape that it was necessary to take me to the hospital.... Having hit it off with Duncan, I was offered a contract for five years.[10]

Audiences seeing *The Fighting Trail* never imagined that some of the feats performed by "the strongman of the screen," William Duncan, were actually executed by Willie Calles.

2. Becoming an Actor in Hollywood

The Vitagraph Company turned into one of the most prosperous film studios. Calles got a five-year contract to perform in William Duncan's action serials. Photograph ca. 1920 (Agrasánchez Film Archive).

Every time a stunt looked too risky for the stars, Willie was available to take their place. When *The Fighting Trail* opened in Ogden City, Utah, the management of the Cozy Theater placed a catchy newspaper ad: "Death Faced Daily by Vitagraph Stars. [This serial] contains more thrills to the foot than anything I have ever seen.... How Mr. Duncan and Miss Holloway survived the many hazardous stunts they undertook in making the picture, I do not know, because it seems to me that they must have taken their lives in their own hands every time they went out to take a scene."[11] Shot at the Sierra Nevada Mountains and the Mojave Desert, the film was released only after seven months of continuous work. Its publicity detailed, "A smashing story of mystery, conspiracy and love, centering about a hidden mine of fabulous value, and its scenes are snatched with fine disregard for life and limb, from the wildest reaches in the Sierra Nevada.... Wild beasts caught in their native lairs match wild settings, and snakes and creeping things imperil the lives of hero and heroine."[12]

Following his first serial, Calles appeared in *A Fight for Millions*, where his name got a fourth credit after Duncan, Edith Johnson and Joe Ryan. According to a newspaper ad, the scenes were shot "in the snow-blanketed mountains of Big Bear Valley, north of San Bernardino, California, where the company was lost for ten days during the taking of them; a heavy snowstorm is seen in the first part, cutting down telephone and telegraph wires."[13] The Cozy Theater of Ogden City announced the movie in September 1918, proclaiming: "Its big, two-fisted hero, and its gentle, though fearless heroine, will win your heart from

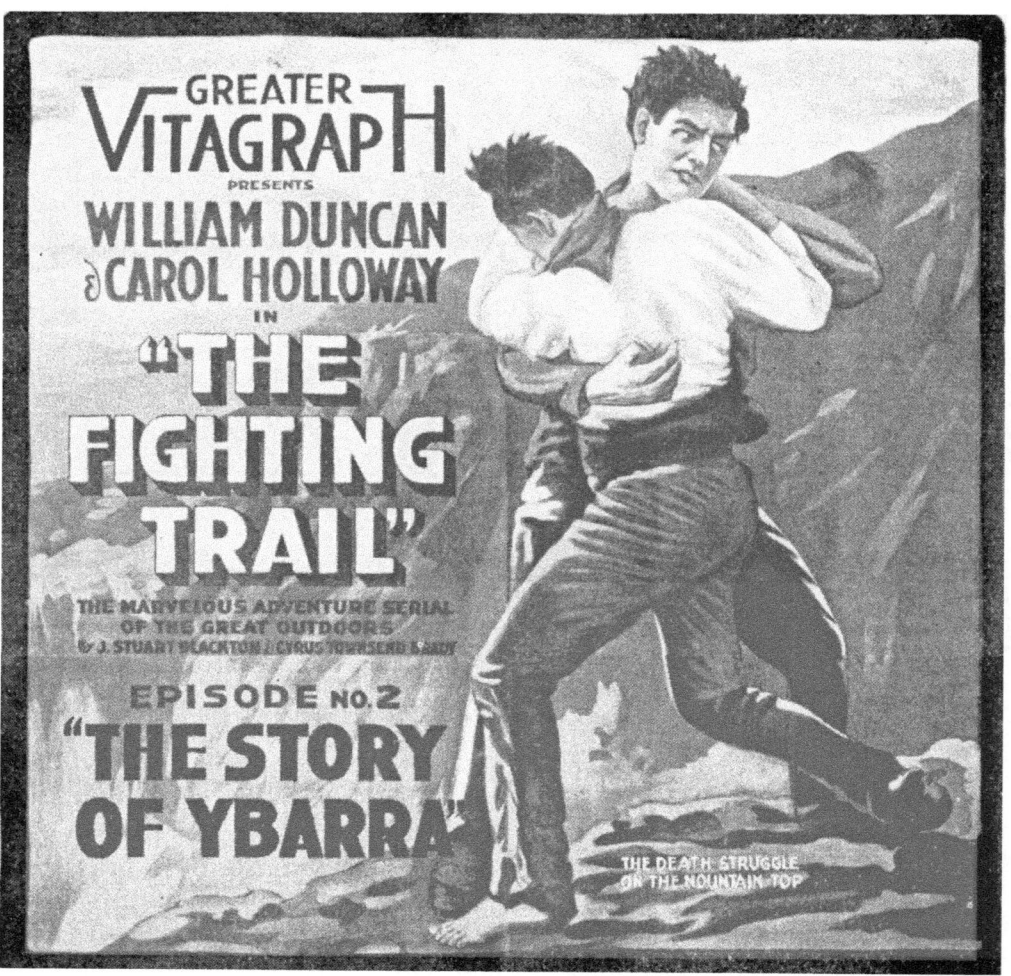

Vitagraph employees were proud of the quality of their movies, "clean, wholesome, action pictures with a real entertainment punch." *The Fighting Trail* was released in 1917 (Agrasánchez Film Archive).

the very first episode. And its thrills will make you forget your troubles. Bigger and better than *The Fighting Trail*, with the same cast." New admission prices for the Cozy Theater went into effect because of the war. With the added war tax, children now paid six cents and adults fifteen cents.[14]

People began to take notice of Calles after his work in *A Fight for Millions*. The actor's amazing characterization of the Indian "Iron Star" won him universal praise. When it played in the Pantages Theater of Winnipeg, Canada, a newspaper reviewer made the following comment:

> Willie Calles, the Indian who plays Iron Star in the serial *A Fight for Millions*, is the champion jumper of Mexico, but never did he do a more perilous jump than he did at the Vitagraph studios to make a thrill for the third episode of their serial. In this chapter, "The Secret Stock-

2. Becoming an Actor in Hollywood

ade," he makes a terrible jump from the roof of a shack to the top of a stockade, more than twelve feet away. No sooner does he reach this than, as outlaws shoot at him, his business is to topple over and fall to the hard ground, 15 feet below.[15]

Calles' other Vitagraph serials included 1919's *Smashing Barriers* and *The Man of Might*. In the highly successful *Smashing Barriers*, "the hero goes out west, gets a job in a logging camp, falls in love with the owner's daughter, and is able to keep a gang from taking possession of the camp." It was released in Mexico as *La eterna lucha*; its publicity highlighted the name of Joe Ryan in the role of a rogue dubbed locally as "Carimarcado." Theaters like the Cine Opera and Cine Royal of Guadalajara typically screened five chapters (ten reels) a day complemented by two Hollywood short comedies. Competing against *Smashing Barriers*, other local venues such as the Allende and Jalisco Theaters exhibited the twelve-chapter serial *Tin Minh: Judex Explorador*, a French import.[16]

Publicity for *The Man of Might* stressed that it had the same cast as two previous Vitagraph serials, the successful *The Fighting Trail* and *A Fight for Millions*. A newspaper ad for the Strand Theater in Salamanca, New York, detailed the cast and also gave the names of

Edith Johnson (as her name is correctly spelled) and William Duncan in a love scene from *Fighting Fate* (1921). None of the serials starring Duncan has survived (Agrasánchez Film Archive).

the characters: William Duncan (Dick Van Brunt), Edith Johnson (Polly Ransome), Joe Ryan ("Scarface" Bender), Walter Rogers (George Teel), Del Harris (Joseph Stebbins), Frank Tokanaga (Chu Cheng Ling), Otto Lederer (Juan Díaz), and Willie Calles (the Indian Tomás). When the New Gem Theater of Olean, New York, played *The Man of Might*, the public got a taste of its unrelenting action through a typical newspaper announcement: "The magic of this super serial will whisk you from mountain to shipboard, from prairie desert to dens of Oriental wizardry. Fights on the heaving decks of storm-tossed ocean vessels, in the deserted cabin — battles of brain and brawn on land, on water, in the air, and threaded through it all a big, human love story. It's a page for you from adventureland."[17]

The Man of Might was partially shot in the Arizona desert as well as in the arid region of Sonora and Baja California. Because the Vitagraph Company put great emphasis on the quality of production, it went to such lengths as to shoot scenes on locations that were far away from the studios. Appraising their merit, author Buck Rainey has pointed out that these films were "served up in a more realistic, palatable fashion in 1919 than was the case with serials in the 1940s and 1950s."[18]

One of Vitagraph's concessionaries in Spain was Cinematográfica Miró, which published the forty-page mini-book *La Novela Film*. To coincide with the release of the movie, one of its issues provided a summary of *The Man of Might*. This pulp magazine not only contained this engaging narrative but also included eleven scene photographs from *The Man of Might*. Perhaps this is the only guide to reconstructing some of the views of the original film. Dubbed in Spanish as *De cara a la muerte*, the sleek narration adopted new names for the movie's main characters. For instance, Joe Ryan's original "Scarface" Bender becomes Leandro Mullen "Puñales" in the Spanish version. William Duncan's mining engineer Dick Van Brunt is now Enrique Carter, and Edith Johnson's Polly Ransome is renamed Sara Benson. Calles' role is only acknowledged as "an Indian that joined the expedition in Los Angeles." An accurate synopsis of *The Man of Might* can be drawn from this foreign publication.

According to *La Novela Film*, the story of *The Man of Might* centers on a buried treasure in a distant island. Several men possess a piece of the map that leads to its location. The hero, Dick Van Brunt, helps the beautiful Polly Ransome in her hunt for this coveted cache. But the criminal "Scarface" Bender arrives at Polly's ranch and kills her father in an attempt to steal the old man's portion of the map. Dick consoles her and over time they get married. After recruiting several people who hold the remaining pieces of the chart, Dick and Polly head an expedition into the sea. "Scarface" and his henchmen try to get rid of the hero and friends at every opportunity. Arriving first at the remote island, the villain is successful in allying himself with an Indian tribe of Aztecs. The tribe captures Dick and his followers; they will be burned in a sacrificial ceremony to the sun god. Only two in the group are pardoned and kept as slaves: "an Indian [Willie Calles] that joined the expedition in Los Angeles and a man of the yellow race belonging to a very old civi-

Opposite: Popular magazines like this one, printed in London, England, attest to the notoriety of Vitagraph's productions overseas (Agrasánchez Film Archive).

The Boys' Herald

Do You Read the Splendid, Long Complete School Stories in the "GEM" Every Week?

The "GEM" is on Sale Every Wednesday, Price 1½d. Get This Week's Number.

AN AEROPLANE CHASE.

Here are some interesting photographs showing William Duncan, the hero of "Fighting Fate," rounding up a number of outlaws by the aid of his aeroplane. In this film there are many thrilling chases, but, of course, the aeroplane wins in the end. In the circle above a bomb from the aeroplane has been dropped upon the enemies' stronghold with disastrous consequences for them.

The bandits have no chance against the aeroplane.

MORE INTERESTING PHOTOGRAPHS FOR YOUR COLLECTION IN NEXT WEEK'S "BOYS' HERALD."

A stampede from the motor-boat when the aeroplane appears above.

The outlaws in full flight across the prairie, pursued by the aeroplane.

lization beyond the sea." The Indian escapes and goes to the rescue of his condemned friends. After overcoming serious obstacles, Dick and companions finally reach the location of the treasure. However, just before loading their boat with the gold, "Scarface" and the Aztecs show up. There is a fierce gun battle and the hero succeeds in taking "Scarface" into custody. Dick and Polly have triumphed over their adversaries and will now be happy together.[19]

The serial reached an all-time high at the box office. After the initial release of their movies, theaters often brought them back to complement newer programs. The Vitagraph re-edited its popular serial *Smashing Barriers* into a feature-length film, thus assuring a continuous exhibition for many years. The company's cliffhangers were very popular in Europe, where the studies had established an effective distribution system for the exploitation of films. One of the regular actors at the studio, James Morrison, recalled the importance of business in faraway Europe: "We used to get paid in cash, and we never knew when we were going to get a raise. We usually got a raise when the Paris office sent word. Yes ... they had great power over there, because we sold so many pictures in Europe. When the raise came, we couldn't count the money."[20]

Calles also appeared in *The Silent Avenger* (1920) and *Fighting Fate* (1921), both directed by and starring the indefatigable Duncan. Billed as "the new million dollar Vitagraph serial," *The Silent Avenger* recounted the tale of a man, sentenced to prison on a false charge, who escapes and assumes a new identity. Once again, Edith Johnson co-starred in this adventure story "of a hard-boiled tenderfoot and the girl who made him fight for her honor against a regiment of thugs."[21]

Magazines such as the widely read *The Boys' Herald* and *Boys' Cinema Weekly* of London, England, attest to the notoriety of Vitagraph's productions overseas. *The Boys' Herald* often included in its pages stunning photographs from Duncan's films, followed by a brief description of each scene. In one, readers could delight in the spectacular action of *Fighting Fate*'s hero, "rounding up a number of outlaws by the aid of his aeroplane." An amazing bombing of a building and the "stampede from the motor-boat when the aeroplane appears above" surely fueled the imagination of youngsters.

Five more images from the same serial appeared in the next installment of *The Boys' Herald*. This time Duncan is seen "escaping from a Mexican prison, after having first trussed up his guard." In a similar fashion, *Boys' Cinema Weekly* advertised Vitagraph's chapterplay *The Man of Might*. As a bonus, this publication offered a detailed account of the movie's plot, complete with dialogue. Readers could follow its story through several chapters until the grand finale was revealed. Thanks to this information, we know that Calles played an Indian called Tomás, whose actions are described at length in the magazine. For today's enthusiasts, both of these publications provide great insight on movies that have been lost.[22]

The amount of work at the Vitagraph studios sometimes required parallel shooting. It was common to see two or three crews finishing different scenes of the same movie. Duncan "seemed to relish the rise in production as he set records for the number of scenes shot in one day; and worked through twenty-four hours straight with three separate companies."[23] The dynamic director often relied on a few collaborators to speed up the shooting

2. Becoming an Actor in Hollywood

Calles did not always play Indians. In this chapter of *The Silent Avenger* (1920) he accompanies William Duncan (right), who "commandeers an automobile for the chase" (Agrasánchez Film Archive).

schedule. One of these was Calles, who had now become his assistant. Calles later assisted director David Smith, a brother of Vitagraph's owner Albert E. Smith.

Calles substituted David Smith when he fell sick during the shooting of a film — probably *Black Beauty*, a Vitagraph special production starring the beautiful Jean Paige and the juvenile James Morrison. It was released in January 1921. Because of his good performance, the producers warmly congratulated Calles and allowed him to continue work as an assistant. Although it is hard to tell which films he helped direct at this time, there is proof of his involvement in several shorts that he later designated in Spanish: *Hermanos, La propiedad única, La bella vaquera,* and *Oasis*. Moreover, he claimed to be the director of *El príncipe rojo* and *El chasis*. With these credentials, he felt entirely capable of making a full feature as a director and star. One day, he asked a Vitagraph production manager to consider his proposition. After consulting with the studio owners, the manager told Calles that his offer would be acknowledged if he acquired U.S. citizenship. Since this condition also implied giving up his Mexican nationality, Calles withdrew his proposal and, disappointed, departed from the company. When *Fighting Fate* was playing in Mexico City in July of 1921, a newspaper article mentioned this incident with a twist on Calles's desire to become a film star:

Willie Calles and William Duncan take a break from the action in this scene from an unidentified film (Agrasánchez Film Archive).

> A Mexican named Guillermo Calles started working in the studios of Los Angeles. He enrolled at Vitagraph three years ago, taking secondary roles in the serials featuring William Duncan. The [physical] type of our fellow compatriot came in handy to do Indian characters; he played admirably a redskin.... Appearing alongside the audacious Duncan, he took increasingly prominent roles in the serial pictures ... demonstrating his talent and unique abilities for the cinema. Recently, Guillermo Calles was offered an excellent bid: his promotion to the category of a star. However, with that illustrious proposition Calles would have to renounce his nationality, he would have to become an American citizen. And of course, in a gesture of absolute self-respect, he chose to remain among the masses, leading a mediocre life rather than paying such an outrageous price for his artistic climb.[24]

In the early decades of the 20th century, the majority of Mexican immigrants saw assimilation into American society as a betrayal to their roots. According to author Francisco Balderrama, even when their original motivation to come to the United States was to find better living conditions, these nationals "continued feeling as Mexicans, with all of their defects and all of their virtues." The 1920 U.S. Population Census demonstrates that a great number of Mexican-born immigrants retained their original citizenship. Balderrama calculated that "only 6,363 or 3.3 percent of 189,974 male and female foreign-born Mexican nationals had pledged American citizenship as compared to 47.8 percent for other foreign-born nationals."[25] In fact, very few people from Mexico applied for naturalization in this year. Of the total number of persons admitted to citizenship in the United States, only 6.5

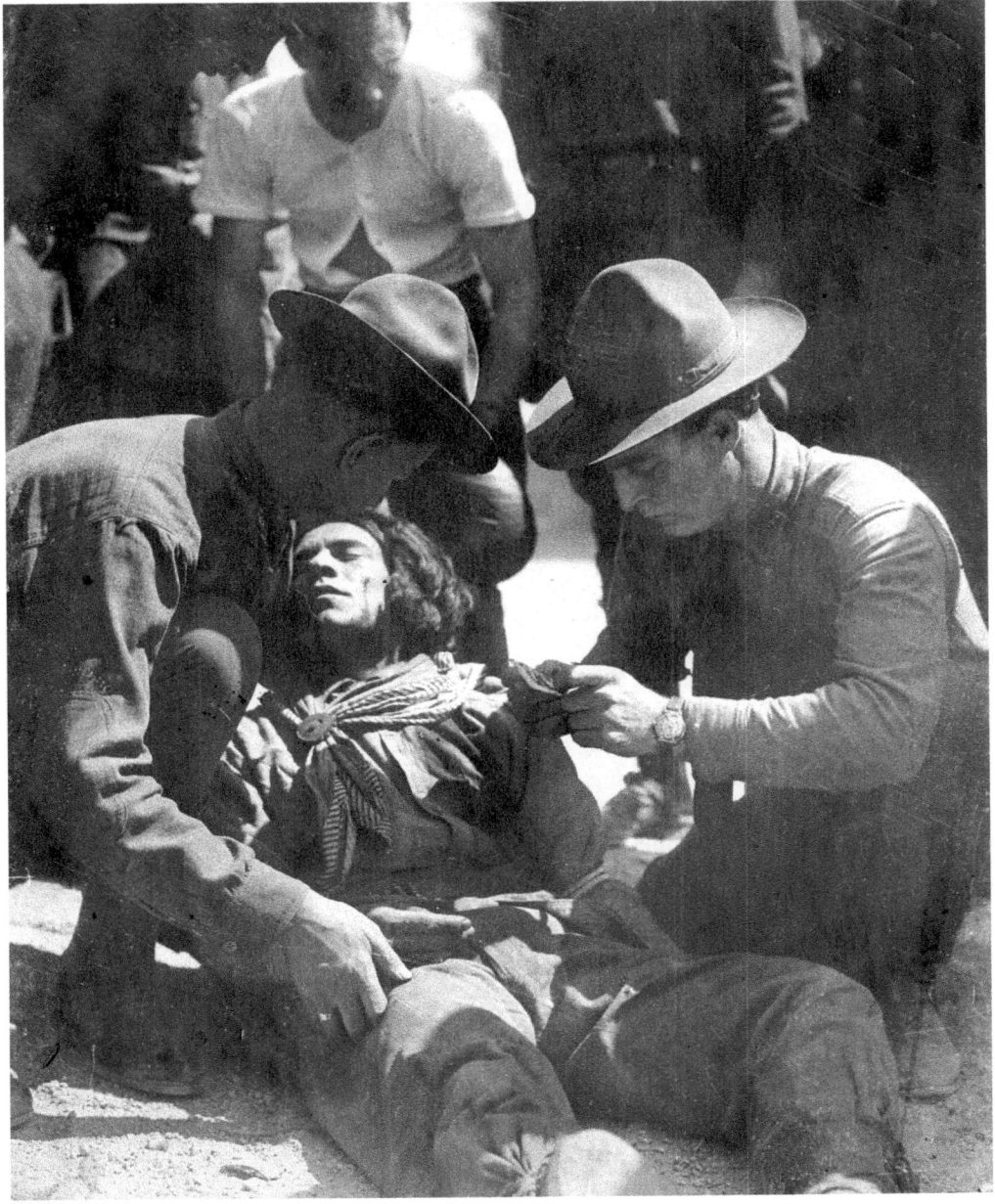

At Vitagraph, Calles (center) was ready to take the place of the stars when doing a dangerous scene. Sometimes he ended up in bad shape. Photograph ca. 1920 (Rudy Calles Collection).

percent were Mexicans. Fewer individuals wanted to become American citizens later in the decade. The naturalization rate for this group reached virtually zero percent in 1928. Loyalty to the homeland prevailed even among those that had achieved status and fame. At the height of her film career in Hollywood, the glamorous star Dolores del Río ardently declared: "Never will I become an American citizen, never!"[26]

The dogged independence of Calles can be weighed against the more practical attitude of other members of his family. His brother Pascual Calles, for instance, was also proud of his Mexican heritage and even became a noted leader of the "Liga Protectora Latina" of Pasadena, California. But he assimilated into American society more easily, seeking U.S. citizenship in the 1920s. Some of his children, like daughter Belén, were supporters of civic causes, helping collect funds for the victims of earthquakes in Mexico. Guillermo Calles's nephew, José "Pepe" Domínguez, started a career as film actor in 1917, later appearing in scores of Hollywood productions. Unlike Willie Calles, who returned to Mexico in the 1930s and had no offspring, Domínguez settled in California and contributed to the growth of the family; he married Francisca Almaraz, with whom he fathered eleven children.

Although Calles was not an American citizen, he had to comply with the official requisites of a resident of the United States. For instance, according to a 1917 army record, he registered for the draft when the country entered World War I. However, there is no evidence that he served in any capacity during the war. According to the same document, he was currently working as an actor for the Lasky studios and signed his name as Willie Calles. In addition, in the Los Angeles Census of 1920 he is listed as William Calles, of Mexican citizenship, single, and having the occupation of an actor. This source adds that he did not read nor write in English, even though he could speak the language. The census shows that he rented a dwelling on 931-C Sunset Boulevard. Living in the same house was John Hauser from Michigan, who worked for the film studios as an electrician.[27]

His activities at the Vitagraph Company unquestionably stimulated Calles's career. After a stream of box-office hits acting alongside famous stars, Calles gained popular recognition. For Mexican audiences, seeing one of their own race executing heroic deeds in movies was certainly important, more so since the cinema frequently portrayed them as the most dreadful characters. Calles could take pride in being a Mexican; his indigenous roots, coupled with a sense of self-worth, inspired the moviegoing masses.

3

Riding the Wave of Nationalism

Serious attempts to establish moviemaking in Mexico began in 1917, the year when the Azteca Film Company was organized by exhibitor Enrique Rosas and the popular stage actress Mimí Derba. They sought to "develop subjects of national interest, inspired by historic ideas that illustrate the true Mexican traditions." In practice, though, the efforts of the Azteca Film Co. tended to imitate the Italian dramas then in vogue. Some of the titles reflecting this trend were *En defensa propia*, *La soñadora* and *La Tigresa*. One of the company's projects that never got finished was *Chapultepec*, a costly movie about the war with the United States. In addition to Rosas and Derba, the task of promoting vernacular cinema fell to Germán Camus, a distributor of European movies.

Camus had the vision of making films adapted from well-known Mexican novels and stage plays. In 1918 he hired Luis Peredo to direct *Santa*, a movie inspired by Federico Gamboa's best-selling novel of the same title. Camus followed with *La banda del automóvil* (a.k.a. *La dama enlutada*), directed by Ernesto Vollrath. After these triumphs, he established his own studios and brought in new equipment from the United States. Other titles that he filmed later were *Alas abiertas* and *En la hacienda*. *Alas abiertas* focused on the Mexican Revolution, portraying the fighting between the Constitutionalist army and the Zapatist rebels. It included stock footage of actual battles taken from an airplane. *En la hacienda*, a rural melodrama, touched upon the exploitation of peons during the Porfirio Díaz regime. Before giving up film production, Camus edited *Las grandes fiestas del Centenario* (1921), a documentary that showcased the festivities of the 100th anniversary of Mexican independence.

One of the most important Mexican movies produced at this time was Enrique Rosas's *El automóvil gris*, a twelve-chapter serial depicting the deeds of a band of thieves operating in Mexico City during the chaotic years of the Revolution. Based on real-life events, the film included footage of the actual execution of the band's leaders. It competed against Camus's *La banda del automóvil*, which premiered a few months before the release of Rosas's serial. In 1919, the historical film *Cuauhtémoc* opened in Mexico City. Inspired by a stage drama, director Manuel de la Bandera recounted episodes of the Conquest of Mexico. The movie paid tribute to the Aztecs and showed "true Indian women whose amazing beauty made them worthy symbols of our bronze race." Similarly, *Tabaré* illustrated the pride of the indigenous people. Uruguay's José Zorrilla de San Martín wrote the poem that inspired this film. No doubt, the influence of *Indigenismo* can be detected in movies like *Cuauhté-*

moc and *Tabaré*. It is also manifest in *Tepeyac*, a story about the miraculous apparition of the Virgin of Guadalupe to the Indian Juan Diego. Whether historical or religious, these movies dealt with subjects of national significance and stressed the importance of the Indian past.

Although the spectacle of the movies reached all corners of Mexico, local productions were hardly noticed by the public. In 1921, for example, a little more than a dozen domestic titles found their way to theaters in the capital. Hollywood motion pictures, on the other hand, dominated the market and enjoyed the favor of exhibitors and public alike. That year, the number of U.S. films exhibited in Mexico City climbed to an unprecedented 406 features. For a country that had recently undergone a social and political revolution, the overwhelming presence of American movies seemed to contradict the nationalist feelings of the day.

With this background, Guillermo Calles "decided to make a pleasure trip" to Mexico City in 1921.[1] He first visited his brother Mariano, who lived in El Paso, Texas. In the same city he contacted Juan de la C. Alarcón, an enterprising theater manager who also filmed short subjects. Recently, Alarcón had produced *Por la Patria*, a documentary showing a parade for Mexican Independence Day in El Paso. Aware of the experience of Calles, the impresario proposed to him making a patriotic movie entitled *Alma insurgente* or *La conquista de México*. Alarcón consulted with his associates about financial support, but they were unable to agree on this matter and the project was canceled. Still, the incident demonstrates that Alarcón and Calles shared a common view and that both were anxious to experiment with the medium of the cinema to celebrate Mexico's history and cultural heritage. As it turned out, ten years later Alarcón became a pioneer of Mexican sound movies when he launched the project to film *Santa* (1931). It is almost certain that the encounter with this impresario from El Paso fueled Calles' enthusiasm for the production of native films.

In Mexico City, another film buff, Miguel Contreras Torres, would soon establish contact with Calles. Contreras Torres had been a military officer during the Revolution but decided to pursue a career in the film exhibition business. In actuality, he desired to become a movie star. With modest resources but huge determination, he managed to produce a couple of pictures in which he starred, *El Zarco* and *El caporal*. In September 1921, Contreras Torres and Calles got together to make the nationalistic film *De raza azteca*. It is probable that its plot had certain similarities with the previous project proposed by Alarcón in El Paso. In *De raza azteca*, Víctor (Contreras Torres) is a noble *hacendado*, a rancher who defends his servants from the abuse of a foreman. Víctor and his fiancée, Catalina (Carlota Santuggini), visit the town of Xochimilco, a bucolic place surrounded by water. They meet the Indian Diego (Calles), a keeper of the customs of the ancient Aztec race who wears a ring that belonged to his ancestors. This ring resembles the one worn by Víctor. Diego saves Catalina when she falls into a canal and later risks his life trying to defend her from some thugs. A series of incredible adventures follow. Víctor and Catalina are thankful to Diego and want to compensate him for his loyalty. Humbly, the Indian tells them: "This act of assistance is really insignificant and I do it because it is my duty. The ring you have on demonstrates that you are a true descendant of my race: you too belong to the Aztec race."[2]

Larry Semon (left) and Guillermo Calles during a casual meeting in Mexico City (1921). Semon was a highly popular comedian at Vitagraph (Agrasánchez Film Archive).

Calles and Contreras Torres made a good team and complemented each other during the course of their joint venture. *De raza azteca* took almost three months to film at the Camus studios and at several locations in Mexico City and nearby towns. One of the first historians of Mexican cinema, José María Sánchez García, pointed out that Calles' involvement in this eight-reeler "was very valuable because he arrived with a knowledge of the latest trends in the field, and his cooperation stood out due to his know-how."[3] In addition, Calles contributed to the story with his romantic ideas. A fusion of the old and the new, the film glorified the Aztec past while praising the virtues of a modern hero played by Contreras Torres. For some viewers, the plot seemed a bit fantastic and critics moved quickly to point out its flaws. A detractor offered his assessment when the picture opened at several Mexico City theaters in February 1922:

> Contreras Torres has just released *De raza azteca*; his third film that he claims is nationalistic, even though we do not see the reason except in the charro hat of the protagonist. Also, because the spectator comes across a band of thieves, dressed as Texan cowboys, who roam around Chapultepec; and witnesses kidnappings and criminal acts in the middle of main avenues in the city, he receives the general impression that throughout the story there are no other decent people than the hero and his aide. All this makes it easy for the observer — one that is unin-

Guillermo Calles (center) joined forces with Carlota Santuggini (the bride) and Miguel Contreras Torres (the groom) to make *De raza azteca* (1921). In a dramatic scene during a wedding, a bullet wounds the Indian hero (Agrasánchez Film Archive).

3. Riding the Wave of Nationalism

formed of the reality of our poor country — to confirm instead of eradicate the ideas sown by a number of Yankee filmmakers, who are ignorant or venomous. Besides this defect, the story is terribly absurd resembling the style of the William Duncan serials....[4]

The unlikely events of the story were in fact what audiences loved most about the movie. Its producers simply wanted to tell a vibrant tale with a touch of local flavor. In doing this, they followed the example of Hollywood's serials that established a formula for action films. Calles and Contreras Torres believed that the essence of movies was their capacity to stir audiences. Putting the formula to the test, they combined a maximum of emotions and a minimum of plausibility in this movie. Although critics complained of the film's incongruous comings and goings, the majority of the public was certainly ecstatic. The line separating reality from fiction seemed to dissolve while the projector was running. Moreover, the implausible happenings on the screen gave audiences an opportunity to break away for a moment from their daily routine.

De raza azteca played in theaters throughout Mexico before reaching the United States in May 1922. The Teatro Colón of El Paso launched a smart publicity campaign and announced a personal appearance by Calles. To tease the public, the Spanish-language newspaper *La Patria* warned that the current movie had sparked a scandal in Mexico City and that a theater impresario in the capital had been rude to the press. "Critics felt insulted and they turned against the picture, saying horrible things," the article read. This type of publicity only fueled the curiosity of spectators who crowded into the Teatro Colón during the four-day engagement of *De raza azteca*. The management gave free passes to the newspaper people who helped promote the picture. In turn, the editors of *La Patria* contributed with more commentaries on the movie and the work of Calles. One read:

> [*De raza azteca*] is a commendable film. It is not the best cinematically, as the photography suffers from imperfection; this is due to the meager resources against which the silent cinema in our country is still struggling. But the simple and realistic plot; the dramatization, the direction and interpretation of the actors are genuinely Mexican. The film presents as its protagonist a courageous charro with a generous heart; the owner of the Hacienda de Lobos, interpreted by Miguel Contreras Torres. It also presents an Indian of Aztec descent, of the stoic race, master of his emotions and soul of the episodes that make this an interesting story from beginning to end. This

Calles sometimes appeared on stage donning Indian costumes, as in this photograph from 1934. He mustered up the audience's support for the progress of Mexican cinema (Agrasánchez Film Archive).

character is played by the young Guillermo Calles, who at the end of the screening appears in person donning a costume with the regalia of the warriors and emperors of the Aztecs. He takes the stage to talk about the development of motion pictures in Mexico. Calles is very convincing in his role as Diego, and he gets a thunderous applause out of the audience. This young Mexican actor ... worked in the studios in Los Angeles where he became an important figure in the films of William Duncan. He did not continue this successful career for the reason that they wanted him to renounce his Mexican nationality.[5]

Across the border, in Ciudad Juárez, the Empresa Samaniego Hermanos turned the local bullfighting arena into an open-air theater for the screening of *De raza azteca*. The impresarios announced the installation of new projection equipment and the setting-up of convenient soda and liquor stands inside the ring. All this added up to a very informal atmosphere. A first-class ticket cost less than half a peso; those wanting to sit on bleachers paid only 20 cents.

Largely, the populace in El Paso enjoyed the few Mexican films playing locally. In addition to *De raza azteca*, they had a chance to see *El hombre sin patria* the same month. Produced by Contreras Torres, this "sensational drama" recounted the misgivings of a Mexican immigrant in the United States. The Teatro Paris presented it four months before its release in Mexico City. *El hombre sin patria*'s sentimental plot found an extremely receptive audience among the working class in El Paso.

Hollywood's pictures shown in El Paso drew a broader segment of the Mexican theatergoers. The costly newspaper ads of *La Patria* promoting these films are an obvious sign of their popularity. The major entertainment circuit catering to Hispanics consisted of the Rex, Eureka, Alcazar, Paris, México, and Hidalgo theaters. In addition to playing the films of Gloria Swanson, Dorothy Gish, and William S. Hart, they also showed William Duncan's serials such as *Where Men Are Men*. Every once in a while, movies provoked heated discussions because they were considered insulting to Mexicans. An example is Cecil B. DeMille's *A Fool's Paradise*, which played at the Palace Theater in April 1922. A local paper mentioned that the film contained "real scenes of a saloon in the border area, with everything from empty bottles of whiskey, to gambling machines, roulette, headlamp, dice, and poker table." It also portrayed "the evil of gambling and drinking" in a room full of "*rurales*, cowboys and partners in crime, Chinese people, onlookers, customers, and visitors." This atmosphere was made even more attractive by the presence of several Mexican female dancers.[6]

The film's saloon sequence immediately caught the attention of prominent people. The Mexican consul in El Paso sent a letter to the local exhibitors, asking them "not to play movies that denigrate Mexicans; because the themes developed in these pictures, besides being unjust and untruthful, are a setback in reestablishing the good relations that should exist between México and this country." One of the exhibitors who complied with this call was the manager of the Teatro Alameda, who promised "not to show the movies that hurt national pride." A newspaper reported that the impresario gave his word that "as soon as he finds out that any film belittles the Mexican people, he will take it back even if this means losing money."[7] In an effort to stop the exhibition of denigrating films, the Mexican government issued a list of over 400 movies bearing the stigma of censorship. It also gave orders to its customs agents to block the importation of any of them. Among the proscribed titles were *A Fool's Paradise* and *The Golden Gift*, which had just played in El Paso. Another picture prohibited was the Aymond Film Corporation's *The Man of Courage*, which "depicted types and customs as if the Mexicans were savages."[8]

Los Angeles's Teatro Hidalgo showed *De raza azteca* on June 24, 1922. This small theater on Main Street attracted a large crowd that had the opportunity to see Contreras Torres in person. The interpreter and producer of *De raza azteca* had come to California to shoot extra scenes for his new film. He visited the Hollywood studios where he met Antonio Moreno and other famous stars. Calles had collaborated with Contreras Torres in the two-reeler *El sueño del caporal*, which was a follow-up to *El caporal*. Contreras Torres played the title role in both of these movies, but Calles's exact role in the sequel is not known. A newspaper ad for the Broadway Theater of Indiana Harbor, Indiana, announced in September 1929 the exhibition of *El caporal* and *Llamas de rebelión* complemented by a newsreel, *Revista mexicana*. The publicity read, "These pictures are interpreted by the noted Mexican artists Miguel Contreras Torres and Guillermo Calles; it is a drama of Mexican charros that can compete with any American Western drama and that reflects the romantic and bucolic life in Mexico."[9]

The warm reception given to *De raza azteca* in the El Paso–Ciudad Juárez area motivated Calles to set up a picture company in El Paso. The bustling border cities seemed to offer an excellent opportunity for the entertainment business, having a significant Mexican population that would welcome movies made by locals. This was no dream. Just a year before, there were three movies produced in the city: *Jane and the Jinx*, *X Back* and *Just a Little Bull*. In order to explore the potential for film production, he launched a publicity campaign in July 1922. A studio photograph of the artist appeared in an issue of *La Patria* alongside a story that highlighted his career at the Vitagraph Company as a participant in the Duncan serials. The paper made known that the Mexican artist was starting a local motion picture company, the Río Grande Film Production Co., and he asked the "Mexican public for their moral support to make his new company a great success." On the opposite page could be seen an attractive portrait of Adela Zambrano, a Mexican actress who was joining the Río Grande Company. In addition, the classified section of *La Patria* promoted Calles as an experienced person working "toward the creation of this brilliant industry in our Mexico." It also emphasized that the cinema would "provide a future for you and the children of your children."[10]

As if these ads were not enough, another section of the newspaper announced that the Río Grande Film Company was seeking "intelligent young men and women desiring to take up the beautiful art of cinematography." The advertisement urged those people interested to "take this opportunity and arrange an interview with Mr. Calles, at 226 Trust Building, El Paso." At the end of the page, another note recommended, "Sales agents with experience needed; we offer a unique opportunity; please no street vendors; if you consider yourself competent, come to us for a talk. Río Grande Film Production Co. Ask for Mr. Barr."[11] The profusion of ads in the pages of *La Patria* probably stirred the curiosity of some readers. Unfortunately, there were no practical results and nothing else was heard of the enter-

TEATRO BROADWAY

LUNES, MARTES Y MIERCOLES
Septiembre 2, 3 y 4

Funciones especiales dedicadas a la H. Colonia Mexicana de este lugar. Estreno de las sensacionales películas

Mexicanas Tituladas
El Caporal
y Llamas de Revelion

La empresa de este teatro desea complacer a la H. C. Mexicana que la favorece y al efecto se complace en anunciar que ha contratado una Serie de Películas Mexicanas que tendrá el gusto de dar a conocer anunciándolas oportunamente. En estas funciones se exhibirán las películas antes mencionadas y una

Revista Mexicana

componiéndose el programa de ocho rollos. Estas películas están interpretadas por los notables artistas Mexicanos,

MIGUEL CONTRERAS TORRES Y GUILLERMO CALLES

Es un drama de Charros Mexicanos que puede competir con cualquiera de los dramas del Oeste Americano y refleja la romántica vida campestre de México a la vez que las pasiones políticas, las envidias, los celos y los egoísmos de algunas autoridades que, excediéndose en sus atribuciones, cometen atropellos que, como el que demuestra esta película, inducen a un laborioso y honrado joven a lanzarse a las aventuras de la revolución. Afortunadamente, la razón y la justicia se imponen y al fin el humillado joven ve recompensada su lucha.

No dejen de ver estas bonitas películas hechas en México por artistas Mexicanos.

Mexican movies shown in Indiana Harbor, Indiana (1929). The exact role played by Calles in this "drama of charros" is not known (Agrasánchez Film Archive).

prise. Adela Zambrano's previous experience in the movies was *Just a Little Bull*, a burlesque bullfighting comedy starring the local actor Charlot Molina. Apparently she also made a five-reel picture called *Regenerado*, a project by El Paso producer Roy Hughes.[12] Afterwards, Miss Zambrano appeared in Neal Hart's Western *The Verdict of the Desert*, which also included Calles in the cast.

Calles's attempt at establishing a motion picture business in El Paso was preceded by the efforts of a group of enthusiasts. In February 1921, Roberto E. Ames, Ignacio Rodarte, Carlos P. Alarid, Manuel Álvarez A., and Miss María Escudero formed the "Juárez Compañía Cinematográfica Mexicana." The company directors planned to have offices in El Paso and a studio in Ciudad Juárez and intended to make films of national interest, as well as "educational, historic, comic, dramatic, artistic and scientific movies."[13] Besides this information, nothing else is known of the enterprise or its participants.

Back in Hollywood, Calles carried on his activities working as an actor in several movies. He appeared in *The Silent Vow*, a William Duncan production shot in 1922 and starring Duncan and Edith Johnson. The role that Calles played in this film is unknown, but a publicity photograph shows him dressed as an Indian. In this scene, he and the beautiful Edith Johnson look worried and perplexed, as if an impeding danger confronted them. The film's advertising read: "A thrilling masterpiece, it is a story of the Northwest Mounted Police, telling of a family feud of two generations." Duncan characterized "a Mountie assigned to track down the supposed killers of his father." This production bragged about an exceptional photography trick which "has been heretofore regarded impossible, that of a character crossing the center line in a double exposure scene." *The Silent Vow* also included a spectacular view where "a gang of dynamite fishermen blow up a stream to stun the fish in it." When Duncan prepared to shoot this part, he was told that the laws of the State of California prohibited dynamite fishing "even when done for picture purposes." After three days of red tape maneuvers, the director "was authorized to blow up as much water as he wished."[14]

Following *The Silent Vow*, Calles joined his old friend Neal Hart, who was directing *The Fighting Strain* (1923). Hart played Jack Barlow, a young soldier who comes home following the war only to discover that his sister (Beth Mitchell) has been kidnapped. The villain is Jim Black (William Quinn), who has also swindled Mr. Canfield (Bert Wilson), the father of Jack's sweetheart (Gladys Gilland), with fake mining stock. Calles played one of the villains, an Indian clad in western clothes and wearing long hair. The first scenes show him in a light mood, joking around with some fellows. At the end of the story, the Indian's ferocity is confirmed when he knocks about one of his victims. *The Fighting Strain* is an enjoyable feature that is about an hour long. It is now available on DVD.

In 1924, Calles came back to work alongside Hart in *The Left Hand Brand* and *Branded a Thief*. It is probable that *Branded a Thief* was filmed in Mexico City and surrounding area. A newspaper account noted that Hart had arrived in the capital to make a movie accompanied by camera operator R. Lesley Selander. Two Mexican actors, Guillermo Calles and Victor Herrera, were also mentioned as being part of this project. Hart and friends went to the nearby town of Xochimilco in search of shooting locations. According to the

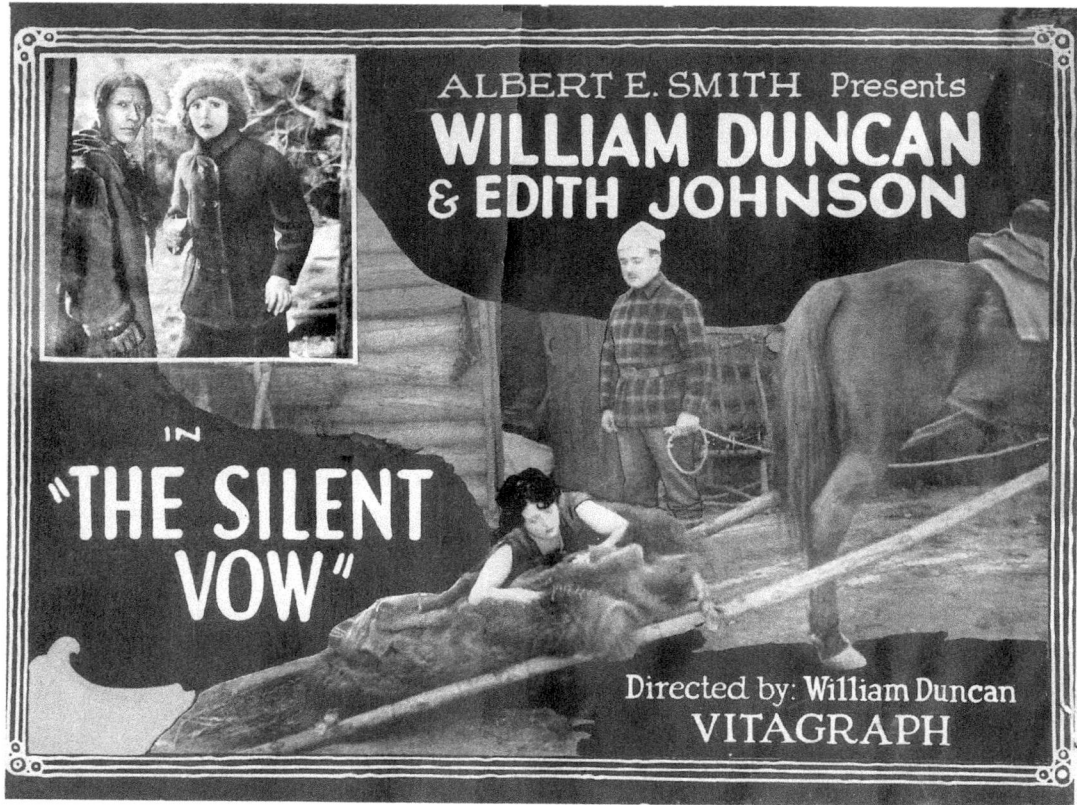

The inset of this lobby card for *The Silent Vow* (1922) shows Calles as an Indian; he and Edith Johnson look perplexed, as if confronted by impending danger (Agrasánchez Film Archive).

news report, the Hollywood star and director intended "to do a movie about Mexican charros, detailing the romantic and extraordinary, but above all presenting México to the outside world as an educated country that is worthy of superior esteem."[15]

Billed as "a powerful human drama of Old Mexico," *Branded a Thief* played in Texas at Galveston's Alamo Theater. A newspaper ad gave a quick summary of the plot: "José León receives a mysterious letter. His refusal to explain the letter to his sweetheart Conchita excites her jealousy and she leaves him. About this time an American cattleman pursued by cattle thieves enters the Bowl of Hell country and is chased into an impassible canyon from which there is but one escape." Hart played the American cattleman. It is probable that Calles took the role of José León but this cannot be established because the film is missing. The program at the Alamo Theater also included a Pathé comedy and an installment of *Wolves of the North* featuring William Duncan.[16]

Staying busy all the time, the Tarahumaran artist accepted a role in *The Dirty Little Half-Breed*, a two-reeler produced by the National Film Corporation of America in 1924. This is an obscure title in the filmography of Calles. A still from the movie shows Calles prominently, wearing long hair and dressed in Indian fashion. He is on his knees clutching a knife and holding down a scared female victim. The image suggests that he is the villain. *The Dirty Little Half-Breed* was a short feature usually programmed at theaters to complement the main attraction. For instance, the Colonial Theater in Lincoln, Nebraska, offered in 1924 a three-part program composed of *Wild Oranges*, the Mack Sennett comedy *The Hollywood Kid*, and *The Dirty Little Half-Breed*.[17]

Calles did not always play despicable roles, as proven by the film *Behind Two Guns* (1924). This was a one-hour Western comedy produced by Anthony J. Xydias and directed by Robert N. Bradbury. The film gives Calles a fifth credit after J.B. Warner, Hazel Newman, Jim Welch, and Otto Lederer. Other actors appearing were Marin Sais, Jay Morley, Jack Waltemeyer, and Emily Gerdes. It became J.B. Warner's last effort, as the "lanky cowboy from Nebraska" died of tuberculosis shortly afterwards. The plot concerns a mysterious criminal, Olaf Ludovic (Lederer), who robs large sums of money from a stagecoach coffer without anyone noticing and while the vehicle is in transit. Dr. Elijah Cutter (Warner) and his aide-de-camp, the Indian Eagle Slowfoot (Calles), arrive in town to solve this puzzle. Posing as vendors of a cure-all remedy, they exchange their automobile for a pair of horses and set out to uncover the criminal. To everyone's astonishment, they reveal that the mysterious stage robber is Mrs. Baxter (Sais), the wife of the owner of the stage-

The Dirty Little Half-Breed is an obscure two-reeler that featured Calles in the role of a villain. It was released in 1924 (Agrasánchez Film Archive).

coach line. Hypnotized by Ludovic and concealed inside one of the trunks carried on top of the stagecoach, the woman is able to steal the money from the coffer. Finally, the hero and his aide discover the hiding place of Ludovic's band and help the local authorities to round up the criminals.

The movie has enough action to keep audiences alert; it also provides lots of comedy through an assortment of funny characters. Called "the *Svengali* of the old west," *Behind Two Guns* is one of the few surviving films of the silent era that features Calles prominently. His character, Eagle Slowfoot, wears pasty makeup and long braids, and he moves at a fast pace on horse and automobiles. In an amusing scene, Eagle Slowfoot puts on a feathered outfit and performs a ritualistic dance at the beat of his drum to attract the villagers.[18]

An obscure silent Western in which Calles appeared was *The Verdict of the Desert*, directed by and starring Neal Hart. One of the actresses was Adela Zambrano, who seems to have played the role of a "dance-hall floozy." Little can be said about this picture released in 1924, although it was considered "a good lively story [containing] good riding, snappy fights, thrills, stunts and romance." According to a synopsis, *The Verdict of the Desert* is a tale "of betrayal and revenge set in the gold mining town of Nugget. Hart played Jack Dawson, who arrives in town to sell his gold, only to run into the man who once defiled his sister. When Jack returns to his mine, the villain uses a dance-hall floozy to lure him back to town. Soon Jack is falsely accused of murdering the villain's henchman over water rights. The real culprit, however, is a half-breed Indian, who Jack brings to justice."[19] There are also some clues to the film in the lobby cards that remain. In one scene, Neal Hart and several other people appear inside a cottage. A longhaired Calles is staring hard at the suspicious "half-breed Indian."

A note published by Los Angeles's *El Heraldo de México* in October 1925, made known that Calles was recuperating from an accident. The actor fell off a horse when filming a movie at the Universal Studios. The doctors recommended that he stay at home for a few days to help heal his bruised left foot. This accident might have happened while shooting *The Verdict of the Desert*, which contained a lot of action performed by actors and stuntmen.

Producer Anthony J. Xydias made another film with director Robert N. Bradbury. *Daniel Boone Thru the Wilderness* (1926) was the title and its cast included Roy Stewart, Kathleen Collins, Bob Steele, Jay Morley, Jim O'Neill, and Frank Rice. Calles and Emily Gerdes, both of whom previously appeared in Xydias' *Behind Two Guns*, were brought back for this one-hour Western. Calles performs a dual role: He comes out briefly at the beginning of the movie as one of the "bad" Indians, and later plays an Indian chief's son who is killed by a white renegade. *Daniel Boone Thru the Wilderness* survived the passing of time, giving us another sample of Calles's performances during the silent era.

Around this time, Calles decided to make a movie. Other people in Los Angeles had already envisioned filming their own projects. One of them was Manuel Sánchez Valtierra, who organized the Anáhuac Film Corporation in 1920 with the explicit intention to "divulge by means of the cinema the refined artistic culture of Hispanic America." Despite his lofty ideal, the enterprise failed to arouse the interest of other capitalists. More successful was

3. Riding the Wave of Nationalism

Neal Hart (sitting on the table) plays a hero in *The Verdict of the Desert* (1925). Calles is standing behind the woman on the right, staring hard at one of the villains (Agrasánchez Film Archive).

Manuel R. Ojeda, a Mexican who worked as an extra in countless Hollywood pictures. He made a film called *La rosa del desierto*, in which he headed a cast that included Helen Winster Howard and Clyde Benson. According to author Ángel Miquel, "when Ojeda returned to Mexico at the end of 1921, he brought from Hollywood the footage and still photographs of a Western that he wrote, directed, and starred in; the hero was a Mexican and the villain an American."[20] Ojeda's production played in Mexico City theaters in March 1922.

Another Hispanic in Hollywood who resolved to make a movie was Chris Pin Martin. Armed with "tons of good will," he produced *Tepee Love*, a romantic story about two Indian tribes facing a dilemma: The son of an Indian chief wants to marry a beautiful woman from the other tribe. The woman's father rejects the fiancé because he seems so foreign and "dresses as an Englishman." Appearing in *Tepee Love* were Martin, Dolores Contreras, and the amateur actors María López, Ramón López and Eduardo Mata. The movie played in Glendale and Burbank in 1922.[21] Chris Pin Martin attempted a second film, *Un feliz vagabundo*, but was unable to complete it. He wrote the story aided by Gabry Rivas, a Nicaraguan poet who appeared in the movie. The female lead was offered to Armida Vendrell, a young artist who had been popular in the Hispanic theaters of Main Street. *Un feliz vagabundo* also featured José de la Cruz, Sánchez Molgoza, Emma Venegas, and others. Its initial scenes were filmed in the barrio of Palo Verde. The artists would only work on Sundays, and then if weather conditions allowed it.[22]

There was yet another film produced by Mexicans in Los Angeles. In November 1926, the Compañía Cinematográfica Cuautla completed *El que a hierro mata*, which played at the Teatro Principal at the end of the month. Several young artists who worked as extras in Hollywood pitched in all their savings to make the movie. Such a scanty budget could not pay for the studio rental. Therefore, they had to improvise their own stage on an empty lot on Figueroa Street. Heading this effort was Antonio M. Ramírez, who photographed the film and adapted a story written by Ana M. Rodríguez. A debutant director, Miguel Ángel Álvarez, gave instructions to the actors Amparo Ramos, Julia S. Provencio, Fernando Parra, David Galván, and Juan B. Quiñones.[23] In spite of their initial success, the Compañía Cuautla quickly dissolved, as very few people were willing to gamble their money on cinematic experiments.

4

"The Vindication of Our Race on the Celluloid"

The severe winter of 1925–26 had a distressing effect on the Hollywood movie industry, bringing most filmmaking activities to a halt. Some production companies, looking for a better climate, left the studios and traveled to San Diego. For example, Robert N. Bradbury's *Davy Crockett at the Fall of the Alamo* was partially shot there in February. Among the few Mexican actors active at this moment was Calles, who performed a small part in this historical drama. A newspaper editorial calculated that during those critical months, over a thousand actors and extras were left without a job. It was not uncommon to see people "living from their savings in the cheapest sheltering homes; others are in their darkest hour, avoiding the rent collector, cutting down on meals or simply taking jobs that are at odds with their artistic talents."[1] Notwithstanding the difficult times, Calles set out to do the impossible: He attempted to produce a film.

Like other Mexicans before him, Calles had a fervent wish to make a movie and star in it. After almost fifteen years of work as an actor and occasional director, his dream became a reality. The idea of filming *El indio yaqui* couldn't have been more promising; the story not only fitted the artist's ethnic profile but also offered him the opportunity to express his romantic and nationalistic impulses. Single-mindedly Calles gathered up $1,500 in savings and began to ask for the support of other enthusiasts. Eager to appear on screen, José M. Duarte, a stage comedian known as the "Mexican Buster Keaton," secured the supplementary funds for the production of the picture. Several Hollywood acquaintances of Calles also rallied round: actors Neal Hart, Betty Brown, Roy Stewart, Joe Ryan, and Walter Shumway. A favorite star in many Westerns, Hart appeared in *Hell's Oasis* (1919), *The Fighting Strain* (1923), *The Left Hand Brand* (1924), and *The Verdict of the Desert* (1925), all of which featured Calles. Hart was already an established actor and producer when he lent a hand to Calles's first effort. He had acquired a reputation for being "a determined and enthusiastic supporter of artists." As in real life, in this film Hart portrays a producer who helps finance *El indio yaqui*. The six-foot-two, blue-eyed actor Roy Stewart was mostly known for his western dramas, appearing recently in *Daniel Boone Thru the Wilderness* (1926). Joe Ryan became the indispensable tough guy in several Vitagraph serials including *Man of Might* (1919), where he portrayed "Scarface" Bender. Walter Shumway had been in the movies since 1918 playing assorted roles. He was the perfect choice for a heartless villain in *El indio yaqui*.

Shooting for *El indio yaqui* started at Universal Studios, concluding with locations in

Sonora, Mexico. As reported by journalist Gabriel Navarro, Calles gathered up his actor friends and gave them instructions to perform "under the intense beam of the studio lamps, in the midst of the expectation of people that are accustomed to scenes of a rather different kind." Navarro continued:

> Calles silently rented a studio, hired a cameraman and two or three American players of prestige that could perform secondary roles. Roy Stewart, a well-known adventure actor, and Neal Hart, who is one of his best friends, both appear in the scenes of *El indio yaqui* briefly conveying their stature to the picture and giving support to the new producer. The rest of the cast, with the exception of the heroine played by the beautiful Betty Brown, was split among Mexican artists that are struggling in Hollywood to succeed in spite of all the prejudices and obstacles. Juan V. Calles, José Duarte, Pepe Domínguez, Enrique Acosta, and Manuel F. Rodríguez play their parts with authentic feeling, cheerfully, free from the restrictions imposed by directors who present Mexicans as they imagine them and not as they really are. A sweet old lady, señora Agustina López, takes the prize for interpretation. She is a mother that remembers past tragedies and recreates them on the screen. Her effort, given that she has never posed for the camera before, is without a doubt the most significant in the film.[2]

Neal Hart was already an established actor and producer when he lent his talents to Calles's first effort, *El indio yaqui* (1926) (Agrasánchez Film Archive).

Calles not only invited friends and colleagues to perform in the movie but also called on members of his family: Acting in *El indio yaqui* were his nephews José "Pepe" Domínguez and Juan V. Calles and niece Margarita Calles. Domínguez had established himself in Hollywood playing minor roles for Vitagraph productions of the early twenties. More recently, he acted in *The Fast Express* (1924). The thirty-two-year-old Domínguez interpreted many villains and eventually worked in more than one hundred movies. Juan V. Calles previously appeared in Universal's *Thundering Dawn* (1923), a drama starring Anna Q. Nilsson and Winter Hall. The young Margarita Calles was the daughter of José de la Luz Calles. Enrique Acosta, a friend of director Calles, appeared briefly as the ill-fated Pancho, the father of the Yaqui Indian. The Mexican-born Acosta acted for the first time in *Don Q, Son of Zorro* (1925) starring Douglas Fairbanks and Mary Astor. He later acted in *The Texan* (1930), a Western featuring Gary Cooper and Fay Wray, continuing a career that included over forty pictures. Another "member" of the cast was Águila, Calles's beloved dog.

Like all Mexican productions directed by Calles in the silent era, *El indio yaqui* has unfortunately disappeared. Only a few scene stills survived the passing of time and are

4. "The Vindication of Our Race on the Celluloid"

Calles had a fervent wish to make a movie and star in it. After almost fifteen years of work in Hollywood, his dream became a reality; he produced *El indio yaqui* in 1926 (courtesy of Dick Domínguez).

included in this book. An account of the plot, written by Homero Lizama Escoffie, has been salvaged by historian Gabriel Ramírez and circulated by author Eduardo de la Vega. The critic Lizama Escoffie originally published this review in Yucatán, Mexico, at the time of the film's release. *El indio yaqui* opens with this evocative scene:

> Mrs. Agustina López wants to sell her screenplay about a typical Mexican tragedy, which begins in Hollywood and continues in the Hacienda Cubanita, in the state of Sonora. After so many hardships, she encounters the Mexican artist Guillermo Calles in the studios of Hollywood. Mrs. López proposes this real-life story to the not-so-fortunate actor in the cinema but who has a stubborn will. He becomes interested in it. She begins to tell her story, taking the role of "Dorotea" and giving Guillermo Calles the role of "Ramón Tollos," El Indio Yaqui.[3]

Having watched the movie attentively, Lizama Escoffie was able to provide a detailed description of *El indio yaqui*. According to his review, the first person appearing in the film is the actor Manuel F. Rodríguez, who plays "a cacique, a despot, whipping and opening bloody wounds in the flesh of his suffering and submissive slaves." When the peon Pancho defends his dog from the cruelty of the despot, he is beaten to death. Before dying, he urges his wife Dorotea and his son Ramón Tollos to run away from the hacienda. After burying him, Ramón, his mother and the dog leave Sonora and cross the border into the Arizona wilderness. Two friendly hunters, Roy Anderson (Juan V. Calles) and Lulú (José M. Duarte), give the refugees shelter in a village where Roy lives in the company of her sister, the fair Betty Anderson (Betty Brown).

Wealthy rancher Morgan (Walter Shumway), bent on possessing Betty, orders his henchmen to intimidate the Indian Ramón by killing his dog. Morgan finally gets his way and rapes Betty. That night Ramón finds her in the wilderness; she is exhausted and feeling ashamed. The Indian improvises a comfortable spot on the grass and offers his chemise to wrap her body. At dawn, Ramón finds out she has killed herself with one of his spears. The desolated Ramón seeks revenge on Morgan but is mortally wounded. Still, the Indian furiously attacks Morgan and makes him fall into an abyss. Because of the fight, Ramón dies; his mother and friends say a prayer by his grave, which lies next to Betty's. As an allegory, the screen is filled with "the heavenly images of Betty and Ramón, reappearing on the horizon and ascending the stairs to the High Throne."[4]

Neal Hart makes a special appearance in the last scene, just as the elder lady, Agustina

Stirring the sentiment of the masses: A cruel rancher played by Walter Shumway (second from left) orders his henchmen to kill the Indian's dog (played by Calles' dog Águila) in *El indio yaqui*. Left to right: José Domínguez, Walter Shumway, José Duarte, Guillermo Calles, Joe Ryan, Augustina Lopez, unidentified, Betty Brown, Juan V. Calles, and unidentified (courtesy of Dick Domínguez).

4. "The Vindication of Our Race on the Celluloid"

López, finishes recounting her tale. At this point, the actor Guillermo Calles introduces her to his old friend Hart, a film director who immediately sympathizes with Agustina's proposal; he thus "welcomes the story and offers to buy the script of this sad Mexican tragedy." The critic Lizama Escoffie points out that although *El indio yaqui* is a dramatic story, it wisely included comic relief provided by José Duarte. Audiences seemed to have enjoyed the comedian's performance because, "with his big and clever gesture, he lightens up the heart and dispels many clouds in the filmic story." The reviewer also commented that *El indio yaqui* was "the first picture that puts our race in its rightful position; therefore, it represents not only a gem of performing art entirely in accordance with the newest developments in cinematography, but also a lofty motivation for Mexico, a country that is usually regarded with scorn in foreign lands."[5]

In some way, the first part of *El indio yaqui* mirrors Calles's real-life experiences. Following his father's death in Chihuahua, he and his mother crossed the border into Arizona, abandoning the homeland. In the movie, a cruel despot is responsible for the death of the head of the family. Later in life, Calles implied that the same happened to his own father.

A scene from *El indio yaqui* (1926). Calles lies on the ground mortally wounded. Agustina López, Juan V. Calles and José M. Duarte comfort the Indian (Rudy Calles Collection).

Mingling facts and fiction, *El indio yaqui* highlighted the exemplary courage of the indigenous race, a theme already explored in *De raza azteca* (1921). The heroism and final sacrifice of an Indian became a model for subsequent screen stories developed by Calles.

Several U.S. films that might have influenced his first effort are *The Yaqui Girl* (1910), *The Yaqui Cur* (1913), *The Lamb* (1915), and *El Yaqui* (1916). This last movie was based on Dane Coolidge's novel and directed by Lloyd B. Carleton. Its story presents the Yaqui Indian chief Tambor (played by Hobart Bosworth), who is separated from his wife (Golda Caldwell) and daughter (Dorothy Clark) by the Indian-hating General Martínez (Jack Curtis). The women are sent to a forced labor camp in Yucatán. Later, "Tambor manages to join his family in their bondage, only to endure the death of his daughter from illness and the suicide of his wife." After killing the white slave owner responsible for these tragedies, Tambor becomes a renegade. Certain similarities exist between Carleton's movie and *El indio yaqui*. In both stories, a nasty boss vents his anger on an Indian and later abuses a woman. Also there is a parallel in the suicide of a female character, which spurs the revenge of the Indian. Adopting an unusual stance for a silent Western, Carleton's *El Yaqui* takes "the side of the Indians in their struggle against white oppression."[6]

Another source of inspiration could have been *The Fighting Trail*, a Vitagraph production in which Calles participated. H. Ducrow played the role of the old Indian "Yaqui Joe" in the first three chapters of the serial. This faithful servant "guards his master and the latter's daughter with his own life." In a climactic scene, some outlaws capture and torture him by burning his feet. When the heroine comes to his rescue, a villain fires at her but the Indian leaps between them and is killed by the bullet. This silent movie presented Indians in a positive light.

An Indian actor who preceded Calles in Hollywood was James Young Deer, who together with his wife, Princess Red Wing, began making a number of one-reel Westerns in 1908. The couple came from the Nebraska Ho-Chunk tribe. Red Wing also acted in Cecil B. DeMille's *The Squaw Man*, and probably met the Tarahumaran actor during the shooting of this film. Young Deer had a successful film career and was able to use "the early flexibility of the industry to exert unprecedented control over popular images of Indians." Author Joanna Hearne has said that the filmmaking couple "rewrote the racial scripts of the western," intentionally giving the plots "a new political center of gravity" that commented "on racism, assimilation, and racial mixture." Some of their films were *Red Wing's Gratitude* (1909), *The Red Girl and the Child*, *A Cheyenne Brave*, and *The Yaqui Girl* (all 1910).[7]

In addition to the cinema, a few Spanish-language plays got their inspiration from the culture and character of the Yaquis. In April 1924, for instance, audiences in Los Angeles attended the Teatro Hidalgo for the debut of Adalberto Elías González's *Sangre yaqui*, a three-act play involving two brothers who fall in love with the same woman. A typical melodrama of jealousy and revenge, the plot has one brother kill the other, only to reveal at the end that they are not actually related. Moreover, the woman discovers that she is really the victim's sister. Very successful, *Sangre yaqui* continued to be in vogue for several years. The Teatro Capitol presented it again on September 8, 1924, during a special gala night. This time, Calles joined the roster of actors that included Enriqueta Almenar, Matilde

4. "The Vindication of Our Race on the Celluloid"

Liñán, David A. Martínez, Daniel F. Rea, Romualdo Tirado, José Chávez, and Fernando Navarro. Calles interpreted the Yaqui Indian Ramón, "a beautiful and noble character," who is also "a sad and somber Indian that leads the play to a climactic tragedy when the traitor dies."[8] Evidently, Calles borrowed not only the name but also the character of this play for *El indio yaqui*.

The Teatro Capitol's advertising of *Sangre yaqui* emphasized the participation of Calles: "For the first time in his life, he will make a personal appearance before the Mexican public of Los Angeles," the ad read. Among the special guests that night were the Mexican consul Juan A. Sáenz, vice-consul Lauro Izaguirre, actor Neal Hart, and Lilia Ortiz, the "Queen of the Fiestas Patrias." The Teatro Capitol invited the public for another reprise of Elías González's play on September 12. An ad mentioned that Calles had been a major draw during the previous show; his performance won the applause of many, including his friend Hart. Four months later, in January 1926, the Hidalgo Theater staged *Sangre yaqui*, giving preeminence to the name of Calles in the publicity.[9] Judging from the ad displays, the actor had quite a number of admirers in Los Angeles and the theaters wisely exploited his popularity.[10]

On May 20, a few days before its release at the Teatro Hidalgo, *El indio yaqui* previewed for the press and special guests at the Bard Theater in Hollywood. Attending were the journalists Gabriel Navarro (*La Opinión*), and Salvador Gonzalo Becerra (*El Heraldo de México*). Following this screening, a guest, who was also a director, approached Calles to congratulate him. Intrigued by a scene in the movie, he asked, "How did you manage to do the trick of the wound?" Calles smiled with great satisfaction, making "his teeth sparkle bright white in contrast to the dark color of his skin." Putting aside all modesty, he answered tersely: "That's a secret I and only I know." The scene in question had the Indian Ramón Tollos firing a gun at one of his opponents. The wounded man bent over while a stream of blood slowly came out of his chest. Critic Navarro commended this trick, done while the camera was running and without any editing. He also affirmed, "We could say in honesty that as far as photography, movement, and editing, it is on a par with the better American pictures."[11] More important than its technical accomplishments was its power to arouse the sentiment of Mexicans. Once again, Navarro spoke in favor of *El indio yaqui*:

> Guillermo Calles has laid the cornerstone of the grandiose edifice that will be the vindication of our race on the celluloid. His initial film, produced partly under the eternally blue skies of California and partly upon the exuberant earth of Sonora, has been the first bugle of the moral freedom of the Mexican, who is perpetually denigrated in American movies, always vanquished by the Herculean fists of a son of North America and typed as a source of evil; from whose brain, dark as his face skin, only a morbid erotic pleasure can sprout.... In *El indio yaqui*, on the contrary, Guillermo Calles has infused the soul of the Mexican with the essence of love, tenderness, and heroism. The image of its protagonist goes past the screen leaving in our mind the impression that everything the magazines and movies have said about our noble indigenous race is a crude misrepresentation.[12]

El indio yaqui's radical departure from Hollywood stereotypes brought forth an enthusiastic reception. It struck a sentimental chord among viewers who saw an Indian turned into a hero, a not-so-common happening in the cinema. Calles's interpretation of the brave

Ramón Tollos received the applause of the public while Walter Shumway, in the role of the hateful Morgan, earned the scorn of all. This turnaround surely surprised (but also delighted) Spanish-speaking audiences, who were continuously bombarded by Hollywood's often-derogatory depictions of Mexicans and Indians. A journalist who lauded Calles' movie after attending the preview was Salvador Gonzalo Becerra. Writing for *El Heraldo de México*, he even associated the identity of the film's hero with Calles, establishing the myth that the actor-director was a Yaqui. In addition to the Spanish-language newspapers in Los Angeles, San Antonio's *La Prensa* sang the praises of the picture: "All Mexicans that have seen it so far agree on its merit: because it's something of their own, because it calls to their feelings, because it reveals to the American people an unknown trait of a race that has been ignored; a race that is idealistic and devoted to beauty, that in critical times comes together under the rallying cry of war...."[13]

Other critics were ready to point out the shortcomings of *El indio yaqui*. Writing for *El Heraldo de México*, Armando Vargas de la Maza observed:

> My applause goes to this new effort of the fledgling Mexican cinematography. *El indio yaqui* is a good film, according to the nationalist point of view, and a promise for the future of the industry in Mexico. Unfortunately, I must make note of a big error. Guillermo Calles's movie has been contaminated by the Anglo-Saxon formula, which is one of annoying stupidity. This recipe only considers the hero, the comic, and the traitor, as well as the woman that is moral or immoral, depending on her sexual actions. *El indio yaqui* suffers from the same defect carried on by certain American producers that only make films to please the people living on farms in the central western United States. This absurd tendency ... has given rise to an endless series of pictures whose only aim is to present Mexico in a tribal condition, where the animal instincts of men and the dissolution of women dominate. The only thing Calles did was to invert the roles in this movie. According to its publicity, it is the first picture "where a Mexican defeats a squad of Americans." If it means a retribution for the thousands of films where "an American beats hundreds of Mexicans," then the movie is justified. But I don't believe this is the way to make art and initiate the Mexican cinema industry.[14]

Because they lacked an adequate cinema that expressed their plight, Mexican audiences raised *El indio yaqui* as a cultural symbol and a banner of national pride. Theater impresarios, quick to recognize the extraordinary pull of this movie, programmed it frequently after its release on June 3, 1926. It played mainly at Spanish-language venues, since American theater circuits "cannot accept anything that is not stated in their contracts with the production moguls."[15] As was customary, the film had titles in Spanish and English. The Pastime Theater in Albuquerque, New Mexico, billed it as *The Yaqui Indian* in 1930. A local newspaper recommended the "adventure, tragedy, courage, humiliation, and nobility of the Indian People."[16] Its exhibition in the Southwest was rather extensive, continuing until the end of the decade when most theaters converted to sound.

In order to promote *El indio yaqui*, Calles traveled along the U.S.-Mexico border carrying a print of the film and some stills. One of the places where he possibly exhibited it, after its opening in Los Angeles, was in El Centro, California. Calles was touring the area in mid–July and headed toward Nogales, Sonora. Immigration records show that Calles and José M. Duarte spent the last week of July 1926 in that city. However, it is only a supposition that the movie played here, as there are no records that would confirm a public show-

4. "The Vindication of Our Race on the Celluloid"

ing. Another place that might have been included in this tour was Douglas, Arizona. In August, *El Heraldo de México* mentioned that Perla Rosa, a movie fan from Douglas, had met Calles. She praised the nationalist character of the Tarahumaran actor and director.

The following year, Calles initiated a second tour with Mexico City as a final destination. *El indio yaqui* played simultaneously in six theaters of the capital starting March 31, 1927. The exhibition of a film made by a Mexican was an odd occurrence, as Hollywood unquestionably dominated the market. Out of a total of 508 movies released in Mexico City that year, 460 came from the United States, 42 were imported from other countries, and the remaining six films were Mexican: *El tren fantasma*, *Yo soy tu padre*, *Una catástrofe en el mar*, *Conspiración*, *El indio yaqui*, and *Raza de bronce*. (Actually, Calles was privileged to have two of his pictures released in Mexico City within a three-month period.)

El indio yaqui also played at several theaters in Guadalajara. The Cine Opera announced it on June 18, while the Cuauhtémoc and Royal Theaters billed the picture immediately thereafter. In the port of Veracruz, *El indio yaqui* was shown at the Eslava Theater on June 3, 1927.

Film critics praised *El indio yaqui*, saying, "It will be the vindication of our race on the celluloid ... the moral freedom of the Mexican, who is perpetually denigrated in American movies" (Agrasánchez Film Archive).

Concurrently, another movie house in the same city announced *El puño de hierro*, a local production directed by Gabriel García Moreno. This simultaneous offering of two Mexican pictures in Veracruz was certainly uncommon. García Moreno's picture is one of the few surviving Mexican silent films. The Filmoteca of UNAM (National Autonomous University of Mexico) has restored it.

El indio yaqui played in Mérida, Yucatán, the following month. The program of the Pathé and Esmeralda Theaters included a stage presentation of comedian José Duarte, who was a member of the film's cast. A local newspaper affirmed: "It is the only picture that presents our race without the stigma of denigration, which is prevalent in other productions. A film of great emotions with thrilling scenes, horrible fights and incredible chases, without omitting scenes of authentic comedy performed by the Buster Keaton of Yucatán, José Duarte."[17]

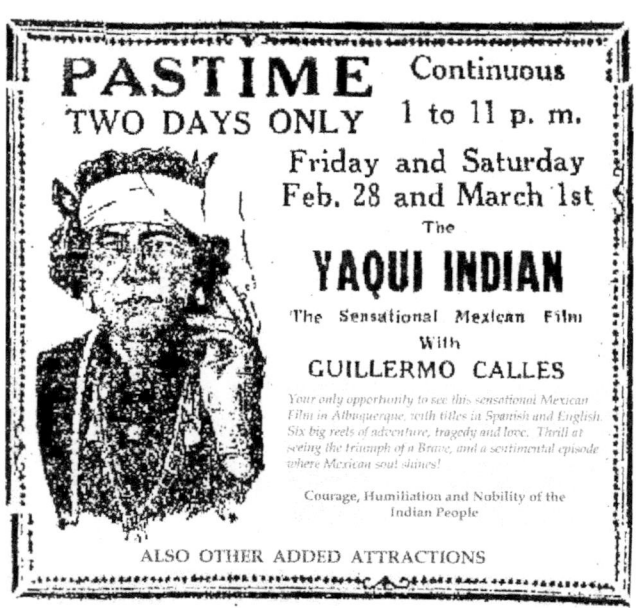

The stoicism of the Indian race was a recurring theme in the movies made by Calles. Newspaper ad for a theater in Albuquerque, New Mexico (Agrasánchez Film Archive).

Prior to making *El indio yaqui*, Calles met Rafael Corella Beltrán, a theater impresario in Mexicali, Baja California. Corella came originally from Guaymas, Sonora, and joined Pancho Villa's army in his younger years. Because he was tall and well-built, people nicknamed him "Corellón." A pioneer in the exhibition business since 1918, Corella established the first permanent movie house in Mexicali in the 1920s, the Teatro México. He also ran the local Teatro Iris, where American pictures often played before their Mexico City release.[18] In addition to the movie business, Corella worked as a public servant for the City of Mexicali in the early 1920s. But his passion was the cinema and he took on the production of several documentaries that highlighted the material progress of the region. He first produced *A través de Sonora* (1924), following with *Baja California* (1925). Presumably, Rafael Corella directed this last film beginning on September 16, 1925, to coincide with the Independence Day festivities. It is assumed that Calles was its principal player. A photograph in the book *Compendio histórico biográfico de Mexicali* shows him surrounded by a crowd and demonstrating his fencing skills. According to this book, the movie "was considered at the time as one of the best made and with more box-office appeal."[19]

Rafael Corella intended to launch a nationalist campaign that could effectively "neutralize the anti–Mexican propaganda" prevalent in the United States.[20] In essence, *Baja California* aimed at publicizing the "natural wonders" of the peninsula to attract tourism. The documentary was part of the broader scheme of Baja California's governor, Abelardo L. Rodríguez, who sought to foment foreign investment and tourism in the region.[21] This was a worthwhile effort, more so since Mexicali had become notorious for illegal activities and rampant crime. Already in 1922, the Spanish-language press in the United States sounded

4. "The Vindication of Our Race on the Celluloid"

the alarm. San Antonio's newspaper *La Prensa* summed up the situation: "Vice constitutes a serious threat to Mexicali. In spite of government regulations, gambling houses and other spots are multiplying. Corruption has taken hold of this unfortunate region since many years ago and [it is] far from diminishing."[22]

Hollywood films of the '20s only contributed to the disrepute of Mexico. An example is Thomas H. Ince's *Shorty's Trip to Mexico* (1922), also released under the title of *Licking the Greasers*. When it played in Los Angeles, an angry newspaper editor exclaimed, "All of the inhabitants of our country are being degraded in an outrageous manner, even calling them by their collective name and without using euphemisms of any kind." This editor continued, "In the movie there is no shortage of the typical Mexican bandits that are completely defeated by the American hero who always comes out victorious; [it is] the same old story."[23] Paramount's *North of the Rio Grande* is another example of this trend. Upon its release, a film critic commented: "In this picture there is an effort to show the Mexican that these people conceive: coward and villain, a professional bandit who runs away at the first gunshot made by an American." Most disturbing was a scene presenting "Mexicans as a bunch of starving cannibals."[24]

Because many films stressed the negative aspects of border towns like Mexicali, Rafael Corella saw the need to counterattack by producing a movie that sang the praises of Baja California. To this end, he sought the patronage of Governor Rodríguez, who had started a transformation of the region. One of the first measures by Rodríguez involved the expansion of the territory's capital, Mexicali. Also of enormous benefit was the elimination of import taxes on building materials, a strategy that led to more construction work in the area. From 1924 to 1927, Mexicali grew substantially, doubling the number of its buildings and increasing the land value of properties. Together with these advancements, the administration supported the creation of labor unions and agricultural cooperatives. In 1923, there was only one labor organization, the League of Chauffeurs, headed by Pablo Burrola. Five years later, this number grew to about 35 unions that included 3,350 members.[25]

Baja California premiered at the Teatro Estella in Los Angeles on March 28, 1926. A few days before, the movie was screened privately at the Rex Theater. Attending this exhibition were the Mexican consul Alfonso Pesqueira, several newspapermen, and some prominent Latin Americans. The press acknowledged that it was "a most instructive and educational film intended to show Lower California as it is." *Baja California*'s release came at a critical moment, while William Randolph Hearst's *The Examiner* made every effort to discredit Mexican politicians like Rodríguez by painting a negative picture of Tijuana and Mexicali. But the *Los Angeles Times* put things in perspective, saying this new movie revealed "Mexico in its true light." The paper also gave some clues regarding the scenes of the film:

> Lower California as a land of progressive cities and developing ranches where respectable businessmen work hard and where lovable home folks have schools, public libraries and sewing clubs is portrayed in a Mexican motion picture that will make its initial appearance in Los Angeles next week. The film was produced ... to offset by a true picture some of the evil and mischief that Mexicans say is being done by certain newspaper interests that give Americans a

sordid and distorted idea of Lower California as a hotbed of vice, corruption and worthlessness.... Vast cotton fields alive with pickers, great cotton gins turning out bales for exportation, extensive cane ranches producing sugar for commerce, flour mills, fishing fleets, water works and many industries are shown in the picture. It shows also well-appearing cities with policed and expansive streets busy with traffic, thousands of cleanly clad children happy in schools, student orchestras and a great agricultural meeting where Gov. Rodríguez is encouraging agriculture.... A considerable amount of explanation and information about the country appears in type in the film. It is in Spanish.[26]

Rafael Corella and Rodríguez knew that the cinema was a superb propaganda medium for the country's material achievements. *Baja California* met with public acceptance, playing repeatedly in theaters along the U.S.-Mexican border. Inspired by this success, Rafael Corella commissioned Alfonso Tovar to write the script for *Raza de bronce*, a film that Calles directed. In November 1926, Corella went to Los Angeles to make the necessary arrangements and to publicize his project. He told the press this movie "would raise the prestige of Mexico but above all, that of Baja California." The producer stated that Calles and Car-

Shot in Mexicali, Baja California, *Raza de bronce* (1927) is considered a lost film of the silent era. This scene shows Calles (back, center) elegantly dressed as the Indian renegade who wants to fit in a different social class. José Domínguez is at left, walking away, and Esther Garcia is at center with Calles (courtesy of Ernie Domínguez).

4. "The Vindication of Our Race on the Celluloid"

men La Roux "will be the main interpreters of the story, in which more that 800 extras will also take part." Tentatively, the female roles were assigned to La Roux and Elisa Araiza, two young Mexican actresses working in Hollywood as extras. La Roux spent a few weeks in Mexicali waiting to appear before the camera but her participation was limited to "a few scenes."[27] The role played by Miss Araiza cannot be established.

Shooting for *Raza de bronce* began in the third week of November 1926. The first scenes were taken at the Agua Caliente resort. As it turned out, another aspiring player, the young Esther García, substituted for La Roux in the female lead. Alfonso Tovar, a journalist for *La Opinión* and an employee of the Mexicali City Hall, not only wrote the film's story but also played the role of a labor leader. Tovar's account tells the dilemma of an Indian (Calles) who falls in love with a young white woman. The Indian gets ridiculed for trying to fit in a different social class; even worse, his own people see him as a renegade. Eventually, the Indian "discovers who he really is, becoming aware of his self worth." Calles's nephew José Domínguez played a humorous villain; a still shows him pompously dressed, imploring the heroine to marry him.

According to historian Gabriel Trujillo Muñoz, *Raza de bronce* included views of "streets

Raza de bronce illustrates the dilemma of an Indian who falls in love with a woman of the white race. Esther García, embracing Calles, played the female lead. José Domínguez tries to jump over the balustrade (courtesy of Ernie Domínguez).

and houses in Mexicali: the interior patio of the Colorado River Land Company building, the house of the Peralta family, the Governor's palace, and empty lots that are now occupied by the Bellavista neighborhood." A small building located along Obregón Avenue and owned by Rafael Corella was converted into a "cinematographic set." According to Trujillo Muñoz, the citizens of Mexicali were extremely enthusiastic and cooperative. He provided more specifics about the film:

> The taxi drivers led by Pablo Burrola (Tarahumara) acted as Indians, wearing wigs brought from Hollywood. Even distinguished gentlemen and señoritas, employees and town's people, participated in social gatherings and other scenes required by the story. The artists that took the main roles: Guillermo *El Indio* Calles, a professional actor and director of the film; Miss Esther García, Sara C. de Villaseñor, José Domínguez, Alfonso Villaseñor, Alfonso Tovar, Eduardo Gastini, Saúl Sanabria ("Cuasimodo"), and others. Some of these people did not have any experience in cinema, and it is surprising that their performance turned out a lot better than what has been the case of some famous artists. Standing out is the participation of the 21st Battalion, commanded by Colonel Juan Castellón under the orders of Captain Fausto Morlett, who executed a praiseworthy job in the "engagements" of the troops.[28]

In addition, Trujillo Muñoz documented several incidents that took place during the making of *Raza de bronce*. While filming the battle scenes, the Indian soldiers were each given five blanks for their guns and certain instructions that they did not understand well. After running out of these innocuous pellets, they started firing the real thing. One gunshot hit the camera, making the photographer jump to the ground; only two people were slightly wounded because of this occurrence. Even more frightening was a violent earthquake that caught everyone by surprise during a banquet given in honor of the film's performers. The anxious guests left the party in a hurry and did not attempt to come back to finish their meal.

A description of an important scene in *Raza de bronce* appeared in the Los Angeles newspaper *El Heraldo de México*. Under the heading "Próximo estreno de una película cinematográfica," a reporter explained:

> One of the key moments of *Raza de bronce* ... was filmed recently in the ravine near the Pasadena barrio of this city [Mexicali]. The 21st Battalion under the command of Captain Fausto Morlett, as well as more than 400 extras, took part in this scene. It simulates an attack by filibusters, who are totally destroyed by three groups united: the army, the organized proletarians with their red and black banner, and the Indians, who likewise feel patriotic love as they leave their hamlets to join in the defense of national integrity. Film director Guillermo Calles, Alfonso Tovar, Alfonso Villaseñor, and First Captain Fausto Morlett, performed the main roles in this scene. In a climatic moment of the battle, señor Tovar, who plays the labor leader Armando, guides his working companions to war, clutching the red and black sign. He and his comrades meet with Captain Morlett to receive orders and they go immediately to the front. Later, when the battle gets tough, [Armando] is shot on the chest; his flag is now picked up by a young student joining as a volunteer, a role performed quite well by Manuel J. Millán. Agonizing, the leader tells him, "Go ahead, save our country!" And the student, waving the flag, leaves Armando and guides the volunteers out of the trench and into enemy territory. No doubt, this scene will be extremely moving when projected on the screen. The role of señor Calles, as the Indian Miguel, was also important in this scene. When the army and the proletarians are fighting from their trench, Miguel appears on his speckled horse fol-

4. "The Vindication of Our Race on the Celluloid"

Another still from *Raza de bronce* helps reconstruct a climactic scene: Guillermo Calles (left) and José Domínguez fight for the love of a girl (courtesy of Ernie Domínguez).

lowed by all the Indians that he picked up from their villages.... Just as he enters the trench, a grenade explodes bringing the horse down and tossing him off into the distance. Miguel gets up with more energy. At the same time a bullet wounds Enrique, played by Eduardo Gastine who is Miguel's mentor. A sad scene takes place. Enraged, Miguel takes the flag from Enrique who is dying; he then comes out of the trench followed by the Indians and they start firing at the enemy.[29]

The debut of *Raza de bronce* took place on February 5, 1927, in Mexicali. The film played for a full week at Rafael Corella's Teatro Iris. An assiduous patron was Governor Abelardo L. Rodríguez, who came to the theater three times to watch the movie. On the first day, box-office receipts amounted to approximately $1,200, an exceptional gross that illustrates the excitement of the locals who went to see themselves acting in a picture. Producer Rafael Corella said he had spent about $7,000 to make the film and that everybody in town gladly helped him to achieve his end, "thinking that Mexicali would become the Mecca of the national cinema." Corella also stated that he obtained $6,000 for the distribution rights of *Raza de bronce* in California, Arizona, New Mexico, and Texas.[30]

Two weeks after the exhibition of *Raza de bronce* at the Teatro Iris, the *Los Angeles Times* gave some more details:

The Bronze Race, a Mexican film with a Mexican plot, was recently released by the Francisco M. Corella Film Producing Company at Mexicali. The show attracted the biggest throng ever seen in Mexicali, it is said. Several Hollywood men engaged in the motion picture business were especially invited to the premiere, among them David Biederman, representing Warner Brothers, who highly praised the production and proclaimed it as one of the best Mexican pictures. The plot deals with the struggles in the early days of Lower California, when several groups of adventurers tried to take possession of the territory, lured by the tales of richness widely spread by fishermen and miners of those days. Love, thrills, the selfish efforts of the villain to marry the heroine, and the constant fight of the hero to turn the events to a successful end, make up this film. Gen. A. L. Rodríguez, Governor of the Northern District, gave every assistance to the enterprise and, on one occasion, allowed 200 troops of the Twenty-first Battalion to assist in the filming of one of the most thrilling scenes, which required an engagement between the adventurers and the organized laborers, Indians and farmers, who fought in defense of Lower California.[31]

That the producer of *Raza de bronce* was paid $6,000 for the distribution of the film in the United States is merely a hint of its extensive exploitation. In Los Angeles, it opened at the Teatro Hidalgo the night of April 4, 1927. The local newspaper, *El Heraldo de México*, ran a series of ads promoting the picture. It also included a dramatic photograph of a battle, in which several men are shooting at the enemy and a woman is seen protecting a frightened child. To heighten the interest of readers, the paper made a few suggestive comments:

> It is expected that the public will like the movie because it entails a great deal of romanticism, both in the merely patriotic subject matter and in the realm where Cupid makes use of his weaponry. The work ... has very engaging moments, above all those dealing with the invasion of Mexican territory by a band of filibusters. The movie shows clearly the great knowledge of Guillermo Calles regarding film technique. We can also appreciate the artistic merit of a fellow compatriot who has gone unnoticed in the performing arts: Esther García. This girl could be a good actress if she is given the necessary [training].... She has a pretty figure and photogenic qualities, posing at ease before the camera. She doesn't seem like a beginner but appears to know already the underpinnings of the cinema.[32]

Several California theaters advertised the movie with its English title *The Bronze Race*. Charging fifteen cents admission, Oakland's Broadway Theater presented it on July 26 and 27, 1927, calling it "the Mexican super-production [with] Esther García and Guillermo Calles; positively different from anything you have ever seen." The following month, *The Bronze Race* played in conjunction with an American film at the Hayward Theater in Hayward. One ad proclaimed, "A special Mexican picture, a novelty picture; titles in English and Spanish; no advance in prices."[33]

When Rafael Corella tried to book *Raza de bronce* in the Mexico City theaters he met with resistance on the part of an important distributor, the Spaniard Germán Camus. Although Camus had been involved in the production of some of the earliest Mexican movies, he was reluctant to promote anything that came out of Latin American studios. Camus had pretentiously stated, "These countries will not be able to make or create movies in a hundred years." Using some political force, though, Corella convinced Camus to distribute the film. When it finally opened in Mexico City, the producer received a telegram informing him of the "resounding success" of *Raza de bronce* on the opening date. It played

José Domínguez was the villain in all the silent films directed by Calles. Still from *Raza de bronce* (courtesy of Ernie Domínguez).

in the capital at thirteen theaters; the reviews hailed it as "the best production so far presented."[34]

Theaters catering to Mexicans in Los Angeles continuously ran *Raza de bronce* long after its initial release. Illustrating its popularity are the many newspaper ads promoting the picture. For special celebrations in the community, exhibitors invariably included a screening of this nationalistic film. Because of the wide exposure of his movies, people regarded Calles as a stanch advocate of "La Raza" (The Race), a term invoking patriotic feelings among Mexican immigrants. From his early days as an extra and supporting actor in Hollywood's serials to his starring roles in *El indio yaqui* and *Raza de bronce*, Calles's career seemed to be on the rise. Driven by the public's acceptance, he designed other stories that were suited to his personality and modest resources.

5

The Popular Appeal of Guillermo Calles's Films

Since the 1920s, theaters on North Main Street in Los Angeles were favorite entertainment spots for Hispanics. These establishments provided movies, plays, and vaudeville to a varied clientele made up mainly of the working class. All year round, there was always a live or filmed spectacle advertised on the marquees of the México, Hidalgo, Principal, Capitol, and Estella theaters. In addition to Hollywood second-runs, they brought the latest films from south of the border. Mexican cinema gathered momentum in 1928, when an avalanche of new and old pictures hit the local screens. Among the most publicized were *Juan soldado, El caballero misterioso, San Juan de Ulúa, El vuelo de Lindbergh a México, Un drama en la aristocracia, El Cristo de oro, El tren fantasma, Los guerreros del aire* and *Sol de gloria*. Besides these melodramas and action pictures, the public had the opportunity to see an assortment of documentaries. For example, *La revolución mexicana* brought to life events of the recent past; *El Niño Fidencio* revealed a miraculous folk healer of northern Mexico; and an innovative Movietone reel presented the king of Spain, Alfonso XIII, whose first recorded message was heard by the audience.

In March 1928, the Teatro México announced *Sol de gloria*, Calles' most recent film, with Spanish and English titles. A company formed by Calles in association with exhibitors Benjamín Aranda and José Elías, Independencia Productions, flamboyantly advertised the movie as the "Non Plus Ultra." It starred Calles, Carmen La Roux, José Domínguez, and Carlos Molina. The good-looking Molina was a musician making his screen debut. Actress La Roux appeared previously in *The Scarlet Brand*, a 1927 serial starring and directed by Neal Hart in which Calles took a small part. Born in Durango, Mexico, La Roux came to Hollywood in 1918 to work as "extra talent," later moving up to starring roles in the early thirties. She also appeared with John Wayne and Mary Kornman in the Western *The Desert Trail* (1935). The performance of José Domínguez stood out in *Sol de gloria*, creating an abominable villain that left audiences in a state of shock. In addition to Domínguez, a sister and a niece of director Calles appeared in the movie: María de Jesús Calles and Belén Espinosa, respectively.

Unfortunately, no print of *Sol de gloria* has survived and the film's plot is equally missing. Calles directed a remake in 1938 under the title of *Pescadores de perlas*. This sound movie has been preserved and can be turned into a useful guide for the reconstruction of *Sol de gloria*'s story. Also throwing light on the silent film are a few scene stills recently uncovered. One shows a machete duel between two adversaries on horseback; one of them is an

Indian (Calles) and the other is a villain (Domínguez). In a second picture, some soldiers appear to be intimidating the Indian and his mother (María de Jesús Calles), while the villain mockingly watches the scene. Finally, a *Sol de gloria* production still reveals the participants of the film during a break, posing candidly for the camera outside of a building. The director is standing next to his brother, Juan Calles, and other unidentified persons. María de Jesús Calles, José Domínguez, and Carlos Molina are also in the group. Several actors and staff members are wearing sweaters and heavy coats, on what was probably a cold winter day.

Conceding that *Pescadores de perlas* closely follows the story of *Sol de gloria*, we can advance an outline of the silent movie's plot. This is a tale of romance and adventure set in a remote village near the ocean. After a shipwreck, the beautiful Rosa (La Roux) is rescued by Nacho, a half–Indian who falls in love with her but keeps his sentiments secret. Paco de Moncada (Molina), a pearl hunter and a loyal friend of Nacho, is also attracted to her. The unscrupulous Lencho (Domínguez) kills Paco's brother and puts the blame on Nacho. Unable to prove his innocence, the Indian hides in the jungle. Some time later, he is caught and sentenced to the firing squad. But the true killer is exposed at the last minute and Nacho is freed. Rosa finds an old letter revealing that Nacho and Paco are in reality brothers. At sunset, and during a fierce battle against Lencho's army, a bullet hits the Indian and he dies in the arms of Rosa.

L.A.'s Spanish-language press at once acknowledged *Sol de gloria* as a prestigious Mexican film. *La Opinión* appraised its "emotional scenes, very colorful, with art, talent, soul, and feeling provided by its actor and author Guillermo Calles." Using striking ads, the Teatro México launched an effective campaign to promote the film. Alluring graphics and sensational phrases tipped off the public: "The best Mexican picture in which the main attrac-

TEATRO MÉXICO
| MIERCOLES 25 | | MIERCOLES 25 |

PENULTIMA DIA.---EXHIBICION DE LA FORMIDABLE PELICULA MEXICANA

'SOL DE GLORIA'

INTRIGA, AMOR, Combates, Fusilamiento, Naufragio, Cocodrilos hambrientos, Voraces tiburones, Panoramas del México bello y mil detalles emocionantes contiene esta portentosa película.

Nuevo y original PROLOGO donde a la vista del público hace explosión un barco yéndose a pique.

YA ESTA UD. PREPARADO PARA CONCURRIR AL HOMENAJE A ROSA FUERTES LA GLORIOSA CREADORA DE LA TRAPERA?

Sábado 28 Debut de la Gentil Artista CARMEN RODRIGUEZ

Sol de Gloria premiered at Los Angeles's Teatro México in 1928. An ad recommended: "Intrigue, love, combats, executions, shipwreck, starving crocodiles, voracious sharks, and a thousand thrills" (Agrasánchez Film Archive).

tions are love, intrigue, mystery, ferocious animals, executions, and thrilling scenes of great excitement." The publicity also capitalized on the names of famous personalities who were invited to the premiere: Lita Grey Chaplin, Edith Johnson, Roy D'Arcy, William Duncan and Barry Norton. For several days, flashy ads kept the excitement high.[1]

Meanwhile, the newspaper *El Heraldo de México* reported on the making of *Sol de gloria* and the people who sponsored it. Calles acknowledged his associate Benjamín Aranda, who advanced the money to produce the film. He also expressed gratitude to Enrique Ferreira, the Mexican consul in San Diego. The consul recommended Calles to the authorities of Ensenada, Baja California, where he shot the scenes of battles between Federal soldiers and "bandidos." On his predicament in trying to manage the aspects of production and direction in *Sol de gloria*, Calles explained:

> I am not able to do what other directors working for big companies are allowed to do. They usually make one or two scenes in a day of work, because they repeat each scene until it comes out perfect. Instead, I have to make sixty or seventy scenes in only one day, because I don't have enough resources. I am forced to finish a movie in a short period, as I wouldn't be able to pay my people if I used more days. Nor would I be in a position to disburse the enormous amount of money [that people] squander on film stock.[2]

A writer for *El Heraldo de México*, Gustavo Solano, whose pen name was "El Conde Gris," highlighted the temperament of the movie's principal character:

> The protagonist of *Sol de gloria* is a descendant of the Bronze Race; an Aztec Indian, proud and dignified; sensitive to the soul's delicate emotions, strong in the fight, unselfish in his love for a woman that is cast by the ocean, fragile and courteous when he approaches the white virgin; so courteous and fragile that he covers his eyes to avoid the embarrassment of the girl, to whom he offers an Indian linen as a shield to her nudity. And if this didn't suffice, the man's subtlety surprises us [when we hear] a parrot summoning him; the Indian walks away daydreaming of the caress of the stars. If this were an American movie, we are certain that the opposite would have occurred. The Indian, lascivious, his nostrils swelling, would have rushed at the provocative woman with an urge to satisfy his animal desires. In the fight, he would have appeared as a coward that attacks from behind, a savage lying in wait for his victim. But Calles, whose inside bears the flashing soul of the race, created an Indian that is a poem of love, sweetness, nobility and heroism. [He says] deliberate phrases like these: "Doesn't an Indian possess by any chance a heart for love?" ... And the public bursts in applause.... Calles has made a work of art with his "Indio Nacho." His allegations are authentic; it is his own life, a life of struggles, dreams and strenuous work, constantly besieged by villains. But [just as] the Indian triumphs over the villain, Guillermo Calles hopes to succeed in the future, overcoming fate like in *Sol de gloria*.[3]

A reporter from *La Opinión* stressed the audience's positive response to *Sol de gloria*. It mentioned that on the first day of showing, "At eight o'clock, there were at the door more than two hundred people swirling about the box office, on which a disheartening sign appeared: 'No More Seats.'" The reporter also declared:

> The picture is worth everything that has been said about it, and the only thing to lament is that it was not produced in an environment more encouraging than ours.... As a director, author, and protagonist, Guillermo Calles has improved himself. In addition to him, the highest honors for the interpretation go to José Domínguez and Carmencita La Roux, who wit-

Calles (center) brought his sister, María de Jesús Calles de Calvillo, to appear in the film *Sol de Gloria* (1928). At left is José Domínguez and at right is Carlos Molina (courtesy of Ernie Domínguez).

nessed from her seat a long and deserved applause by the audience. Carlos Molina has a good look, but we deemed his expression a little timid, revealing a beginner in contrast to Domínguez, who would surely stand out in American productions of first class. His villain was certainly convincing. A live prologue, arranged by one of the theater's actors, preceded the film's screening. Calles, who got a prolonged applause, took part in this act, as well as [Romualdo] Tirado and the rest of the stage company.... It is a pity that the theater does not have sufficient capacity to hold everyone in our community in Los Angeles, so that they could see a young artist of brilliant future like Guillermo Calles.[4]

It is estimated that more than 10,000 spectators attended the screening of *Sol de gloria* during its first five days at the Teatro México. Targeting the people's longing for the homeland, an ad recommended, "The movie ... has a fully Mexican atmosphere, the members of the army in our country having participated in it, with the location scenes entirely shot in Baja California." The success of *Sol de gloria* in Los Angeles brought instant recognition to its cast. La Roux, for example, presided over several social events in her honor. Producers began to pay attention to her and offered her a number of movies. Domínguez made another film with Calles and later appeared in dozens of Hollywood productions.

5. The Popular Appeal of Guillermo Calles's Films

A high point in *Sol de Gloria*: The noble Indian engages in a machete duel with an opponent (José Domínguez, left) (Rudy Calles Collection).

Taking advantage of *Sol de gloria*'s initial success, the Teatro México reprised it the following month, as a special presentation in honor and for the benefit of the main interpreters. Leading the list of special guests were Antonio Moreno and Neal Hart, two of Calles's most famous friends. Also attending were the producers of the picture, Benjamín Aranda and José Elías. *La Opinión* reported on the highlights of this presentation:

> With the presence of the prestigious Spanish film artist Antonio Moreno and other screen luminaries like the star Neal Hart, Joe Rickson, and Mr. Lloyd Ingraham, a pleasant party took place at the Teatro México last Thursday night, in honor of the cast of the great Mexican picture *Sol de gloria*. Señor Moreno and the rest of the special guests remained in their reserved seats throughout the night and left only when the event concluded. Following the exhibition of the film, and with a full house, Gabriel Navarro took the stage to give a brief speech and introduced Antonio Moreno and his famed companions. The public honored all of them with a massive applause and the orchestra cheerfully sounded the reveille…. The salient musical number was without a doubt [the one performed by] the orchestra of the "Gigolós," a real surprise for all of us. The director of the orchestra is Carlos Molina, who portrays the young Paco de Moncada in *Sol de gloria*. Alfonso Bussón, spokesperson of the Teatro México, introduced the

cast of the movie. At the end of the festival, Carmencita La Roux and José Domínguez danced the typical "jarabe tapatío."⁵

The film's popular appeal seemed to be on the rise, as it played once again in the same theater "on the occasion of the inauguration of the superb building of the City Hall" and to accompany the festivities of downtown Main Street. In order to draw a large clientele, admission was lowered to 20¢ adults, 15¢ children. Newspaper ads continued to target the public, giving a few more hints about *Sol de gloria*: "Intrigue, love, combats, executions, a shipwreck, hungry crocodiles, voracious sharks, panoramic views of beautiful Mexico, and a thousand moving details." To top it all off, the theater's April 25 program included a "new and original prologue where the audience witnesses an explosion followed by the sinking of a boat." Such dramatic acts on the stage were inspired by the famous prologues of Sid Grauman's Chinese Theater in Hollywood. Under the direction of Romualdo Tirado and Ernesto González Jiménez, the Teatro México adopted this strategy to draw attention to the exhibition of a new movie.

Parallel to the exhibition of *Sol de gloria*, a new Hollywood production starring Dolores

Production still taken during the shooting of *Sol de Gloria*. Guillermo Calles (second from left) standing next to his brother Juan (fourth) and his sister María de Jesús Calles de Calvillo (fifth). Betty Brown and Carlos Molina stand beside María, while José Domínguez (wearing hat) kneels in front and Carmen La Roux stands third from right (Rudy Calles Collection).

del Río was released in Los Angeles. The United Artists Theater, located on Broadway and Ninth Street, announced *Ramona*, touted as Edwin Carewe's "supreme romance." An ad for the movie read: "Loved by a white, loved by an Indian; she loved both of them." Obviously, there was an underlying theme in *Sol de gloria* and *Ramona*: the defense of the Indian race. Both films romantically described the plight of aboriginal cultures, threatened by the "overwhelming thrust of the whites." Although they possessed distinct personalities, a journalist regarded Guillermo Calles and Dolores del Río as the standard-bearers of ethnic pride among Hollywood's Hispanic artists.

Competing for a share of the Mexican audience, Charles Chaplin's *The Circus* played at Sid Grauman's Chinese Theater, enhanced by a stage prologue that featured clowns and acrobats. A film that spurred a controversy was a documentary about the folk healer "El Niño Fidencio." The Spanish-language press denounced this Fox production as offensive. Seemingly, some intertitles were made "with the intention to prove that Mexico is a hungry, ragged, degenerate, and wretched country." Even the Mexican consulate protested its exhibition, but the film company refused to pull it out, alleging that a lot of money had gone into its promotion.[6]

Sol de gloria continued playing in Ensanada, Baja California, where Calles personally presented it in May. Many people were attracted to this exhibition because some of the film's scenes were shot there. In August, its director went to Fresno, California, for a showing at the Lyceum Theater, where more than 1,410 persons bought tickets to the movie and many more did not get a seat because of the theater's small size. Calles addressed the public briefly after the exhibition of his film. In the nearby town of Delano, the Star Theater took advantage of Mexican Independence Day and exhibited *Sol de gloria* on the night of September 15. A second Mexican production, *El Cristo de oro*, was also shown. Following the screening of both movies, Calles was invited to speak to the audience, culminating his speech with the traditional "Viva México!" a patriotic cry in honor of Mexican Independence. Lastly, a band played the Mexican and American national anthems.

In October, the Teatro México requested Calles's film *Raza de bronce* as the main attraction for the festivities of "Día de la Raza," or Columbus Day. In addition to the screening of the picture, a stage act entitled "Homenaje a la Raza" was presented. That same month, audiences had a chance to see *El indio yaqui*, which was brought back to the Teatro México. Other establishments like the Teatro Principal met the current demand for grass-roots spectacles by programming *Sol de gloria*. A few days later, the Principal offered to its clientele *La Virgen del Tepeyac*, a melodrama with religious overtones. (It was released in Mexico as *El milagro de la Guadalupana*.) Celia Montalván, a popular vaudeville actress, headed its cast interpreting a devoted Catholic woman whose love redeems a man who had lost faith in God. To bolster its prestige, manager Dionisio Acosta promoted the Principal as "El As de los Teatros de la Calle Main" (the Ace of theaters on Main Street), while also stressing it was the only theater on North Main Street "in the hands of a Mexican company."

Because of the extensive exhibition of his movies, Calles prevailed as the leading Mexican filmmaker in the Los Angeles community. His productions were in great demand at Spanish-language theaters on Main Street. These movies attracted audiences that gathered to celebrate holidays and patriotic events. They also drew crowds at philanthropic shows and other fund-raisers. In no small way, Calles's association with several exhibitors added to the commercial success of his films. For example, behind the financing of *Sol de gloria* was Benjamín Aranda, who had a theater circuit in Brawley, California. Similarly, the producer of *Raza de bronce*, Rafael Corella, was Mexicali's most important exhibitor.[7]

Calles was not the only one producing independent films in 1928; a few other modest filmmakers also tried their luck. Oriel Lester Adams, for instance, took his crew to Sonora, Mexico, and directed *El caballero misterioso*. Debuting in this movie was the singer Laura Espinoza de los Monteros, who was accompanied by the popular orchestra of Adolfo Girón. Julieta Marks and Enrique Aguilar performed some of the other roles. Ann Newhardt Adams wrote the story and a photographer from Paramount Pictures, Frederick E. Kalfer, was responsible for the camerawork.[8]

At the beginning of June 1928, Calles announced that he was preparing to shoot a new movie, *Dios y ley*. The plan called for filming in one of the Hollywood studios, with outdoor scenes in the coastal area of Oxnard. The newspaper *La Opinión* gave a few tidbits: "Its story will be Mexican like the previous ones, and it will have an all–Mexican cast....

On Main Street, Los Angeles, the Teatro México (formerly the Grand Opera House) was the center for Spanish-language live entertainment and films. Photograph April 1936 (Agrasánchez Film Archive).

5. The Popular Appeal of Guillermo Calles's Films

Probably, as was true of his previous film, this one will be backed by the Aranda enterprise and it will include Carmen Castillo as its principal female star."⁹ In the end, Castillo, who had recently appeared in *El Robin Hood mexicano*, did not act in the movie because shooting was postponed.

Plans for *Dios y ley* were constantly changing during the following months. Early in July, Calles announced a trip to Mexico City, where he would seek support for this new project. The press said that other artists were to accompany him in his journey, among them Carmen La Roux. Calles later mentioned that another performer, Carmen Guerrero, would star in *Dios y ley*, now scheduled for production before the end of the year. *La Opinión* made known that the beautiful Guerrero was "ready to leave for Colombia in order to make a movie under the auspices of the government of the Sister Republic." However, Guerrero decided to stay in Los Angeles. It was also suggested that Calles's next movie would include Carlos Molina in a leading role. Molina was a musician from Colombia who had just debuted as an actor in *Sol de gloria*. The name of a Brazilian performer, Oliverio Guillermo, popped up in this discussion, hinting that he would play a heavy.¹⁰ As it turned out, neither Molina nor the Brazilian actor took part in Calles's upcoming venture.

The director went back to Mexico City for the premiere of *Sol de gloria*, which took place at the Teatro Palacio on November 14, 1928. Well in advance of its release, a local daily ran several photographs of scenes from the film. Barely two months later, Calles started a tour of Texas accompanied by Carmen La Roux and the business agent T. Contreras. They carried with them prints of *Sol de gloria* and *El indio yaqui*. After a screening in Houston, the movies opened at San Antonio's Teatro Nacional in January 1929.

The Nacional was the top entertainment house for Hispanics in that city. Among the people invited to the premiere were the Mexican consul and the staff of the Spanish-language newspaper *La Prensa*. This publication explained that Calles and La Roux were traveling in the U.S. Southwest "promoting two of their best pictures, as well as making personal appearances in which they talk about their work and their goal of creating a Mexican cin-

Because of the wide acceptance of his movies, Calles prevailed as the leading Mexican filmmaker in the U.S. Southwest. Newspaper ad for the release of *Dios y ley* (1929) (Agrasánchez Film Archive).

ematographic industry." Commenting on *Sol de gloria*, the paper noted, "Its theme is beautiful and filled with emotion; its landscapes are all Mexican.... In one word, it is a movie that had it been put out by the American studios, it would have traveled the world around by now." *La Prensa* also stated that the film "synthesizes the abnegation, valor, suffering, and dignity of the battle-hardened Aztec race. It is the story of an Indian who fought against the adversities of life, finding a way to provide happiness to the woman he loved." Finally, an ad invited the public to come to the theater and see "the intelligent little dog Águila that performs admirably in the picture."[11]

The Teatro Nacional screened *Sol de gloria* one more time the last week of February. To complement this exhibition, Calles and La Roux presented an amusing live show entitled "De San Antonio a Hollywood." The audience had the opportunity to see the actress execute several songs and dances. Other local talents also took part in this performance. Apparently the movie drew the attention of a large segment of Mexicans in San Antonio, including restaurant owner José López, who decided to name his business Sol de Gloria. It served Mexican food and was located near the Nacional Theater, on Santa Rosa Avenue. López announced it profusely in the pages of the local daily *La Prensa*: "Here you can taste the exquisite Mexican food; our menu is the least expensive and our service is the best; lunch, coffee and desert for fifteen cents."

During their stay in San Antonio, the interpreters of *Sol de gloria* shared with the press some of their immediate plans. La Roux intended to go to Spain to show her film. Calles indicated his wish to travel to Colombia, where he would take charge "of the principal motion picture studios in that Republic." (None of these plans materialized.) A more pressing task for the director was to continue touring other Texas cities. In February, he exhibited *Sol de gloria* and *El indio yaqui* in Galveston and Corpus Christi. The personal appearance of Calles and La Roux attracted large crowds. Corpus Christi's Teatro Azteca was in short supply of seats for three consecutive nights. The theater was packed with people, and "a multitude had to watch the picture standing up for two or three hours."[12]

Calles's itinerary also included the Rio Grande Valley. He went to Brownsville and crossed the border to exhibit his films in Matamoros, Tamaulipas. An immigration record shows that Calles re-entered the U.S. at the Brownsville International Bridge on March 20, 1929. At the end of April, *Sol de gloria* played at the Teatro Independencia in Nuevo Laredo, Tamaulipas. The following month, it had a run in San Diego, California. The local Germania Hall announced its exhibition but at the last minute there were some difficulties with the Fire Department and the show was canceled in spite of the public's enthusiasm to see the film. A few weeks later, the picture played at the same city's U.S. Theater, with the added participation of Carmen La Roux. The theater's management made it known that the actress "would perform several acts and explain a few incidents that took place during the filming of *Sol de gloria*."[13]

With fresh enthusiasm, the resolute Calles embarked on a new cinematic adventure. Proclaimed as a "Mexican story and with some new surprises in its technical aspect," *Dios y ley* started production in Los Angeles at the end of June 1929. Although originally planned as a silent feature, its director left open the possibility of eventually incorporating a musi-

5. The Popular Appeal of Guillermo Calles's Films

cal recording simultaneous with the film. The cast was made up of Calles, Carmen Guerrero, José Domínguez, Juan Martínez, and Plácido Siqueiros. Some members of the director's family appeared in the film: doña Anatolia Guerrero, María de Jesús Calles de Calvillo, and Margarita Calles, the director's mother, sister, and niece, respectively. Prior to *Dios y ley*, Carmen Guerrero was only known for her roles in a Spanish-language two-reeler, *Un fotógrafo distraído*, and the feature *Ruben Goes West*. Afterwards, she became a leading star in several Mexican talkies. The popularity of José Domínguez as a baddie was already established in *Sol de gloria*; it was no surprise that his interpretation in *Dios y ley* made people loathe him.

Fidel Murillo, a critic writing for *La Opinión*, lauded the film and said of Calles that his "eternal faith in the future" alone made possible this new project. Murillo also declared that *Dios y ley* "is worthy of praise because it represents an endeavor of a group of Mexicans who with no money, in a place where gold buys everything, and without resources, where competition is formidable, equipped only with their enormous faith, have set out to conquer."[14] During an interview for the magazine *Ilustrado*, Calles spoke of the difficulties

To keep production budgets low, Calles often invited friends and relatives to collaborate in his films as in this dramatic scene from ***Dios y ley***. At left is mother Anatolia Guerrero de Calles, fourth from left is sister María de Jesús Calles de Calvillo, and behind her is niece Margarita Calles. Belén Calles de Espinosa is the third girl from right (courtesy of Ernie Domínguez).

he encountered as an independent filmmaker and hinted at how much money was invested in *Dios y ley*: "Tell our fellow countrymen that they should take into account, more than my artistic skill, my enormous effort. I am absolutely sure that for a picture that costs no less than $50,000, I have been forced to make it with only a quarter or a fifth of that amount." Loreley, who was reporting for *Ilustrado*, suggested to Calles that he should approach the big companies and pre-sell them his film projects in order to obtain ample funds for production. Calles only smiled and answered: "It seems that you don't know this industry. To sell means to become a slave: altering the story, using inadequate clothes, etc. I am more familiar with my country and I know how to make movies. Seeing over and over the same distortions of the truth make me sad."[15]

Following four weeks of incessant work, the filming of *Dios y ley* culminated with scenes taken at Malibu Beach, a favorite summer spot among Hollywood stars. Visiting the set was journalist Gabriel Navarro, who arrived in time to watch a climactic moment of the story. The description of what he saw offers excellent information on the plot of this lost movie:

> The scenes are supposed to be taking place in Mexico, opening with the wonderful views of the Tehuantepec Isthmus and closing with the catastrophe caused by the volcano of Colima, in 1900. The production includes more than a hundred people, counting the main cast and the extras.... The story has developed from a discreet beginning, growing in interest toward the final scenes. Here, panic prevails in every corner, while the Colima volcano throws up fire and the nearby villages fall down like castles in the air.... The last scene of *Dios y ley* was filmed near the sea.... In the background, [I saw] the ruins of a former splendid residence, now destroyed by the fury of the volcano. Dead people cover the fields and villagers are running in panic. The flames from the ruined house illuminate the scene with a macabre and tragic blaze. Daniel is on the ground, cast by the earthquake. Jenaro, his eternal rival, has arrived opportunely to take revenge. Assisted by two of the bandits, he performs a sinister act on the unfortunate Indian: With a burning stick, and in the middle of a savage scream that mixes the murderer's anguish and pleasure, he blinds forever Daniel's eyes.... The scene is so real that, without a doubt, it will make spectators shiver in horror when projected on the screen. Calles (Daniel) acts in a way that we have never seen; Domínguez's (Jenaro) facial expression is one of ferocious madness.... The performance of Carmen Guerrero (Elisa) is one of pure anguish, while the gesture of Juan Martínez (Ernesto Ochoa) reveals a definitive resolve.[16]

Three days prior to its formal opening, *Dios y ley* previewed for a selected number of viewers at the Teatro México. There were several newspaper reporters and the film's main cast: Calles, Guerrero, Domínguez, Juan Martínez, and Plácido Siqueiros. Also present were Xavier Cugat, Carmen Castillo, Delia Magaña and other local artists. On August 30, 1929, the México opened its doors to the public for the exhibition of *Dios y ley*. The theater had just been renovated and re-decorated, adding some detail work "that make it look like an Aztec temple." At the entrance, there were paintings symbolic of Mexican folklore, the charro tapatío and the china poblana. The management designed an attractive publicity campaign for the occasion. Newspaper ads were fancier and larger than usual, adorned with eye-catching displays and phrases: "Better than *Raza de bronce*, more beautiful than *Sol de gloria*, superior to *El indio yaqui*." Emulating the opening of Hollywood movies, six powerful searchlights outside of the theater drew the attention of people in the streets. An ad read, "Follow the light beams that will take you directly to the doors of the theater." To make the opening more glamourous, the management invited several Hollywood luminaries and hired a photographer to film the event. Maestro Ernesto González Jiménez wrote a musical accompaniment specifically for the movie, and Romulado Tirado designed a lively prologue featuring thirty artists on stage. Record-breaking attendance during a ten-day showing of *Dios y ley* obliged the exhibitor to bring the picture back the following month. This time, the proceeds went to the participants of the movie, who appeared on the stage accompanied by all the extras.

Sound films in the Spanish language were beginning to be produced, not only by Hollywood's principal studios but also by a few daring Latin American artists seeking a place in the industry. For instance, the Cuban-born René Cardona debuted as an actor and participated as a co-producer in *Sombras habaneras*. Put out by the Cuban International Films and Hispania Talking Films, this five-reel picture featured Jacqueline Logan, Juan Torena, Paul Ellis and Cardona. Concurrently, an enterprise known as the Sono-Art Company made a Spanish-language version of the film *Blaze O'Glory*; entitled *Sombras de gloria*, it starred the Argentine singer José Bohr and Mona Rico. Cardona's movie was released in December of 1929 and the Sono-Art picture opened in January of 1930. Apparently, theater entrepreneurs set out to win the public by converting to sound pictures. In a hurry, the Teatro México made plans for the release of *Sombras habaneras* on December 4. Electrical engineers quickly went in and provided the theater with wiring and amplifiers. On opening night, though, the sound system failed and the program was postponed. The audience had to come back a few days later to watch the movie, but "they could not resist their desire to laugh because of the weird noise that was heard." Some people complained about this deficiency and criticized the dialogue, which was "translated directly from English, infested with incomprehensible French, and the actors speaking in all the languages except in Spanish."[17]

Meanwhile, Calles was moving swiftly to provide sound to *Dios y ley*. By doing this, he became the first Mexican to add synchronized sound to a feature-length movie. Thus, *Dios y ley* was innovative because it included background music and dialogue recorded on a disc. Stage actors lent their voices for the film's soundtrack. In early December, the movie with sound was presented to a selected audience at the Eastman labs in Hollywood. The experiment, however, did not please some of the viewers. A journalist not only yelled at the film's inaccurate depiction of reality but also disapproved of its sound improvements. Dissatisfied, he let it known in an article for the newspaper *La Opinión*.

> In *Dios y ley*, we notice the simulation of a regional story: a Tehuantepec and a Colima in the style of Hollywood. It is an improbable plot that has many humorous situations brought forth by the fantasy of Calles. In the middle of Tehuantepec, we see "charros" from Tamaulipas and "tehuanas" lacking in their characteristic hieratic attitudes; a social order that does not exist and a conflict of the sexes that is not known, adding to it a caveman who has been transplanted from the Stone Age. Captivated by the craze of talking pictures, Calles decided to synchronize *Dios y ley*, and that is what we saw. Instead of improving it, the effort damages the film. During its nine reels, there are barely two or three with dialogue, but the dialogues are done without talent, using phrases lacking meaning or emotion, and the musical accompaniment is monotonous.[18]

"For a picture that costs 50,000 dollars, I have been forced to make it with only a quarter or a fifth of that amount," Calles said. One of the participants in *Dios y ley* was the dog Águila (Rudy Calles Collection).

5. The Popular Appeal of Guillermo Calles's Films

José Domínguez played an obnoxious villain in *Dios y ley*. His characterizations really made people loathe him (courtesy of Ernie Domínguez).

More criticism was voiced in January 1930, when *Dios y ley* played in Phoenix, Arizona. This time, someone in the audience took offense because the film did not reflect local customs. M. Gavila, a resident of Phoenix, wrote to the editor of *La Opinión* protesting the exhibition of the picture at the Teatro Plaza. Vehemently, he said that the movie was "degrading for Mexico because the settings and characters do not correspond to the reality of our customs and our life." Gavila rejected the picture outright:

> A movie that pretends to be about traditions in our country and is presented as the first Mexican picture spoken in Spanish, follows a false storyline in which there is nothing Mexican.... It portrays savage and criminal lives; just as it was done before by Hollywood when they set about to discredit us. In my humble opinion, it is necessary to take precautions so that these pictures are not exhibited in theaters in the United States because, unfortunately, they are bad propaganda for our country and for our fellow compatriots.[19]

Unaware of the heated discussion, Calles started on a promotional trip south of the border. At the beginning of February, the director arrived in Guadalajara and exhibited *Dios y ley* at three theaters: Lux, Cuahutémoc, and Juárez. A local newspaper ad billed it "one

The beautiful Carmen Guerrero starred in *Dios y ley*, one of the first movies with synchronized sound made by a Mexican (courtesy of Dick Domínguez).

of the first singing and spoken pictures in Spanish.... [I]t has been appropriately added some music, and the majority of its scenes have been printed in color, so that the optical effects are all pleasant." This suggests that parts of the movie were tinted, a common method used to create a specific mood. The film represented a true novelty as the majority of the theaters in Guadalajara were still playing silent movies. The theater's publicity made it known that "Señor Calles will personally take charge of the exhibition of his picture; he will appear in person to greet the public, and his intelligent dog Águila will be on the stage."[20] Another ad affirmed that this was the first Mexican movie set in Tehuantepec. Tickets for the first-class Lux Theater cost one peso, a rather pricey admission considering that local theaters showing silent films only charged thirty cents for children and sixty cents for adults.[21]

In Mexico City, Calles programmed his film for a simultaneous release in six theaters starting on March 8. An ad for the Rialto Theater called attention to "the first national effort in talking pictures." Attractive handbills emphasized, "The first Mexican movie provided with music, songs and spoken in Spanish." Immediately, *Dios y ley* played in San Antonio,

Texas. The Teatro Nacional exhibited the silent version on March 24, three months before the theater officially converted to sound. Later, it re-ran *Dios y ley* touting the movie as "the first production in Spanish made by Mexican artists."[22]

Sound movies were picking up in popularity in Los Angeles and some newsreels captured people's attention too. The Teatro México, for example, announced in April 1930, "The first great review of our country, spoken and synchronized by Mexicans with perfect sound; hear and see the new president of Mexico speak to his country; military maneuvers, infantry, cavalry, artillery, and air force in extraordinary drills." The publicity did not give the name of the newsreel but in all probability, it was a Paramount Sound News production of the inauguration of Pascual Ortiz Rubio. Throughout the year, silent motion pictures alternated with some of the first talkies. After exhibiting the reel of President Ortiz Rubio, the México Theater offered a silent movie made by Miguel Contreras Torres, *El león de la Sierra Morena*. A vaudeville show with the comedian Don Catarino complemented this program. Meanwhile, at the popular Teatro Hidalgo, José Bohr's *Sombras de gloria* was hailed as "the first picture completely spoken in Spanish."

A year after its release in Los Angeles, *Dios y ley* came back enhanced "with dialogues in Spanish and a synchronized musical score." The Teatro México scheduled a screening of the movie together with a personal appearance by Calles on July 18, 1930. Providing added appeal, Elena Landeros took the stage previous to the screening to present several Mexican songs. Following this engagement, the picture had a second run at the Hidalgo, a theater that charged lower admission prices and implemented all kinds of strategies to lure the public. It announced, for instance, "A great number of flour bags will be given away to our patrons during a draw." Movies featuring Calles seemed to be a sure shot for this theater, which recycled *El indio yaqui* for the umpteenth time. To help raise funds for the flood victims of Nogales, Sonora, the Teatro México organized in August a special screening of Romualdo Tirado's *La jaula de los leones*. Reyna Vélez, a sister of the famous Lupe Vélez, performed a dance during the function. Also appearing on stage was Calles, who came to the theater with Águila.[23]

September and October were months of particular significance for the majority of Mexicans in Los Angeles. Despite the economic crisis, theaters found ample pretext to celebrate Mexico's Independence Day. The Teatro Estella offered three movies featuring Calles: *De raza azteca*, *Raza de bronce* and *El indio yaqui* were scheduled for September 15, 16 and 17, respectively. The Estella appropriately complemented the billing of *Raza de bronce* with a stage act entitled "Águilas mexicanas." The box office success of *El indio yaqui* motivated the management to hold it over for an extra day. More movies targeting Hispanics came in October, starting with the world premiere of Miguel Contreras Torres's *El águila y el nopal* at the Teatro México. The theater repeated the movie a few days later to celebrate "El día de la raza," or Columbus Day. This time, the management added a special prologue performed by Romualdo Tirado and the popular vaudeville artist La Chata Noloesca.

The patriotic festivities of Mexicans in Los Angeles were not complete without the exhibition of movies with ethnic flavor. On October 17, the México programmed two features. The first one, *Serenata mexicana*, was a two-reeler advertised as "a movie spoken and

Very little is known about *El charro*, a film featuring Guillermo Calles and his wife Angelita Salcedo (Rudy Calles Collection).

sung in Spanish" with Carlota Cortés and José Arias's orchestra. The second was a silent production entitled *El charro*, "by the famous actor Guillermo Calles." Intriguingly, this last movie of six reels is not listed in any filmography of the artist. The appearance of Calles in charro costume is even more unusual because he consistently portrayed Indians in films. This represents perhaps the only time in his career when he played a traditional charro. A couple of stills that were recently found show the actor wearing flashy charro outfits. In a romantic scene, he is offering a flower to his sweetheart, Angelita Salcedo, who was Calles's wife in reality. Guillermo's niece, Margarita Calles, appears in another still of the movie dressed as a China Poblana. *El charro* must have drawn the attention of local audiences because two months later the same theater showed it again.[24]

At the time, Calles was filming a melodrama called *Regeneración*, a.k.a. *La mujer que supo amar*. This five-reel Spanish-language talkie was produced in Hollywood in 1930 with the collaboration of the Areu brothers. Its shooting probably took place during the fall, when the popular Areu stage company gave a series of presentations in theaters of Los Angeles. The cast consisted of the dancer-singer Dorita Ceprano and brothers Enrique, José,

5. *The Popular Appeal of Guillermo Calles's Films*

and Roberto Areu. Also taking part in the film were Oscar Guisado, Juan Aristi, Ramón Muñoz, and Angelita Salcedo de Calles. As with so many Spanish-dialogue Hollywood productions, this film is inaccessible. A transcript of its dialogue has been located in a public archive and consulted for the following synopsis.[25]

The story recounts the life of Roberto (Enrique Areu), a former singer, now an alcoholic who is recovering in a mental hospital. A young actress, Julieta (Dorita Ceprano), and her father visit Roberto and are impressed by his singing abilities. After obtaining consent from the hospital, they arrange for him to perform at their theater. Julieta and Roberto fall in love, but her ex-boyfriend, Carlos (José Areu), is jealous and plots against the newcomer. He makes Roberto drink from a bottle spilled with a drug. Enervated, the young singer loses control and provokes a riot during the show, effectively ending his career. Roberto and Julieta go their separate ways. Years later, she comes across the regenerated Roberto, who has triumphed as an author. Reconciled, they start a new life together.

The original dialogue transcript of *Regeneración* suggests this is a typical urban melodrama with several stage numbers interspersed. Romantic songs illustrate the mood of the

In all probability *El charro* was a silent movie with a length of one hour. It opened in 1930 at Los Angeles's Teatro México. Margarita Calles is at left; her uncle Guillermo is at right (courtesy of Dick Domínguez).

story: "New York, New York, you are the owner of love and illusion." There are a few shabby gags performed by a sanatorium intern who poses as Emperor Napoleon. It is a characteristic of the film to shift continuously from comedy to drama. *Regeneración* was really a project that Enrique Areu and Dorita Ceprano wrote and financed. Thus it seems to have been simply an assignment for the director. By all accounts, it represents an oddity in stark contrast with Calles's own brand of nationalistic pictures.

The company of J.H. Hoffberg was in charge of marketing *Regeneración*. Besides selling silent and synchronized motion pictures and equipment, Hoffberg handled other Spanish-dialogue pictures like *La jaula de los leones* and *Las campanas de Capistrano*. It also distributed the popular Mascot serials, which featured Rin Tin Tin, Tom Tyler and Walter Miller. Calles directed another movie for the Hoffberg Company. It is difficult to find this movie today; all we know about it is its Spanish title, *La venganza del indio*, and that the story dealt with "Redskin Indians."

Regeneración was double-billed at all times because of its short length (50 minutes).

The Areu brothers and Dorita Ceprano produced *Regeneración* (1930), a Spanish-language melodrama directed by Calles in Hollywood (Agrasánchez Film Archive).

5. The Popular Appeal of Guillermo Calles's Films

It previewed at the Teatro California Internacional in December 1930, but few people took an interest in it. Its distribution was extensive; it played in New York City and Mexico City in 1931. The Pastime Theater in Albuquerque, New Mexico, combined *Regeneración* with the comedy *Anen La Berara*. The Palace Theater in Key West, Florida, paired the movie with the Poverty Row melodrama *Docks of San Francisco*. The film came back to Los Angeles a year and a half after its initial preview. The inaugural program at the California Theater gave the picture a stage prologue featuring the tenor Manuel Maytorena, the orchestra of Ernesto González Jiménez, and "a group of eight nice-looking girls." By 1940, Dorita Ceprano was still touring Texas with her vaudeville show. Interestingly, she came to Brownsville bringing along a print of *Regeneración*, which played at the Dittmann Theater.[26]

6

On the Road: From Los Angeles to Mexico City

The 1929 collapse of Wall Street's stock market led to a serious financial crisis that reached all corners of the United States economy. As the new decade started, masses of people from coast to coast lost their jobs. The spread of unemployment affected mostly the lower and middle classes, which paid the price of uncontrolled economic growth of the previous years. Finding work in Los Angeles became extremely difficult for Mexicans and other minority groups, a situation that opened the door to discriminatory policies. According to historian George J. Sánchez, the recently enacted California Alien Labor Act "displaced many Mexican workers from construction sites, highways, schools, government office buildings, and other public works projects."[1] While the crisis was raging, a number of theater establishments closed down. Those that catered to Hispanics were among the first casualties, typically overwhelmed by a high rent or an excessive payroll. People began to take notice of the alarming rate of failures in the show business at the end of 1931, when an editorial of *La Opinión* wearily declared:

> The theaters are feeling the effects of the so-called Depression, a specter that frightens those with a weak spirit inside and outside of the United States.... During the weeks before Christmas, seven theaters closed their doors to the public.... An equal number of enterprises are seriously considering following such a discouraging example, fearful of the growing deficit that has its roots in a number of factors, all adding up to a formidable total.[2]

The entertainment venues that were hit hardest by the crisis included the California, Hidalgo, México, and Orange Grove theaters. A major exhibition house for Spanish talkies was the California Theater, which struggled to obtain pictures in this language and forced its management to show Russian, German, Japanese, and even Jewish films temporarily. Still, the house had to slash its list of expenses in order to continue in business. Romualdo Tirado, a well-known stage author and actor, opened the Orange Grove Theater to provide a forum for local talent and to give work to the many unemployed. A few weeks after its inauguration, it went bankrupt and more than twenty people working for Tirado lost their jobs. The same fate befell the Teatro México, which was barely surviving as a burlesque spot. Miraculously, the old Teatro Hidalgo kept functioning thanks to its vaudeville acts and the screening of "westerns that greatly please a segment of our public who like terrifying adventures and thrilling moments." The populace went to the Hidalgo because it was more affordable. Almost anyone could enjoy a matinee show for only fifteen cents.

Movie houses that offered English-language talkies did not fare well either. The sump-

6. On the Road: From Los Angeles to Mexico City

tuous Chinese Theater announced on December 25, 1931, a new film starring Clark Gable and Wallace Beery. A stage prologue featuring a cast of one hundred artists complemented the program. Marlene Dietrich was one of the stars invited for the opening night; the lavish event that was made even more attractive by reducing the admission price by one-half. In spite of all these efforts, the theater only sold half of the seats, making this premiere a terrible flop.[3]

Throughout this year, Mexicans headed south as there was simply no place for them in the impoverished economy. The United States government initiated a deportation program targeting more than fifty thousand nationals residing in Southern California. This exodus included countless people who had been working for the Hollywood movie industry. Among them was the journalist Roberto Cantú Robert, who boarded a train packed with six hundred repatriates bound for Mexico City. They not only left behind a job, but also a property and in some instances their own family. According to Cantú Robert, there was little choice but to emigrate in search of better economic opportunities. Prior to his departure in May, he wrote an article describing the state of affairs in Hollywood:

> Great confusion reigns among the Hispanics in the movie business because of the latest actions taken by the studios, which have suspended their production in Spanish. First National and Warner Brothers have delayed production for three months; Universal has not produced since January; Columbia is inactive after the completion of *Ten Cents a Dance* [*Carne de cabaret*]. Upon finishing the comedy *El príncipe gondolero*, Paramount is canceling Ramón Pereda's contract and sending Chilean actor Roberto Rey to its branch in Paris. The situation is complicated by the arrival in Hollywood of Spanish artists that Fox studio has brought in from Spain; according to them, they will be producing films for our audiences. But I tell this again: If the producers continue their policy of merely adapting works originally written in English, it will be very difficult to conquer the Latin American market.[4]

During the Depression, immigration authorities in California put into practice a deportation program that sent fifty thousand Mexicans back home. Los Angeles, ca. 1931 (Agrasánchez Film Archive).

Most of the Spanish versions of Hollywood movies proved unpopular, despite having dialogue and songs in Spanish and a cast composed mostly of Latin Americans. A movie like *Don Juan Diplomático*, for example, followed exactly the same script as the original English-language picture *The Boudoir Diplomat*. This romantic comedy directed by George Melford blended the accents of Spain's Miguel Faust Rocha, the Brazilian Lia Torá and the Mexican Celia Montalván in a story of deceitful politics and love affairs. Everything in the film took place in an imaginary kingdom called Luvaria. One could only guess the reaction of the public to this peculiar jumble. In all probability, they got bored with its complicated situations. More annoying was the Spanish-language version of *Resurrection*, titled *Resurrección*; both starred Lupe Vélez and Gilbert Roland. In the original English-language movie, the Mexican actress's broken English helped make her character more convincing; audiences enjoyed seeing her as the tormented heroine Katiusha Máslova. By contrast, the Spanish edition met with scorn and critics found the rendering of dialogue very disappointing. Gilbert Roland's performance was not appreciated either, as "he was a tolerable comedian under the auspices of Norma Talmadge; but now that he is making movies in Spanish using his real name [Luis Alonso], he is simply detestable."[5]

Producers gradually recognized the audiences' distaste for Hollywood's Spanish-language talkies. By the mid–1930s, after churning out approximately 180 films of diverse length, the studios discontinued their production. Concurrently, the film industries in Mexico, Argentina, and Spain were engaged in a race to conquer the Hispanic public, offering more palatable fare.[6]

Foreseeing a new era of Spanish-dialogue movies, the Teatro California reopened its doors in January 1932, announcing the world premiere of *Soñadores de la gloria*. A Miguel Contreras Torres production shot in Spain, Morocco, and Hollywood, it attracted a large crowd to the California Theater during its two weeks of exhibition. The theater billed the picture as the "first Mexican super-production, all spoken in Spanish." Its cast included Lia Torá, Miguel Contreras Torres, Medea de Movarry, Paul Ellis and Alfredo del Diestro, as well as a group of fearless "bullfighters and thousands of soldiers."

Meanwhile in Mexico City, the production company Nacional Productora de Películas concluded the shooting of *Santa*, the first sound-on-film effort made south of the border. *La Opinión* published "for the first time in the United States" a still from *Santa*; in this historic image were shown the leading actress Lupita Tovar and the Rodríguez brothers, who invented the sound system used for *Santa*. Roberto and Joselito Rodríguez were young Mexicans who lived in Los Angeles when they created this innovative sound-on-film recording system.

Observant of his compatriots' recent achievements, Calles grew impatient to start on a new project. Yet many things were holding him back, among them the costly sound technology and the retrenchment of his former financial backers, the exhibitors. Theater owners were feeling the effects of the Depression and could no longer afford to invest in the production of movies. Following a prolonged seclusion, the restless Calles came out in the open at the start of 1932 and announced his plan to make an innovative film that would show the towns, scenery and local customs of Mexico. Apparently, the Mexican government had endorsed him through the consul in San Diego, California, Enrique Ferreira. An influential man whose brother-in-law was the former president Plutarco Elías Calles, Ferreira had "ready access to high officials in the Mexican government."[7] These connections proved helpful for Calles's project. On January 13, the movie kicked off with a take of Mayor John C. Porter handing Willie a letter addressed to the president of Mexico. Also

6. On the Road: From Los Angeles to Mexico City

appearing in this first scene were the Mexican consul, Rafael de la Colina, and other bureaucrats who posed for the camera in front of City Hall. A street crowd gathered to watch the filmmaker shake hands and chat with the mayor and the consul.[8]

Not until that day, however, did the press take notice of Calles's intention to make a movie. He pulled together "a couple of thousand dollars" for the road expenses and developed a rough itinerary of the places to be included in his "travelogue." Joining him was the camera operator Ernie Smith, an old friend and a nephew of Vitagraph's co-founder. Ernie had been an assistant photographer in that company in the early twenties. Calles's wife Angelita and their dog Águila were also part of the team. Hauling portable camera equipment, they drove away in their automobile. A banner attached to it proclaimed, "From Los Angeles to Mexico City." All together, the trip lasted three months, starting in January and going to April, when the filmmaker returned to Los Angeles and entered a Hollywood editing room to splice together his film. Only after finishing the soundtrack did the director choose to name it *Pro-Patria*, a title that captured its nationalistic intention. Reflecting on the genesis of the project, Calles explained:

> I was aware of the activities of several Mexicans in the realm of sound film production and I could not stay inactive, simply because the cinema has always been my passion and I have lived the best years of my life dedicated to it. Other people have worked hard and made pictures of various themes, all in the fictional genre. After going through numerous difficulties, I then decided to do my first talking picture concentrating my efforts on something that they had neglected: to reveal to the outside world the many beautiful aspects of our Mexico.[9]

Rafael Corella had already made a number of travelogues illustrating life in Mexico. In 1925, he filmed the "revistas" *A través de Sonora* and *Baja California*, which represented the first efforts at promoting the progress of northern Mexico. In addition to the Fox newsreels of the late twenties, which described political and military developments, theaters exhibited movies like *México auténtico*: "Where beautiful things of our homeland that are unknown to Mexicans can be seen."[10] A short film made by Gustavo Sáenz de Sicilia in 1929 was *México, país de romance*. Also, *Así es México* aimed to promote the country as "the paradise of tourists, because it presents a diversity of beautiful views, always selecting the most famous." Of special

In spite of the economic crisis, Calles set out to make a film of the towns and scenery along Mexico's Pacific Coast, *Pro-Patria* (1932). He is shown here with his dog Águila, his wife Angelita Salcedo de Calles and the maid (Agrasánchez Film Archive).

significance was a series of shorts called *Viajes de Bernal a México*, shot along the border and produced by Alberto Méndez Bernal. From January to March 1931, the California Theater of Los Angeles exhibited *Viajes de Bernal a México*, complementing the program with several Hollywood Spanish talkies. Presumably, these reels were synchronized with sound, as author Eduardo de la Vega has suggested.[11]

Long before Calles made his travelogue, a group of people from Oregon State drove to Mexico City with the intention of studying the country and recording with a camera the scenery and tourist attractions along the way. Four Americans driving two cars launched a "Hawley Motorcade" arriving in Torreón, Coahuila, in April 1924. Before continuing to Zacatecas, they told the press that their mission was to deliver a letter from Secretary of State Charles Evans Hughes to the president of Mexico. One of the travelers, John Straigth, was a journalist reporting his impressions of the trip. Paird Robert, an expert in photography, filmed the towns and scenery. News of this automobile excursion appeared in Los Angeles's *El Heraldo de México* on April 12, 1924.

Newsreels and travelogues were an integral part of the spectacle offered by theaters in Los Angeles. Thus, it is not surprising that Calles decided to experiment with this medium. Beyond the imaginary tales of the cinema, he saw the need for non-fictional pictures that could spark the audience's interest in Mexico. Others before him had publicized several aspects of the country, but he was sure there were incalculable marvels still waiting to be revealed. His enthusiastic undertaking of *Pro-Patria* demonstrates a profound faith in movies as a tool for educating the masses.

This film is not available today; a description of it was found in the pages of *La Opinión*. This Los Angeles daily published the chronicle of Calles's cinematographic excursion into Mexico in the spring of 1932. *La Opinión*'s critic Gabriel Navarro worked out an engaging narrative based on the letters that the director of *Pro-Patria* wrote during his trip. The recounting provides historical information about a vast geographical region, also offering suitable commentary on a pivotal period of modernization of the country. A number of photographs taken during the shooting of *Pro-Patria* were included in the publication. The letters written by Calles are of significance because they represent the only report of the shooting of a Mexican documentary that is on hand.

The route followed by Calles and his companions started in Los Angeles on January 16 as they headed south to the border city of Nogales. Three days after departing, they crossed into the state of Sonora. Authorities allowed them to film the passage of the frontier line, with scenes of tourists filling out immigration papers. Because of cold weather, the members of this excursion wore thick coats at the beginning of their trip. A more benevolent climate welcomed them a few miles south in Magdalena, the so-called "Paradise of Sonora." Driving on a highway in good condition, Calles's vehicle reached the capital of the state, Hermosillo. In spite of the Depression, the visitors noticed a hectic pace of business and a multitude of people working at the beer and soda factories, and at the cracker and flour mills. Local authorities greeted the travelers, who started to record on film several aspects of the city including meetings with state officials.

Continuing south, they arrived in the port of Guaymas on January 27 and collected

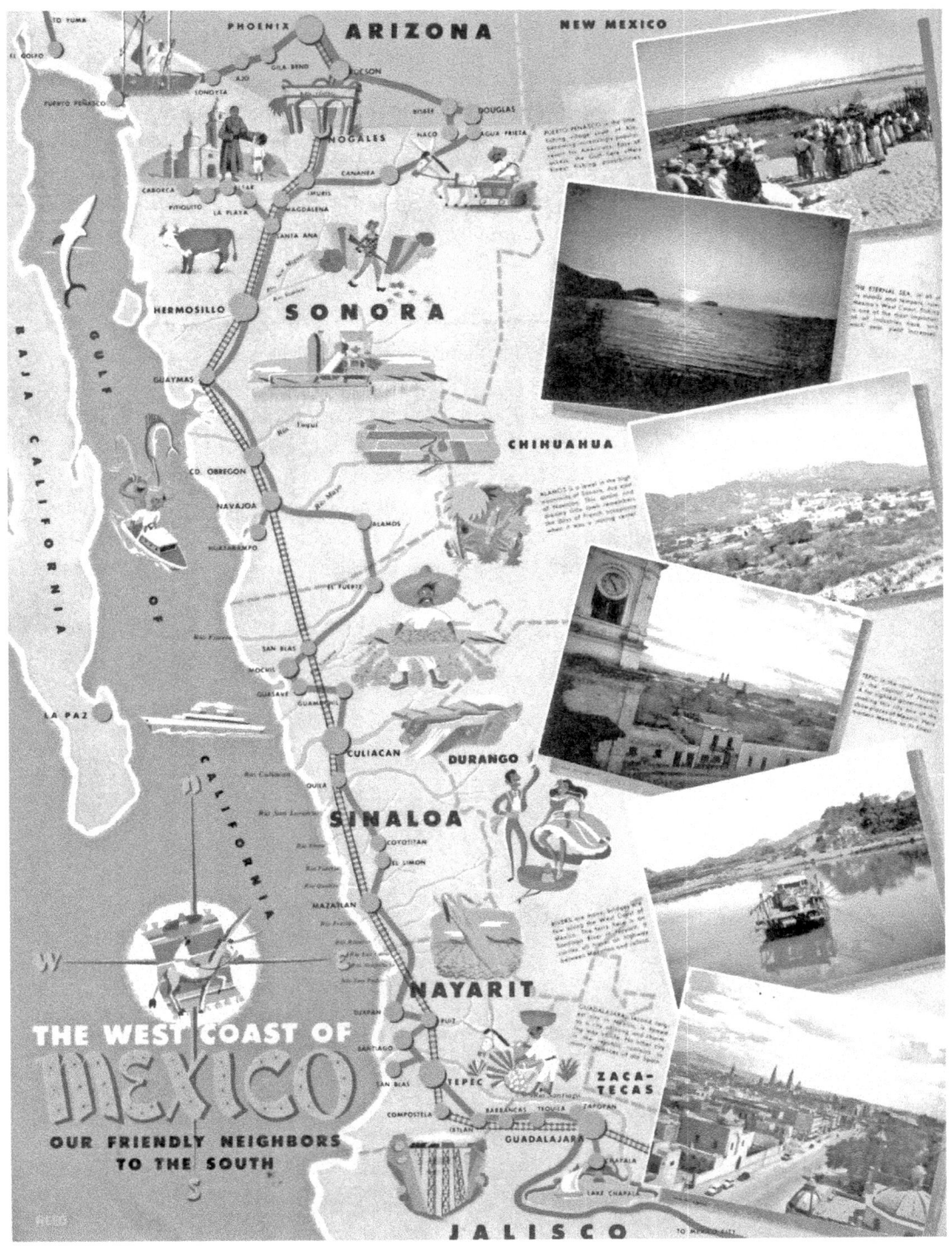

The excursion from Los Angeles to Mexico City lasted three months. After splicing together his travelogue, the director chose to name it *Pro-Patria*, a title that captured its nationalistic intentions (taken from the November 1950 *Arizona Highways* magazine).

timely information on the economy of the bay and its harbor. The next day, the filmmakers set out for the plains that lead to the Sierra del Bacatete, a region populated by the Yaqui tribes. They made a stop near Cruz de Piedra to photograph the beautiful terrain, having as background the mountains of the Sierra. A few miles further, Calles noticed the absence of his dog Águila and drove back to try to find her. They saw a group of Yaqui Indians near the highway who had secured the dog. Gladly they returned it to its owner. Up the road, the travelers met a regiment of soldiers in Pitahaya, who exercised strict vigilance to protect the roads and make them safer.

In order to cross the Yaqui and Mayo rivers, efficient "pangas," or ferry-flats, carried the travelers' vehicle. The road then took them through Los Mochis, a busy coastal town on the Gulf of California. Another port of importance was Mazatlán, known for its charming atmosphere. They stayed there for four days photographing several points of interest. Their excursion continued to Nayarit, a state possessing exuberant vegetation and plenty of wildlife. One of the things that Calles valued the most was the hospitality of the locals. "It is not an exclusive virtue of those who are in authority here," he explained, "but it springs from the people themselves, who are different from other folks in the country; and they are highly attentive and polite. Even the least inquiring person cannot fail to notice

A similar view of Guadalajara's cathedral appeared in *Pro-Patria*. When the film was exhibited in Los Angeles, the singer and movie star José Mojica praised this scene saying it reminded him of his homeland. Photograph ca. 1940 (Agrasánchez Film Archive).

their instinctive sense of good manners." This characteristic of the inhabitants of Nayarit was most evident in the state's capital, Tepic, where common people in the streets "never use immoral language."

Upon their arrival in Tepic, Calles and companions received a warm welcome from the locals; a crowd of shouting youngsters followed their automobile from the outskirts of the city to the Hotel Palacio. Because the festivities of the Carnaval had just started, the visitors had the opportunity of filming a colorful parade. A strikingly beautiful, darkskinned woman dressed in "Huichol" garb, who was leading this parade, impressed them. They also attended a rodeo, where Calles refurbished his bull-riding abilities only to be shoved away by the bull. Ernie Smith had a taste of a luscious homemade wine called mezcal, "of which he drank more than one glass, in amends for the torture of Prohibition." A tour to the nearby towns provided Calles with a wealth of information regarding natural resources. The region had optimum potential for the development of several industries, including arts and crafts.

Views of the construction of the road linking Los Angeles with Mexico City were included in the documentary. The magnitude of this infrastructure project came to the attention of the filmmaker when he arrived at the state boundary of Nayarit and Jalisco. Here he encountered Colonel Filiberto Gómez, governor of the State of Mexico and the man in charge of building the highway. After greeting him, Calles explained the objective of his excursion. He stressed that his plan "had been to present a film that could provide the best vision of the highway, the creation of which has been undertaken with so much enthusiasm; showing the local scenery of each region that this road traverses." Also, the filmmaker said with confidence that his film "will generate new waves of tourism, awakening the interest of businessmen who want to contribute to the economic progress of Mexico." Above all, Calles concluded, "it will help thousands who ignore us or have a false opinion of us, to make a better appraisal of the invaluable wealth of the country and of the culture of the Mexican people."[12]

Before Calles' group arrived in the town of Tequila, Jalisco, local authorities greeted and guided them to a summit on the road. Looking down from this point, Ernie Smith was able to photograph the landscape of Tequila at the precise moment when "the sun rays bathed the town in its entirety, producing a marvelous effect of light." One of the most prominent families in the locality invited them to see the mezcal factory of José Cuervo and the "taberna," a place of enormous size with thousands of gallons of liquor stored in barrels. A few minutes later, the visitors stepped into a regal mansion, the Quinta El Retiro, where they met José Cuervo's widow. The exquisite surroundings of the Quinta and the hospitality of its owners greatly impressed them. After a few toasts and a sampling of aged tequila, the guests took pleasure in a banquet of mixed foods.

Refreshed, the travelers got in their automobile the next day and headed for the capital city of Guadalajara. Calles and his companions visited the governor of Jalisco at the State Palace; the administrative chief had words of encouragement for the filmmaker and offered his support. Following two days of shooting in Guadalajara, they continued to Morelia, the capital of Michoacán. A striking sight was the Tarascan Indians, who carried on their backs large wooden cages full of pottery. The Tarascans habitually walked long distances from dawn to sunset in order to sell their wares. After a visit to Lake Pátzcuaro, the travelers went on driving until they reached the state of Mexico. Colonel Filiberto Gómez, whom they had previously met in Nayarit, arranged for a stopover of the group at the mining town of El Oro. Three days "enjoying social gatherings, banquets and excursions" were enough for Calles and companions. Colonel Gómez also invited them to his hacienda on the outskirts of Toluca, where they shot quite a few feet of film that captured the magnificence of the volcano Nevado de Toluca.

Calles recognized that the unreserved support of Colonel Filiberto Gómez was vital for the success of his cinematic venture. Because of the colonel's personal contacts, many doors were opened; authorities in different towns offered their hospitality and showed enthusiasm for the project. While in Toluca, Calles seized the opportunity to ask the colonel about the best way to get an interview with the president of Mexico. Without hesitation, Colonel Gómez offered to escort the filmmaker to Mexico City and arrange to see the chief of state. Early the next day, they took the highway covering the distance from Toluca to the country's capital in a few hours, arriving at the presidential residence of Chapultepec Castle punctually. As their automobile passed through the main gates, Calles might have felt with emotion that one of his dreams was becoming a reality. Within minutes, Colonel Gómez introduced him and his companions to President Pascual Ortiz Rubio.

After explaining his cinematic project to the chief executive, the Tarahumaran artist begged him to appear in it. Outside of the castle, a small group of officers gathered around Ernie Smith's camera. The photographer skillfully manipulated his equipment, capturing the images and sounds of this episode. Excitement ran high for the director of *Pro-Patria*, who later recounted that the president "performed with striking naturalness, as if he were accustomed to the chores of film studios." Before packing up, Calles asked the president to pose with him for a still shot. Three months later, this photograph appeared prominently in the Los Angeles newspaper *La Opinión*, in advance of the opening of the documentary.[13]

Calles stated that during this interview, "the president showed genuine interest in knowing the situation of highways; the guarantees and security of travelers; what kind of assistance is provided to them, and in particular the assistance granted to us; the condition of my automobile upon arrival and the characteristics of the scenery where we passed through." The president deemed profitable the visit of Guillermo Calles and Colonel Filiberto Gómez. In fact, one of his aspirations was to propel the creation of the country's infrastructure. The president once declared, "Building is the magical word of our era." Even before taking office, he emphasized the necessity of focusing on economic goals, prioritizing "the task of national reconstruction." While carrying out this mission, he said, "[A]cademics as well as laborers should contribute with the same energy; the wealthy and the poor will have an equally important job; all the aptitudes and all the opinions could be utilized beneficially."[14] This philosophy explains why the president listened to the account of Calles with so much interest and consideration.

During their stay in the capital, Calles, Angelita, and Smith carried on a busy schedule filming points of interest in and around the capital. Among the many attractions that

6. On the Road: From Los Angeles to Mexico City

Calles's enthusiastic undertaking of *Pro-Patria* demonstrates a profound faith in movies as a tool for educating the masses. This photograph, taken around 1932, shows fishermen on Páztcuaro Lake, in Michoacán, with the famous Janitzio Island in the background (Agrasánchez Film Archive).

they photographed were the scenic waterways of Xochimilco, the gardens of San Ángel, the ancient pyramids of Teotihuacán and, finally, Tepeyac, the hub of pilgrimage to the Virgin of Guadalupe. They even had time to visit the film studios where Antonio Moreno showed them a trailer of *Santa*, a film with optical sound that he had just finished directing. Quite impressed by this accomplishment, Calles ventured to say that the movie would be "as famous as the novel written by Gamboa."

In mid–April, Calles and companions returned to Los Angeles hauling several cans of film. Immediately, the director shut himself at the Eastman studios and proceeded to edit his documentary. The first cut resulted in a version "over eight thousand feet long, having some parts with dialogue and natural noises, as well as some parts in color." Its opening titles of "daring originality" were done by the Mexican artist Machado. Expressing satisfaction, Calles told the press that his job was now complete, giving credit for much of what he had achieved to the assistance of Mexican political and military authorities, as well as ordinary citizens in that country. He also acknowledged the support of the press in Los Angeles. "It might not be anything sensational; nevertheless it represents the hard work of a Mexican who wants to do something for his countrymen," the director added. Initially two versions of the film were planned: one in English and another in Spanish. Yet, the English edition was not finished. Gabriel Navarro, who provided the narration for the Spanish version, knew the *Pro-Patria* project quite well, as he had helped publicize it through the pages of *La Opinión*.

When Calles arrived in Mexico City, he and his wife went to visit President Pascual Ortiz Rubio at the Chapultepec castle. Los Angeles's *La Opinión* published this photo in 1932 (Agrasánchez Film Archive).

Calles put the last touches to his film at the end on June. At this time, the manager of the Teatro Hidalgo announced a special program in his honor. It included the premiere of *Alma Yaqui*, a stage drama written by Navarro, and the screening of *Dios y ley*, which now played with synchronized sound. Calles appeared on the stage once again accompanied by the participants of his movie. Following the live and filmed attractions, a group of twenty artists performed several musical numbers. For this occasion, the theater raised the admission charge to fifty cents for adults and twenty-five cents for children, as compared to the regular fare of fifteen and ten cents, respectively.

In the face of a widespread economic crisis, a marathon show helped provide work for many unemployed actors and musicians who were "two steps from starvation." A publication mentioned that many artists lacked a place to live. Some were seen at cheap cafés on Main Street, "killing time and waiting for someone to buy them a cup of coffee or give them shelter." People who usually earned eight or ten dollars a show were currently paid less than two dollars. Attesting to this poignant reality was the experience of a stage company that at last found work at a nearby town: After their performance, the actors returned to Los Angeles with just enough money to buy a couple of inexpensive meals.[15]

Considering the difficult circumstances, it was positively a miracle that Calles finished one more film. Like the rest, he also had to work hard to earn a living, accepting small roles here and there in Hollywood pictures. For example, he played a tropical island native in RKO's *Bird of Paradise*, a movie starring Joel McCrea and Dolores del Río. Calles's earnings served only one end: the completion of his travelogue. A special screening of *Pro-Patria* took place at the beginning of July 1932. Attending were writers José María Sánchez García, Gabriel Navarro and Fidel Murillo. Praising the documentary's informative and artistic features, Sánchez García said:

> After seeing *Pro-Patria*, I found its title completely justified. Although it has been created without a plan, this enjoyable film is strung together with great skill. It does not have a plot, but it does not need it to keep the audience's interest. It takes us from one surprise to another, as if we were browsing around in the treasures of a fairy country. The voice of its narrator, clear and pleasant, acquaints us with extraordinary landscapes and personalities, carrying us comfortably like the magic carpet of a famous tale. Many times, his words capture the irreplaceable adjective, which gratifies both hearing and sight. Good judgment pervades Gabriel Navarro's monologue and it highlights the work of the photographer.... For many years, people in Mexico have worked on this kind of filmmaking. Garduño, Tinoco, Carrasco, and Turnbull (citing only the best local talents), each have memorable accomplishments. Now comes the modest Calles, along with the equally modest [Ernie] Smith, and they show us something new, when we thought the subject was exhausted. [These are] nine reels of itinerant spectacle, so entertaining and beautiful that it seems short, too short.[16]

Another reviewer, Esteban V. Escalante, spoke of his old friend Calles as "the indefatigable champion of Mexican cinematography in the land of Uncle Sam." Putting aside all pretenses, Escalante said that he did not intend to do a critique of the film: "I am miles away from considering myself a critic of an art that is as difficult and intricate as the motion pictures." Accordingly, he contributed only this on the subject.

> Calles, with Angelita Salcedo, his sweet and lovely wife, have accomplished what I consider a good shot with this picture that was needed long ago; not only to wipe out the impression that other nations have of our "Mexican curios," but also to foster tourism in that land so full of color that is the West Coast of Mexico.... The camera operator Smith deserves special praise for the skillful photography; Angelita Salcedo earns applause for her discretion; and Calles's exertion and willingness to pay tribute to Mexico, make him worthy not only of applause but also of a military salvo. If my perception is right, *Pro-Patria* is a picture that will become part of the history of Mexican cinema.[17]

A third journalist, Fidel Murillo, mentioned that everybody in Hollywood was talking about *Pro-Patria*. He regarded Calles as "one of the most obstinate fighters of the cinema industry, who in the end has gotten his way." Murillo remarked that the director, "after a long period of reserve in the artistic and economic field, has succeeded in producing a rather unique film in the history of Spanish talkies." The journalist went on to explain:

> In the first place, the picture has been made on an almost individual basis. It is one of those quixotic adventures that we often see in our people, who are so prone to dreaming. With a couple of thousand dollars at the most, several rolls of stock film, an automobile and a camera with its operator, Calles left Los Angeles one day to carry out an adventurous trip along the Pacific coast of the Republic of Mexico. He must have had a plan, of course, but confesses that he "didn't know for sure what to shoot, or how long the journey would take." Probably, as long as the money collected with difficulty by him and Ernie Smith lasted. More than two months of wandering about the coastal towns, exploring the cities, spending the night at any place and sometimes sleeping under the skies, next to their automobile.... A month later, the film came out of the laboratories converted into an artistic thing.... [Although] only presenting a series of views naively captured on film, what sparks behind them is a superior intelligence. That's the way we saw it a few days ago at the Eastman Kodak studios.[18]

The Teatro México boasted the finest stage facilities in the area. For the release of *Pro-Patria* on July 22, 1932, it welcomed Hollywood luminaries, lesser known actors and Latin American consuls (Agrasánchez Film Archive).

6. On the Road: From Los Angeles to Mexico City

The Teatro México was closed for a while due to the economic slowdown, but it got ready for the opening of *Pro-Patria* on July 22, 1932. A theater that boasted the finest stage facilities in the neighborhood, with a capacity for one thousand people, welcomed Hollywood luminaries, lesser-known actors, and Latin American consuls. Among the special guests was singer-actor José Mojica, who said enthusiastically: "I love to see when a Mexican, one of my own race, makes a great effort to excel in any career and especially in cinema." Mojica also commented that one of the reasons he went to see the movie was because he wanted "to get a glimpse of the [cathedral] towers of my homeland, Guadalajara, which appear in one of the scenes; I have not seen them in such a long time!" People gathering at the México gave Mojica a standing ovation that night.

The Teatro México management announced a special prologue performed on a stage that boasted "a brand new artistic decoration." To entertain the public, the orchestra of Antonio González Alfonso played the musical overture "Guaraní," featuring the pianist José I. Medina. A fancy first-tier box was reserved for the mayor of Los Angeles and the consul of Mexico. Outside, the beam of a powerful searchlight attracted a curious crowd. Spurred by the images and sounds reminiscent of old Mexico, the audience gave free rein to patriotic sentiment:

> The movie started with the exhibition of a flag in colors, which the public saluted with a lengthy applause.... The insistent clapping frequently interrupted the screening. It seems that a great number of people from Jalisco occupied the auditorium, because when the familiar landscape of Guadalajara appeared we heard not only applause but also enthusiastic cries. The public very much liked the rodeo scene in the hacienda San Cayetano and they got excited to see the arrival in the city of Mexico, as well as the beautiful sights of Xochimilco with which the film ends. President Ortiz Rubio's interview was difficult to hear, unfortunately, due to unending clapping that drowned the words coming from the screen. The same occurred at the sight of several monuments to the heroes of Independence, in particular when the film showed the statue dedicated to Don Miguel Hidalgo at the Colegio de San Nicolás, in Morelia.[19]

Admission to the Teatro México during the exhibition of *Pro-Patria* was 75 cents for special seats and 25 cents for general admission. The program included a cartoon as a complement to the film. As stated by the management, more than five thousand tickets were sold in the first week. The audience's only complaint involved the run-down condition of the sound equipment, one observer pointing out: "It is a pity that the reproduction machines are not of the best kind; in spite of this, the photography comes out reasonably clear and the voice is heard adequately, being able to understand all the words of the description."[20] In August, working-class audiences had a chance to see the movie playing at a theater charging lower admission prices: the Hidalgo.

With *Pro-Patria* gaining public acceptance locally, Calles announced to the press his intention to travel to Mexico City to promote the film. As soon as he recovered from a bad bout of bronchitis, the artist boarded the train on August 11, 1932. A small group of friends went to the station to see him off. Staying at home in Los Angeles were his wife and his mother. Calles made a stop in Nogales and Hermosillo, Sonora, continuing on to Sinaloa State. *Pro-Patria* arrived in El Paso, Texas, where it played at the Teatro Colón on Mexican Independence Day, on September 16–18. Located downtown, the Colón was the most important movie house catering to Mexicans in that city. Its owner, Rafael Calderón, operated several entertainment venues in El Paso and across the Rio Grande. It is very likely that Calderón programmed *Pro-Patria* at other theaters of his circuit. After this showing, Calles' itinerary took him to Guadalajara, where he made a personal appearance on October 13. Four theaters exhibited his film: the Lux, Cuauhtemoc, Juárez, and Rialto. The next day, the picture went to the Regis, Royal, María Teresa, and Montes theaters. On the third day, the Juárez and Rialto played it again. Several newspaper ads described the undertaking as "a commendable nationalist effort designed to reveal to the world the beauty of our Mexico."[21]

In spite of Calles' enthusiasm, exhibitors in Mexico City were reluctant to show his film. Apparently, theaters in the capital rejected *Pro-Patria* due to monopolistic practices. Exhibitors had exclusive contracts with American distribution companies and were not free to program any other material from independents. This reasoning is supported by some statistics. With the exception of one movie from England, all 28 new releases announced in the capital in September of 1932 were Hollywood productions. The thirty-plus exhibitors in the capital did not accept Mexican pictures for fear of retaliation from American companies.

In November, a group of local filmmakers openly criticized the monopolistic attitude of film exhibitors. Coming together, they petitioned the authorities to implement a policy by which they could exhibit their films for at least two days a week. They also asked that the exhibitors pay them a minimum of ten pesos for each reel shown. This measure, the producers argued, should be extended to all the theaters in the country in order to advance the national film industry and to "impede its demise in this early period, or its falling into strange hands." Finally, their petition appealed to the patriotic sentiment of exhibitors, as they could benefit from the showing of Mexican pictures because "these movies would be more attractive, as the people value the progress of local films by virtue of the nationalistic feelings that are so widespread in the country."[22]

It was a year before Calles was able to exhibit his documentary in Mexico City. By then, regrettably, a faded welcome was awarded to *Pro-Patria*. This turned into a major disillusionment for its director, who lamented "having placed in it all my patriotic feelings, the same feelings that I thought were aroused in every Mexican." He added, "As a payment for my toil, I only got a few stimulating reviews from my friends, the journalists Esteban V. Escalante, in Los Angeles, and Alejandro Aragón, in this capital."[23]

Calles did not detail the problems surrounding the exhibition of his documentary, but only attributed them "to reasons that are obvious." This vague explanation might be a subtle reference to the exhibitors' discrimination against Mexican films. The political atmosphere when Calles arrived in Mexico City also had something to do with this incident. At the beginning of September 1932, President Pascual Ortiz Rubio resigned because of political pressure. As a result, a degree of uneasiness prevailed in the government, and many public servants who wanted to preserve their jobs turned their alliance to the new administration. Under the circumstances, it is entirely possible that censors discouraged the exhi-

6. On the Road: From Los Angeles to Mexico City

bition of *Pro-Patria*, a film that seemed to exalt the deposed president. At any rate, the issues surrounding the ill-fated release of the documentary in Mexico City are complex and it would be necessary to review the actual film if one were to make a final judgment. It is also hoped that the eventual re-surfacing of *Pro-Patria* would translate into a better understanding of Calles's nationalistic sensitivity.

7

A Pioneer of Mexican Talkies

The fledgling sound film industry in Mexico surprised everyone when it turned out more than twenty pictures in 1933. Considering that there were six films made in 1932 and only one the previous year, the prospects for this Spanish-language motion picture business seemed to be bright. Yet many entrepreneurs were reluctant to invest in an activity that they perceived as too unsafe. This cautious attitude was even more pronounced because of the economic crisis, a fact that explains the budgetary limitations for local productions. A movie that took three or four weeks to shoot usually cost between 30,000 and 50,000 pesos (equivalent to $8,000 to $13,000). A good part of the budget went to paying the salaries of the director, stars, a dozen supporting actors, and approximately thirty people in charge of production. Some films cost as little as 17,000 pesos (less than $5,000). On *Mano a mano*, for example, the producer employed only a few inexpensive actors and paid no studio rent. Shot entirely on location, this adventure movie took only two weeks to complete.[1]

The allure of the talkies attracted a mixture of artists and technicians with Hollywood experience. The Depression made most of them travel to the southern neighbor. Spanish, Cubans, Mexicans and even Americans set out to conquer the local stage and film scene. Among the actors arriving in Mexico were Ramón Pereda, Carmen Guerrero, René Cardona, Emilio Fernández, Alfredo del Diestro, Julio Villarreal and Adolfo Girón. The crowd of directors also started to grow with the arrival of Ramón Peón, José Bohr, Chano Urueta, David Kirkland, John H. Auer and Calles. In addition, the local scene drew other people with various talents: sound engineers, production managers, photographers, makeup artists, and journalists.

Although possessing a résumé that stretched to the early days of Hollywood, Calles's admission to the Mexican studios was not smooth. Being a director of a dozen films did not impress the producers either. Humbly, he spent several months knocking on doors. In April 1933, he was selected to direct the short feature *La Chillona*. Financed by the Compañía Nacional Productora de Películas, this four-reeler was a parody of *La Llorona*, a recent thriller. The comedy included in its cast José M. Duarte, Carmina de la Llata, Flora Martínez, and the veteran radio actor Jesús Graña. For the second time, Calles and Duarte collaborated on a movie, after working together in *El indio yaqui* seven years earlier. Billed as the first Mexican comedy, *La Chillona* required only three days of shooting at the studios of the Compañía Nacional. Ezequiel Carrasco took charge of the photography; he and the director were able to devise interesting "tricks" for the movie. The Cinelandia, a Mexico City theater that specialized in short subjects, frequently billed *La Chillona* alongside other popular comedies starring Cantinflas, Laurel and Hardy, Chaplin, and others. All that remains of this film are the magazine illustrations of a couple of scenes, in addition to a lobby card poster advertising a program at the Cinelandia Theater.[2]

La Chillona (1933) was a parody of the popular Mexican "talkie" *La Llorona*. Like other films directed by Calles, it is now lost. Left to right: José Duarte, Carmina de la Llata and Flora Martínez (Agrasánchez Film Archive).

After spending almost a year in Mexico, Calles went back to Los Angeles in August to take care of some personal matters. The press made it known that he was only visiting his relatives and did not intend to stay in the country more than a few days. Apparently, he had entered the United States on a non-resident status. Without delay, the artist returned to Mexico City where he had been assigned to direct *El héroe de Nacozari*. The film was based on an incident that occurred in 1907 in Nacozari, Sonora. Jesús García Corona, a railroad engineer, saved a village from destruction when he hauled a dynamite-loaded train into the fields. García Corona drove away the burning freight but, minutes later, an explosion killed him. Starring in this drama were Ramón Pereda, Antonio R. Frausto, Lucha Díaz, and Conchita Banuet. *El héroe de Nacozari* utilized locations near Mexico City and this worked to the film's advantage. It was successful in recreating the mood of the daily routine of railroad workers.

The shooting was plagued with problems. The studio first contracted an aspiring actress who had no idea of how to perform in front of the camera. Thus, she had to be replaced by Conchita Banuet in the middle of the picture, altering the timetable and increasing production costs. In addition, actor Antonio R. Frausto suffered an accident, almost getting electrocuted. But the most visible matter involved the director; Calles's authority on the set was challenged because of the constant interference of his colleagues. A writer for the magazine *Filmográfico* reported:

> The start of *El héroe de Nacozari* has been so unfortunate that we dare to predict it will be the last effort of its producers when it is finished. A Mexican director of ample experience and justified prestige, Guillermo Calles, was designated as the man in charge of directing. Yet, do his credentials matter when everybody in the company, starting with the engineer Sáenz de Sicilia, tries to direct and does not acknowledge the personality of the director? Movies aren't

The story of *El héroe de Nacozari* (1933) involved a real-life event. Ramón Pereda (top) characterized a railroad engineer who sacrifices his life to save a village from the explosion of a dynamite-loaded train. The other actor is Antonio R. Frausto (Agrasánchez Film Archive).

done like this, here or in China, and the only outcome is ridicule. Dear Sirs of the Compañía Nacional Productora de Películas, with such mischief you cannot make progress. The result has to be inevitably disastrous in a movie where everybody gives orders and the cameraman gets offended because his suggestions are ignored and then leaves the set in anger.[3]

Gustavo Sáenz de Sicilia, production manager of the Compañía Nacional, was a man who loved the movies and dreamed of becoming a director. Because he represented the producers, his decisions on the set often prevailed over the opinions of others, including the director. The behavior of cinematographer Antonio Fernández had no justification and can only be attributed to his bad temper. Although he had worked many years in Hollywood, his career in Mexico was cut short after doing only two movies. In *El héroe de Nacozari*, he experimented with special effects and did the railroad miniatures. In order to quiet down any scandal, Calles declared that he had not been obstructed nor had his status as director been ignored. To further clarify the situation, he explained that the producers were simply "exchanging opinions with him in order to shoot such and such scene, but they never imposed their

7. A Pioneer of Mexican Talkies

authority." Apparently, these observations helped restore the reputation of the Compañía Nacional. Still, *Filmográfico* added that Calles had not been given a full opportunity as a director in this film. In order to do this, the magazine concluded, "It would be necessary to provide him in advance with a screenplay; to allow him to alter some of the camera shots, if this would improve the picture, and to let him finish the movie without stifling his creativity."[4]

Following a private exhibition of *El héroe de Nacozari*, the editors of *Filmográfico* expressed their positive opinion of the movie. They pointed out some of the spectacular scenes like the one showing the collision of a train. The photography and sound recording impressed the people attending the screening. The soundtrack's flawless quality was due to the recording system of the Rodríguez brothers. Comparing similar pictures made in Hollywood, the magazine concluded: "We never imagined that filmmakers in Mexico were sufficiently equipped to undertake movies in the style of *El héroe de Nacozari*, because of its technical difficulties."[5]

Nevertheless, Calles declared that he was not entirely satisfied with his performance on this movie. The director acknowledged the producers for giving him a chance, but demanded that a true "opportunity be offered to me so that I can prove with facts, not

El héroe de Nacozari was almost entirely shot on location. This enhanced the realism of a film that showed views of the tracks and the daily routines of railroad workers. B.J. Kroger, sound engineer, stands in back (wearing tie), and next to him (left to right) are staff member Martín Caballero, cinematographer Antonio Fernández, Calles (in white suit), actress Lucha Díaz, leading man Ramón Pereda, leading lady Conchita Banuet and make-up artist and actress Dolores Camarillo (Agrasánchez Film Archive).

words, the things I'm capable of doing." Not just the director remained skeptical of his work. When *El héroe de Nacozari* played in theaters the following year, it became a target of acerbic commentaries. An unsympathetic critic, Luz Alba, complained that the movie's heroic theme and patriotic intentions could not make up for its blatant deficiencies. Mrs. Alba's conclusion was that "we are still playing at making movies."[6]

Within a week of its release in Mexico City, the Teatro California of Los Angeles announced *El héroe de Nacozari*. Following a period of inactivity, this theater reopened in May 1934 with Calles' new film. The names of Calles and Ramón Pereda were familiar to the public and probably guaranteed a good turnout. An ad mentioned that the premiere was "attended by top personalities, [which] constituted a boost for this center of entertainment that begins a new season of Spanish-language films, sent directly from Mexico."

Upon the completion of *El héroe de Nacozari*, Calles co-directed with Jorge Bell *El pulpo humano*. This was "an old-fashioned mystery melodrama" about "a heartless, miserly money-lender." While it was being shot at the studios of the Compañía Nacional in September of 1933, a fire destroyed one of the sound stages, forcing the production to resume at the México Films studios. Calles did not feel happy with this job either, complaining some time later: "Being forced to work as co-director, that is, as a helper, does not inspire or encourage anyone. I am firm that they should give me a chance to direct and, if I do not meet the terms, they can just forget about me." The person taking that offer seriously was the actor Ramón Pereda, who immediately called on him to direct *El vuelo de la muerte*.

Pereda's fame started in Hollywood, when he appeared in several Spanish-language movies. His celebrity was put to good use from the day he set foot in the Mexican studios.

Shooting a scene for *El pulpo humano* (1933; a.k.a. *Infraganti*) in Mexico City's downtown. Calles co-directed the film (Agrasánchez Film Archive).

7. A Pioneer of Mexican Talkies

In 1933 alone, he performed in five films, becoming one of the best-paid actors. Given his status, it was not surprising that he wanted to produce his own movies. Playwright Antonio Guzmán Aguilera, better known as "Guz Águila," supplied Pereda with an original screenplay entitled *El vuelo de la muerte*, a melodrama recounting the tragedy of the Spanish pilots Joaquín Barberán and Esteban Collar. They had already established a record during a two-day flight from Spain to Cuba. Upon resuming their journey into Mexico, their plane crashed in the middle of the jungle. The Mexican Air Force sent several rescue missions. However, Barberán and Collar were never found. Being opportune, another actor, René Cardona, quickly put together a two-reel film depicting the event. He included in it the song "El corrido de Barberán y Collar," which the Trovadores Tamaulipecos had made popular. Capitalizing on the notoriety of this tragedy, Cardona's short feature premiered at once.

Pereda's *El vuelo de la muerte* was adorned with many folklore songs and stage performances. Its plot revolved around a courageous pilot, León (interpreted by Pereda), and his fiancée, Adriana (played by Adriana Lamar). She has promised her dying father that she will marry León. During a party, Adriana sings accompanied by the famous composer Jorge del Moral. Impressed by her talent, the composer offers to turn Adriana into a successful artist. León foresees the end of his romance with Adriana and is concerned by the news of the disappearance of pilots Barberán and Collar. Adriana's debut as a singer is acclaimed; she and the composer spend a lot of time together and become enamored. In an attempt to rescue the lost pilots, León takes to the air and suffers an accident in which his face is deformed. Bound by her previous promise, Adriana has no choice but to marry León. Immediately after their wedding, though, the troubled León puts an end to his life in a suicidal flight.

Overcoming a period of waning self-confidence, Calles set out to work enthusiastically on *El vuelo de la muerte*. The movie's most spectacular episodes were the flight scenes, which the director did with a great deal of pleasure. A newspaper detailed the exploits of director Calles and his first assistant Carlos Cabello: "They managed to do great feats when tied to the fuselage of an airplane flown by Captain Chagoya; they shot scenes at the same time that the plane executed turns, spins, and loops-in-the-loops. Fortunately, there were no tragic incidents to regret."[7] The aerial views of downtown Mexico City and stock footage of the Mexican Air Force's failed reception of Barberán and Collar are elements that increase the film's historical value.

To emulate the polish and glitter of Hollywood's film premieres, the producer of *El vuelo de la muerte* selected a high-class theater for the opening of his movie. The small but beautifully ornamented Cine Regis stood on one of the main avenues of Mexico City, next to the historic Alameda Park. Honoring the Mexican Air Force, the event brought together numerous personalities and artists. Magazines like *Filmográfico* ran articles and ads designed to arouse public interest in the new picture.

> Following its premiere in the exclusive Cine Regis, the first movie made by Producciones Pereda continued its exhibition at the circuit theaters; thus providing a lot of work to the box-office employees. A recently inaugurated house and one of the largest in Latin America, the Máx-

Adriana Lamar and Jorge del Moral (center) starred in *El vuelo de la muerte* (1933), a melodrama that included the performance of popular songs. Sara García is at left (Agrasánchez Film Archive).

imo Theater, attracted such a throng that in fact it was necessary to ask the police for help, so that the crowds who wanted to enter the theater by force could be contained.[8]

As soon as it concluded its exhibition in Mexico, the movie went to Spain; it played in Madrid in December 1934. *El vuelo de la muerte* gave the Mexican Embassy and the Spanish Air Force an excuse to celebrate and promote the solidarity between the two nations. Representatives of both institutions attended the screening.

Calles' activities as a director were postponed and he went back to acting in local pictures. Although he felt comfortable as a performer, he longed for a chance to again direct his own movies. People began to call him *El Indio*, a name that emphasized his racial origin and fervent nationalism. One of his friends, the journalist Esteban V. Escalante, put it on the record: "He became in Hollywood what no other Indian has become: a director of motion pictures." Escalante further pointed out Calles's virtues and shortcomings:

> Ten years of contact with Guillermo Calles grant us the authority to say that, among the people in our studios who work behind the megaphone, he is perhaps one of the best prepared. Although nobody will find a fluid conversation, an encyclopedic culture, or things of that sort

7. A Pioneer of Mexican Talkies

In *El vuelo de la muerte*, Ramón Pereda played the role of a troubled pilot who puts an end to his life in a suicidal flight (Agrasánchez Film Archive).

in Calles; as a practical technician, as an expert of the hidden secrets of cinematography, and as a keen observer of human psychology, we think that there is hardly a competitor for him. Like in all Indians, what affects Calles negatively is his excessive modesty. If he liked to show off and command the attention of everyone, his luck would be different; but it is the other way around, he spurns all flattery and is one of those who believe that silence is more eloquent than a noisy pompousness.[9]

Willie Calles was not the only Indian in the movie industry. His friend Emilio Fernández, although of mixed blood, also took the name of *El Indio* because of his strong ethnic look. Fernández's mother came from a Kikapú tribe. While struggling as an extra in Hollywood, he met the already-established Calles, who helped him to get a job in the studios. Back in Mexico, they appeared together in two 1934 films, *Corazón bandolero* and *Tribu*. The first was an adventure story set in nineteenth-century Mexico. Taking secondary roles, he and Fernández portrayed two heroic fighters, "often more bandits than soldiers." During the shooting, Calles fell from a horse and suffered a minor head injury. At the time, the friends shared an enthusiasm for the show business that went beyond the movies. A popular magazine, *Revista de Revistas*, mentioned in a light tone that "the Cholula

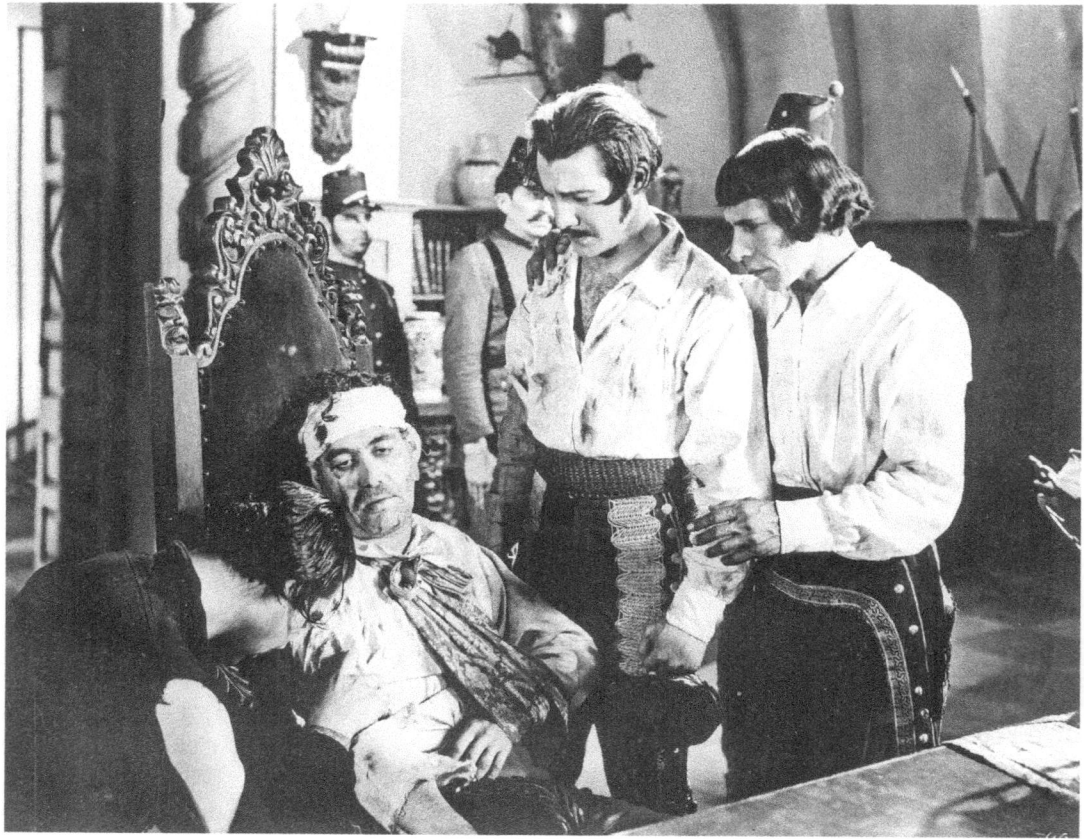

A scene from *Corazón bandolero* (1934), directed by Raphael J. Sevilla. It is an adventure movie set in nineteenth-century Mexico. From left to right: Emilio Fernández, Domingo Soler, Juan José Martínez Casado and Calles (Agrasánchez Film Archive).

Indians, Guillermo Calles and Emilio Fernández, are making plans for a troupe of charros to tour Mexico and the United States." It is not known if they ever carried out this idea. *El Indio* Fernández later directed films during the golden age of Mexican cinema, becoming one of the first directors to gain international recognition.

Calles and Fernández collaborated again in *Tribu*, joining the "group of capable secondary actors." The film told the story of a rebellious tribe that was eternally engaged in war, "defending the integrity of its territory, the freedom of its people, its religious rites and customs." Miguel Contreras Torres wrote, produced, and directed *Tribu*, idealizing the clash between the indigenous tribes and the Spanish Conquistadors. Contreras Torres also played an Indian chief whose abrupt death is avenged by a loyal Indian warrior portrayed by Calles. This show of solidarity is reminiscent of *De raza azteca*, the 1921 silent movie made by Contreras Torres and Calles. The Indian interpreters in *Tribu* spoke in Zapotec, an ancient language still in use in Oaxaca State. This fact added an element of authenticity to the film.

Not content with merely appearing in films, Calles set out to explore the possibilities of making a movie independently. There was mention of *Placer y venganza*, a project he intended to produce at the beginning of July 1934. *Revista de Revistas* revealed the title of this project and the name of its principal actor, C. Cueto González, whose photo appeared in the pages of this publication. The same magazine had reported earlier that Calles finally had the joy of seeing again his beloved dog Águila. After many months of separation, Águila was brought from Los Angeles by a relative. A reporter said: "Although the dog is well beyond her canine youth, Calles affirms that she can still do clever tricks and will soon be employed in a local movie."[10] Two months later, Calles visited the port of Acapulco, "accompanied by his inseparable nephew and his female dog"; they had gone there in search of locations. The artist's desire to produce *Placer y venganza* seems to have faded quickly, though. At the start of 1935, he was called to join the cast of *Martín Garatuza*, a swashbuckler adventure in which he made a cameo appearance. Almost immediately, Calles prepared to take one of the main roles in *María Elena*, a romance-action picture starring Juan José Martínez Casado, Carmen Guerrero, Adolfo Girón, Pedro Armendáriz, and the dog "Águila." *María Elena*'s 180,000-peso budget placed it among the most expensive Mexican pictures of the year.

Location scenes for *María Elena* were shot in the port of Alvarado, Veracruz. Though increasing production costs, filming in the tropics gave the movie a more realistic atmosphere. Hollywood's influence in the story was noticeable, especially during the second half that shows a mysterious island inhabited by primitive women. Some adventurous men fight for the possession of the pearl-rich island. An army of aggressive and scantily clad women subdues the men and takes them hostages. To their rescue comes Indalecio (played by Calles) who, aided by his dog Águila, sets his friends free. A number of musical performances, like the regional dance "La Bamba," contributed to the success of *María Elena*. Emilio *Indio* Fernández, who was an accomplished dancer, joined the cast and executed the famous "La Bamba" rhythm. Columbia Pictures released the movie in the United States as *The Devil's Island*. One of the places where it played was the Terminal Theater in Newark, New Jersey. Presumably, the movie did very well there, grossing $7,000 in one week. In Texas and California, *María Elena* broke many box-office records for a Mexican picture, thus becoming one of the first blockbusters of the era. A measure of its lasting popularity was the fact that in 1948 a distributor ordered new prints of the movie for a re-release in Mexico City.

One more 1935 film in which Calles participated as an actor is *El tesoro de Pancho Villa*. Compared to the costly *María Elena*, this picture had an extremely low budget. Director Arcady Boytler once said, "It is my best picture; considering how it was put together, with little money, little time, and almost without a screenplay, it turned out a neat film."[11] The story centers on a treasure that Pancho Villa and his men hide in a remote cave. After burying the gold, Villa orders his bodyguard to kill everyone who helped bury it, to ensure total secrecy. Calles played a greedy soldier who wants to steal the gold but is gunned down by Villa's guard. Other actors performing in *El tesoro de Pancho Villa* were Antonio R. Frausto, Victoria Blanco and Raúl de Anda.

The name of Guillermo Calles came up as a possible candidate for directing *Judas*, a melodrama that touched upon the theme of betrayal. In the end the job was given to Manuel

Guillermo Calles (center) plays a greedy rebel soldier who plots to steal a fortune in gold in *El tesoro de Pancho Villa* (1935) (Agrasánchez Film Archive).

R. Ojeda, a veteran actor who started his career in Hollywood. Produced by the REMEX cooperative, *Judas* is an interesting example of the participation of Mexico's ruling party in the movie industry: The Partido Nacional Revolucionario (P.N.R.) financed it. Imbued by the ideology of the Revolution, the story depicted the social struggle of the peasants, who find an ally in a new generation of educated middle-class young men and women. *Judas* became a propagandistic tool for the party in power: "Its principal goal," it has been surmised, "was to support the program of the agrarian reform instituted by the regime of President Lázaro Cárdenas."[12] The cast included Carlos Villatoro, an actor who befriended Calles and worked with him in several movies of the thirties.[13]

During the presidency of General Lázaro Cárdenas, the cinema industry expanded rapidly. Such films as ¡*Vámonos con Pancho Villa!*, *Cielito lindo*, *La Golondrina* and *Judas* all had as a background the Mexican Revolution. The stirring of patriotic sentiment was evi-

Opposite: The production budget for *María Elena* was very high for a Mexican movie. It included locations in the tropics and was enhanced by beautiful music (Agrasánchez Film Archive).

dent in *El cementerio de las águilas*, a movie about the Mexican American war. Focusing on the indigenous past were *Janitzio*, *El indio* and *La noche de los Mayas*. The Cárdenas administration also fostered the production of short reels and documentaries that sought to promote tourism, informing the public about Mexico's material progress.

This period saw the emergence of organized labor and the formation of cooperatives in all sectors of the economy. Motion picture workers followed suit and began producing their own movies with the aid of government agencies. Some of the movies financed under this system are *Rosario*, *Más allá de la muerte*, *¿Qué hago con la criatura?*, *El superloco* and *Judas*. Inspired by these developments, Calles envisaged his return to directing. Since 1933 he had been pondering the idea of making a film called *Oro mexicano*, about which there is very little information. In June 1936, the artist went to Tijuana to organize a cooperative for the production the film. According to the newspaper *La Opinión*, the cooperative "was established for the purpose of ameliorating the state of misery in which the people have fallen since the business enterprise of Agua Caliente closed its doors on July 20 of last year." The displaced workers of the Agua Caliente casino decided to form a film company, inviting Calles to be its director.[14] *Revista de Revistas*'s Esteban V. Escalante reported:

> Guillermo Calles, our old and unrelenting filmmaker friend, now living in Tijuana, Baja California, writes us from that border city. He tells us that he has established a motion picture producing company, under the name of "Producciones Cinematográficas Baja California, S.A." It has been formed by several groups of workers and peasants of that distant region, and will initiate its moviemaking business with a capital of 100,000 pesos. Calles discloses in his extensive letter that there are in the region vast opportunities for the production of movies; because Tijuana has a free trade zone, an incomparable climate, beautiful scenery, and is located very close to Hollywood, which means a great deal since the importation of technicians and equipment can be done easily.[15]

Many people believed that Tijuana had the potential for an alternative moviemaking center. Already in 1932, the actor Ramón Pereda visited the border city with the intention of shooting a movie and "to organize a motion picture company that can establish its own studios in town." Foreshadowing Calles's own project, Pereda conveyed to the press the reasons in favor of creating such an industry in Tijuana and posed the question: "What publicity would be more effective for the Northern Territory [of Baja California] than to become the Mexican Hollywood?"[16] At the time of Pereda's visit to Tijuana, the region was still enjoying an economic boom due to the influx of tourists from the United States. It attracted many people who wanted to escape the austerity of Prohibition. One of the most popular places in the area was the hotel-resort of Agua Caliente, where tourists could enjoy hot springs, a splendid casino and a racetrack. Even though prohibitionists constantly attacked the dissolute life of this border city, the more liberally minded defended Agua Caliente because "it is neither a dive nor a gambling hell, but a resort that is orderly, as quiet and as comfortable as any first class hotel in Los Angeles or San Francisco."[17]

The idea of a filmmaking business in Tijuana seemed to have enticed many artists. One was Carmen La Roux, the star of *Sol de gloria*. In August 1936, U.S. news agencies released a photograph showing La Roux and Dolores del Río together. The photograph was accompanied by a short paragraph that read: "Hollywood. With the prospect of achiev-

7. A Pioneer of Mexican Talkies

ing stardom in her own right, Carmen La Roux, for eight years 'stand-in' for Dolores del Río, film star, listens to a few pointers which Miss Del Río is giving her.... Miss La Roux's chance arrived with the formation of a Mexican film company, said to be subsidized by the Mexican government. The new company will shortly start production in Tijuana." There is no doubt that Calles's cinematic project was getting enough publicity by now. Although not mentioning him by name, an enlightening article in *The Hollywood Reporter* detailed these efforts:

> Local businessmen are raising cash in an attempt to make this spot the Hollywood of Mexico and steal Mexican production thunder from Mexico City. Claiming promise of government subsidy to aid in the erection of studio, a group has incorporated as Producciones Cinematográficas Baja California with a capital of 100,000 pesos, declaring that as soon as its first picture is finished, additional capital will follow. Plans are for films to be made in both English and Mexican. The first story, *Águilas doradas* (*Hills of Gold*) is already in script form with leads tentatively set for Juan José Martínez Casado and Inés Aguirre. Almost all of the material will be filmed outdoors, but with a minimum of interiors shot in a building now being transformed into a temporary stage. If plans proceed as anticipated, the group will endeavor to get Hollywood secondary names to give added impetus to the scheme. Morris Landres, of the Century Film Corporation of Hollywood, was approached on the production deal and spent the weekend here in conferences on the project.[18]

Although Calles painted a rosy picture of the project, the actual situation in Tijuana was more complex. The atmosphere was anything but reassuring, as few people had the energy and optimism to follow through with such an enterprise. As he kept busy organizing his motion picture company, an editorial of *La Opinión* in Los Angeles made known the political chaos prevailing in Baja California. The paper denounced the incompetence of governor General Gabriel Gavira, who was blamed for many erroneous decisions that led to a serious administrative crisis. In 1936,

Dolores del Río (left) and Carmen La Roux in 1936. The young La Roux was a stand in for Del Río in several Hollywood productions (Agrasánchez Film Archive).

115

Baja California saw the coming and going of three different governors, an indication of the instability afflicting the area. Furthermore, rumors that some members of the U.S. Congress were plotting to purchase this territory from Mexico fueled the debate.

With the repeal of Prohibition in 1933, many border towns lost their appeal to foreigners. Another blow came when President Lázaro Cárdenas decreed the abolition of gambling throughout the country. In addition to this, the government announced the expropriation of land and properties that had been under foreign control. The Tijuana economy suffered because of these measures, resulting in "the shrinking of space for the glamour of Hollywood."[19] Against all odds, however, some enthusiasts proposed the establishment of filmmaking in the area as a way to alleviate the current unemployment crisis.

These plans met with many obstacles, and it must have been frustrating for someone like Calles to see that his dream of making films here was fading. Yet he still believed in the improvement of the situation when he called on other actors to join him in Tijuana. Two popular comedians, Antonio R. Frausto and his wife Fraustita, were currently touring the country and made a stop in that city to collaborate with Calles. As the days passed, however, the plan to film *Oro mexicano* became more entangled. Calles's financial situation was growing dimmer and family members living in San Diego had to bail him out several times. Things worsened when Águila, Guillermo's steadfast partner in the movies, died of old age. A magazine article said that cinema idol Rudolph Valentino had given this pet to the Indian artist in the mid-twenties. Águila's final performances were in *María Elena* and *El tesoro de Pancho Villa*, two films that were still playing in theaters in Los Angeles. After dying in a San Diego clinic, the pet's remains were sent to Los Angeles to be buried. No doubt, this loss hastened Calles's decision to return to Mexico City, where he wound up acting in several films.

A last attempt to rescue this motion picture project in Tijuana was made a year later. In November 1937, two members of the cooperative "Producciones Cinematográficas Baja California" sent a telegram to the president of Mexico to ask for help. Representing the company were Serafín Jiménez and Fidencio García, who stated that they planned to film *Oro mexicano* under the direction of Calles. They solicited from the government a loan of 100,000 pesos for this purpose. In addition, the group requested tax-free incentives for the "production of commercial films, artistic and educational features, and a complement of short subjects dealing with geographical themes." Not content with merely sending a dispatch, Jiménez and García traveled to the capital in the hope of obtaining an interview with the president. This not being possible, they were informed in writing that their business matters had already been turned over to Baja California's governor.[20] Nothing is known about the fate of their project after this date.

Prior to Calles' experience in Tijuana, another film enthusiast pursued the possibility of building a studio in Baja California. According to the findings of author Esperanza Vázquez Bernal, the impresario Roberto Farfán had plans for the construction of the "Imperio Azteca" motion picture studios in El Rosarito, a town near the city of Tijuana. Twenty hectares of land were purchased for this purpose. Furthermore, the project contemplated the use of 180 additional hectares "for the development of lots where the Azteca City will be established and the living quarters of the employees and staff workers will be located." Farfán unsuccessfully sought aid from Mexico's president. Finally, when the government decreed the closing of gambling establishments, the backing of this project by foreign capitalists collapsed. In June 1936, Farfán was still counting on the assistance of the Mexican government to reach his goal.[21]

Upon his return to the capital, Calles went on to perform in three films: *Así es mi tierra*, *A la orilla de un palmar* and *Almas rebeldes*, all made in 1937. This year saw a significant increase in the production of Mexican movies, with thirty-eight features produced compared to twenty-five the year before. More than half of them were rural melodramas that incorporated a variety of musical numbers in their plots. Catering to the audience's preference for comedies, the industry cultivated a new genre that later came to be known as "comedia ranchera." In *Así es mi tierra*, for instance, a revolutionary general (played by Antonio R. Frausto) plans on retiring to his ranch to lead a peaceful life. What he encounters instead is the burdensome task of fixing the love affairs of his servants. In the end, the general decides it's better to stick to the revolution. Two popular vaudeville actors, Cantinflas and Manuel Medel, provided the comic relief. Calles appeared briefly in the role of a soldier taking orders from the revolutionary general.

Directed by Raphael J. Sevilla, *A la orilla de un palmar* was partially shot in Veracruz. Its main cast included Carlos Villatoro, Alberto Martí, Vicente Oroná and Marina Tamayo. Inspired by a popular song that gave the film its title, it centered on the beautiful but hostile Paula (Tamayo), whose confidant, the old and wise uncle Goyo (Calles), counsels her to be distrustful of men. There are three males who are attracted to the shrewish young lady; only one survives Paula's fury and ends up marrying her. The picture contained musical numbers composed by the well-known *Charro* Felipe Gil. A commercially successful release, it enjoyed the advantage of an extensive publicity campaign.

Perhaps one of Calles' best performances was in *Almas rebeldes*, a film produced by Raúl de Anda, directed by Alejandro Galindo and featuring de Anda, Nancy Torres, Eduardo Arozamena, Pedro Galindo, Jorge Treviño, and others. By coincidence, the actors of Indian extraction Emilio Fernández, Alfonso Bedoya and Calles appeared together in this movie. The

In another film set in the tropics, *A la orilla de un palmar* (1937), the old and wise Uncle Goyo (Calles) counsels the hostile Paula (Marina Tamayo) to be distrustful of men (courtesy of Dick Domínguez).

plot involves a band of horse-riding revolutionaries who plan to buy arms in the United States. A young woman joins them by accident. Aware of their secret plan, the government sends a detachment of soldiers to capture them. During their painful journey, most of the rebels die and others are left behind. The only survivors are the woman, the captain of the group (de Anda), and his loyal aide, Avendaño (Calles). When they are about to cross the international divide, the approaching army fires upon Avendaño and he dies. Standing safely on U.S. ground, the rebel leader asks the Mexican federal soldiers to fulfill Avendaño's last wish of being buried on Mexican soil.

Almas rebeldes is an engaging movie, with well-developed characters and believable dialogue. Calles' performance is very convincing, more so since he typifies an Indian soldier. In fact, Avendaño mirrors in some ways the artist's own straightforward manners. This character is as devoted to his companions as he is toward the animal world. He thinks highly of the captain of the rebels because of his impeccable conduct and good manners. For example, the Indian draws attention to the fact that his superior "eats meat using a carving fork and wipes his mouth off with a cloth." Avendaño is also shown scrubbing the

Nancy Torres and Calles in *Almas rebeldes* (1937), a movie populated by real-life characters and endowed with down-to-earth dialogue (Agrasánchez Film Archive).

back of an exhausted horse, an attitude suggesting a practical knowledge of animals as well as closeness to them.

According to producer-star de Anda, *Almas rebeldes* cost him his ranch, together with several cows. He spent all his savings in order to finish this movie. In 1938, he appeared in the rural melodrama *La virgen de la sierra*, directed by Calles. The following year, he took part in the revolutionary tale *Los de abajo*, which reunited the three *Indios* of Mexican cinema: Calles, Emilio Fernández and Alfonso Bedoya.

Mexican film production prospered in 1938, when nearly sixty features came out of the studios. During the year, eighteen new directors entered the industry, prompting the film workers union (UTECM) to establish a separate guild for this category of professionals. The creation of the Directors Union entailed the spelling-out of its rules of admission for new members. Before obtaining full membership, an applicant had to have directed at least three features. Also, a minimum wage for the directors was fixed at 7,500 pesos (about $1,500) per movie. At this moment, the union did not yet have the power to ban a producer from hiring non-members; with the passing of time, restrictive rules adopted by the guild made it almost impossible for non-members to direct a movie. No one could have imagined in 1938 that sixteen years later the Directors Union would block *El Indio* Calles — one of its founding members — from directing a movie.

8

Last Films as a Director

Hoping to repeat the success of his silent film *Sol de gloria*, Calles returned to the director's chair to start on a new version. He reshuffled the story but kept its suggestive title for the duration of the shooting. At the time of release, however, producers Guillermo Calderón and his cousin Virgilio Calderón changed its title to the more descriptive *Pescadores de perlas*. The journalist Alfonso Patiño Gómez wrote the dialogue. He had previously supplied dialogue for the silent serial *El automóvil gris*, which was re-released with sound. The 1938 production of *Pescadores de perlas* is of historical significance because it throws light on a lost silent picture. Unless *Sol de gloria* is ultimately recovered, the information on its plot will be subject to the review of the sound version.

Pescadores de perlas was shot in the port of Acapulco and the nearby Pie de la Cuesta. Production started in January 1938 and continued at the sound stages in Mexico City. Due to interruptions, it took three months to complete. The main actors and the characters they interpreted were Victoria Blanco (Rosa), Víctor Manuel Mendoza (Ignacio), Carlos Villatoro (Ernesto), Ángel T. Sala (Tiburcio), Efrén Buchelli (Gustavo), Sara García (Juana), Alfonso Bedoya (Simón) and Eufrosina García (Sofía). A synopsis of the story follows.

The beautiful Rosa is the only survivor of a shipwreck. The mulatto Ignacio finds her on the beach and takes her to the village. The brothers Ernesto and Gustavo, who head a group of pearl hunters, give her shelter. Ignacio falls in love with the young woman but keeps his feelings secret. Meanwhile, the good-looking Ernesto straightforwardly declares his love for her. The wicked Tiburcio, who steals pearls from others, kills Gustavo and then blames the mulatto for this crime. Ignacio cannot defend himself and hides in the wilderness with his dog. In his absence, his sick mother Juana dies. Ignacio's dog delivers a written message to Rosa, but when it returns to the wilderness, Tiburcio and the police follow. They apprehend the mulatto and sentence him to die at dawn. Rosa discovers a letter revealing that Ignacio is the half-brother of Ernesto. At the last minute, Sofía declares the mulatto's innocence, saving him from execution. Tiburcio tries to escape in a boat with his brother Simón but is captured and put in jail. Simón gets a band of criminals to attack the town's fortress and liberate the prisoner. Tiburcio is finally freed, but a shark later swallows him. During the assault on the fort, Ernesto is wounded. Rosa goes to his assistance and kisses him. Ignacio observes this scene from his cover position and gets distracted. He is fatally shot. Rosa and Ernesto see him die while the sun is setting.

This synopsis is particularly useful because it helps identify the characters and events

8. Last Films as a Director

of the original silent movie. Clearly the most developed figure in *Pescadores de perlas* is the mulatto Ignacio, who corresponds to the Indian Ignacio (Nacho) interpreted by Calles in *Sol de gloria*. Carmen La Roux, Carlos Molina, and José Domínguez most surely interpreted Rosa, Ernesto, and Tiburcio, respectively. Further, a review of *Pescadores de perlas* substantiates the slogans in the publicity of *Sol de gloria* when it was released: "Intrigue, Love, Combats, Execution, Shipwreck, Hungry Crocodiles, Voracious Sharks, and Panoramic Views of Beautiful Mexico."

Pescadores de perlas shows how much its director was influenced by the style and technique of the silent era. For example, the comings and goings of the characters during the attack on the fort remind us of the action serials starring William Duncan and Neal Hart. In all probability, the footage of a crocodile-infested pool was from a Hollywood silent picture, perhaps from *Sol de gloria* itself.

Some of the scenes in *Pescadores de perlas* are indicative of the romantic view that permeates the work of the Indian director. An example is the love triangle between Rosa, Ignacio and Ernesto, which inevitably ends with the tragic death of one of them. Although the heroine loves both men, she chooses Ernesto because he is akin to her race and social class. Painfully aware of this fact, Ignacio stoically renounces Rosa's love; at the same time, a bullet from an unknown assailant cuts through his chest. To emphasize the poetic nature of the story, the image of a splendid rose bush frames the agonized mulatto. The movie ends with a view of a sunset on the ocean's horizon. Thus the film's original title, *Sol de gloria*, echoes Ernesto's moving commentary on his brother's death: "He died with the setting of the sun, the sun of glory."

According to the romantic paradigm, the hero sacrifices himself for the good of others; his death ultimately stands as a proof of his nobility. In Calles's view, the racial status of the hero only adds to his moral fiber; being an Indian means staying free of the iniquity of whites. Already, the 1921 movie *De raza azteca* proposed a brave Indian who endangers his life in an attempt to defend his friend's fiancée from an attack. A similar model is used in *El indio yaqui* and *Sol de gloria*, where the hero endures persecution and unrequited love. In both movies, the male protagonist dies during a ferocious battle. Yet the perfect example is found in *Dios y ley*, which portrays a stoic Indian who sees no end to his torment. The movie highlights the suffering of the hero when a villain burns his eyes; this is followed by the Indian's renunciation of the woman he loves. Adding to it, the dreadful action takes place in the midst of an earthquake provoked by an erupting volcano.

A hint of the narrative style of *Sol de gloria* can be discerned in *Pescadores de perlas*. The resort to written messages is a typical feature of silent films; there are plenty of instances where this happens in the sound movie. First, the mulatto sends out his dog with a message to Rosa and she immediately responds in the same manner. Later, she gets an anonymous note revealing the true identity of Gustavo's assassin. On another occasion, Rosa finds by accident a letter explaining that Ernesto and the mulatto are half-brothers. At the last minute, when the mulatto is about to be executed, Rosa arrives bringing a dispatch that declares him innocent, thus saving his life. As was true of many films of the period, *Pescadores de perlas* typically utilizes written messages to speed up the action or to clarify various dilem-

Carlos Villatoro and Victoria Blanco form the romantic couple of *Pescadores de perlas* (1938), a remake of Calles's silent film *Sol de Gloria* (Carlos Villatoro Collection).

mas in the story. It was only natural that Calles exploited this technique following closely the models found in silent movies like *Sol de gloria*.

Pescadores de perlas is a rather short film, less than sixty-five minutes in length. Although its plot is simple, the linking of some scenes is awkward and the build up of the intrigue is weakened by the overload of letters and written explanations. Some characterizations are lacking in development, which perhaps is a consequence of the simple replication of the silent version. Ángel T. Sala's villain is too schematic and he utters his lines without much conviction. A similar problem afflicts Victoria Blanco, who at times seems to be reading her lines from cue cards behind the camera. On the other hand, the camera makes the most of her anatomy when she is emerging from the sea at the beginning of the story. Her dripping dress clinging to her body reflects the glow of a tropical sun. Also worthy of mention is the view of the shipwreck that utilized stock footage and miniature recreation in some parts.

Calles proved some of his skills by designing an apparatus for the submarine photography in *Pescadores de perlas*. A reporter who went to Acapulco to see the shooting observed: "What stood out and impressed us the most in the movie were some scenes taken at the

8. Last Films as a Director

bottom of the sea, for which they used a special underwater piece of equipment created by *El Indio* Calles, and in which there were fights with authentic sharks."[1] Two incidents in connection with these scenes endangered the lives of actors Carlos Villatoro and Víctor Manuel Mendoza. While doing a submarine dive, Villatoro risked being drowned by the current and the crew had to rescue him. On a separate occasion, Mendoza went into the water to perform a scene and nearly lost a foot to a shark bite. Because there were no adequate hospitals in Acapulco, the actor was driven to Mexico City. Mendoza's recuperation and other setbacks delayed the completion of the film, causing director Calles and the producers great anxiety.

Even though the movie included attractive songs performed by the *Charro* Felipe Gil, the release of *Pescadores de perlas* seems to have gone unnoticed. This author could find no printed records of its exhibition in Mexico City. In the United States, many theaters showed it under its original title, *Sol de gloria*.

Almost without a pause, in April 1938 Calles began preparations to direct *La virgen de la sierra*, a rural melodrama that depicted Mexican traditions. Originally, Emilio Gómez

In this *Pescadores de perlas* production still, Carlos Villatoro is second from left and next to him is sound engineer José B. Carles. Director Calles is in the center, between actresses Victoria Blanco and Eufrosina García. The rest are unidentified staff members and one actual Mexican soldier (standing, at right)(Carlos Villatoro Collection).

Muriel had been selected as director but producers Alejandro Seyffert and Carlos E. Amador substituted Calles. Although *La virgen de la sierra* is considered a lost film, we can get an idea of its plot by examining a transcript of dialogue deposited at the New York State Archives.[2] This transcript was used for censorship purposes during the film's release in 1939. At that time, a writer for *The New York Times* mistakenly ascribed the role of the villain to actor Raúl de Anda. Books and filmographies that relied solely on that writeup perpetuated this error. Thanks to the discovery of the dialogue transcript, we can identify with more accuracy the roles played by each actor: Anita Campillo (Juanita), Carlos Villatoro (Miguel), Raúl de Anda (Roberto), José Eduardo Pérez (Enrique), Armando Soto la Marina *Chicote* (Nicasio), Carmen Rivas Cacho (Chole), Pepe Martínez (Bernardino), Antonio Díaz (Pablo), Victoria Argota (Doña Elodia), César Rendón (Fernando) and Jesús Navarro (Jerónimo). A young woman appearing in the movie but not mentioned in the credits is Carolina Barret (Remedios). A movie still shows her in a scene in the town's cantina. Several stills have surfaced recently thanks to the research of historians Federico Dávalos and Esperanza Vázquez. These images are an indispensable aid in elucidating the story's plot and characters.

To be able to film underwater, Calles created a special piece of equipment. One of the *Pescadores de perlas* actors suffered an accident while doing a submarine scene. Here Carlos Villatoro is being lowered into the water as Ángel T. Sala (back right, in white shirt) looks on. The other men in the photograph are actual fishermen of Acapulco, cast as extras (Carlos Villatoro Collection).

8. Last Films as a Director

The story takes place on a Mexican ranch surrounded by mountains, where the virtuous Juanita lives in the company of her mother Doña Elodia and her brothers Roberto, Fernando and Jerónimo. Juanita also has a boyfriend, the noble and good-looking Miguel. A couple of servants work at the ranch, the amusing Nicasio and the *nana* Chole. Roberto receives Enrique and Pablo, two friends from the capital who arrive accompanied by their chauffeur Bernardino. Enrique, who is fond of women, has come "in search of a little adventure." He immediately focuses his attention on the beautiful Juanita. During a lively fiesta at the ranch, the deceitful Enrique plots the rape of Juanita; he prepares coffee mixed with a drug and gives it to Juanita and her boyfriend Miguel. Later in the night, the seducer poses as Miguel and convinces Juanita to join him in the dark.

The following morning, Juanita awakens obviously depressed and confesses to Doña Elodia what happened to her the night before. Enrique and Pablo have left the ranch with-

Flyer for *La virgen de la sierra*, a rural melodrama that opened in Mexico City in 1939, now a lost film. The ad at left shows Anita Campillo and Victoria Argota (Carlos Villatoro Collection).

out saying goodbye. Roberto is enraged with Miguel, who he thinks has seduced his sister. Miguel tries to prove that Enrique has committed the crime and that he should be brought to testify. By chance, Miguel finds an empty bottle labeled opium, confirming that he inadvertently drank this drug with the coffee during the fiesta. He goes out to find Enrique. In the town's cantina, the villain takes out a gun and kills Jerónimo. The locals want to take revenge on Enrique, condemning him to the "law of the Sierra." Enrique tries to escape at the same moment that Miguel arrives. They engage in a fistfight until Enrique falls off a cliff and dies.

Prior to the 1939 exhibition of *La virgen de la sierra* in New York, the state's censorship office eliminated some of its scenes. A document that accompanied the film's dialogue transcript gave specific instructions to this end. The censors ordered that prints for New York State theaters should remove "all views of Juanita and Enrique from point where they walk away after meeting, until girl is shown later in house. This will eliminate all scenes: back of carriage wheel, kisses, and awakening of girl." No doubt, the censors perceived the rape scene as scandalous. Another remark in the censor's document made it imperative to "eliminate all views of bottle labeled opium, a drug used for purpose of accomplishing

Juanita (Anita Campillo foreground, center) and her fiancé Miguel (Carlos Villatoro) attend a fiesta at the ranch in *La virgen de la sierra* (1938). Angelita Salcedo de Calles stands to Villatoro's left (Carlos Villatoro Collection).

seduction." Some of the reasons given for the rejection of these scenes were tersely quoted: "Would tend to corrupt morals" and "Immoral." New York's censorship of movies was in fact one of the most stringent. Throughout the thirties, several Mexican films were mutilated prior to their public showing. This practice continued for a long time, lessening somewhat in the mid-fifties.[3]

A note published in *La Prensa* of San Antonio, Texas, described an outdoor bathing scene in *La virgen de la sierra*. Partially nude, young actress Anita Campillo posed for the camera in the midst of a lake. (Reference to such a view is absent in the dialogue transcript at the New York censorship office. In all probability, the print examined by the censors had already been purged of the suggestive footage.) Witnessing the shooting, Esteban V. Escalante reported on this scene:

> Here we are, on the banks of the imposing Lake Zempoala, watching *El Indio* Calles direct some pleasant scenes of a movie that will be called *La ley de la sierra*. The scenery is magnificent; there is water all around, we see pine trees, and the exuberance of the Highlands. We spent almost all day looking with admiration at the sculpted body of Anita Campillo, as her scene simulated the bathing of a daughter of rich landowners. It was a moment of intimate contemplation for us and for all the artists. We will stay here for approximately five days, lost in the middle of the Sierra of the State of Morelos; and afterwards we will return again to the studios to finish this film of Producciones Seyffert, which promises to be an important effort, artistically and economically.[4]

For the opening of *La virgen de la sierra*, distributor Jorge M. Dada selected one of the most exclusive theaters in Mexico City, the Balmori. The publicity campaign included eye-catching flyers adorned with photos and original art. One of these leaflets proclaimed in a typical fashion: "An intense drama, tinged with pleasing songs, beautiful scenery, superb acting, and evocative music!" Certainly, a key ingredient in *La virgen de la sierra* was its music, composed and performed by *El Charro* Felipe Gil. Also, its authentic settings and fresh depiction of traditions earned the movie positive commentaries. Critic Juan M. Durán y Casahonda established the faults and virtues of the movie:

> A lot has been said about the excessive use of *charros* in Mexican movies. This new film directed by Guillermo Calles does not succeed in steering clear of the provincial theme. The story takes place in a *hacienda*, with the forceful guitar strumming, the local fiesta, and the domestic fauna. Yet, perhaps because the ranch is embedded in the most rugged country, we can feel the fresh air of the altitude and the scent of the people living in the fields, who are alien to the vices that corrode urban centers. In this, as in most local films, the director does not know how to move his characters; he is not aware of the technique that joins the action with the dialogue. Spectators get the impression that, in order to talk, the characters must pause and stand still in front of the camera. The dialogue is simple and pleasing, though. With a quicker pace and more smoothness, the story's bucolic zest would have been enriched.... The essence is there, in the Mexican *charros*, without ornament or other pretension, in a toast that looks so real, and in the dance of the girls at the neighboring village, which has such a simple elegance that it seduces us.[5]

The Latino Theater in New York City announced the opening of *La virgen de la sierra* in 1939. Writing for *The New York Times*, Harry T. Smith provided a tantalizing comment about the film:

The exuberant Sierra of the state of Morelos served as a backdrop for *La virgen de la sierra*. The film's crew and actors paused for a publicity shot. Back, left to right: Carlos Villatoro, unidentified, Raúl de Anda, José Eduardo Pérez, Antonio Díaz, unidentified, unidentified, Armando Soto la Marina ("Chicote") and Pepe Martínez. Front, left to right: unidentified, Guillermo Calles, producer Alejandro Seyffert, unidentified, Anita Campillo, film journalist Esteban V. Escalante, unidentified (Carlos Villatoro Collection).

> Americans contemplating a visit to the picturesque mountain country of Central Mexico and fancying themselves Don Juan would do well to see *La virgen de la sierra*, now at the Teatro Latino, and get an idea of what is likely to happen to young men taking unfair advantage of the innocent maidens of that region. Even the attractiveness of Anita Campillo fails to excuse the use of doped coffee by the city slicker [José Eduardo Pérez]. Consequently, the audience is happy when he gets his just deserts at the hands of the hero [Carlos Villatoro], who relieves the indignant rural folk of the job of applying "the law of the Sierra." Guillermo Calles ... added some pleasing music and pretty views to the routine action.[6]

La virgen de la sierra is just one example of numerous movies produced in 1938 that portrayed Mexican ranch life. Out of approximately sixty features completed that year, twenty-seven employed rural settings or tropical backgrounds. Because of the increase in production, the four studios in the capital worked at full capacity and the available pool of directors expanded considerably. Raúl de Anda, for example, made his debut directing a story full of folklore, *La tierra del mariachi*. Carlos Véjar was offered an opportunity to

8. Last Films as a Director

direct *La rosa de Xochimilco*, which was the second production of Alejandro Seyffert after *La virgen de la sierra*. Veteran actor Alfredo del Diestro joined the group directing *Nobleza ranchera*, a bucolic film in which he also starred. A Spanish immigrant, Martín de Lucenay, tried his luck and managed to make a couple of rural melodramas, *La Valentina* and *A lo macho*. Luis Lezama, who had only directed silent features, made *Un viejo amor*. An artist working as a set designer, Fernando A. Rivero, turned to directing in 1938. His movie *El fanfarrón* featured the virile singer Jorge Negrete and offered views of the Hacienda de Tetlapáyac, where Russian director Sergei Eisenstein shot part of his celebrated *Que viva México!*

Parallel to the growth of the industry, a sad reality emerged in the dishonest practices and corruption of some of its members. A highly visible case involved the leader of the UTECM (Union of Workers of Mexican Film Studios), Enrique Solís, who was accused of accepting bribes and exploiting workers. An organization of theater employees threatened to boycott films made by members of the UTECM. Workers took to the streets to protest this and other measures. A magazine described the procession of "artists with makeup on their faces, dressed in old, modern, and futuristic clothes; garbed in evening attire in the middle of the day, or sporting Emperor Maximilian's costumes, who arrived at the headquarters of the labor union to ask for the support of either this or that faction in the conflict."[7]

In spite of all these problems, the production of movies continued at a steady pace. At the end of 1938, Calles co-directed *La justicia de Pancho Villa* (aka *El gaucho Mújica*) with Guz Águila. This popular vaudeville author probably met Calles in the mid-twenties, when he was working on the Hispanic stage in Los Angeles. *La justicia de Pancho Villa* represented his debut as motion picture director and producer. He also wrote the script. The film's main cast included the Argentine singer Vicente Padula, Stella Inda, Amparo Arozamena, Loló Trillo, and Luis Álvarez, who took the role of Pancho Villa. The story recounted the adventures of a *gaucho* who leaves his beloved Argentina to join the revolutionary army of General Francisco Villa in Mexico. Enhancing *La justicia de Pancho Villa* were many musical performances and several stock shots with panoramic views of Chile, Perú, Ecuador, Colombia, and Panama. Viewer interest gets a boost when the *gaucho* (Padula) arrives in Mexico and comes face to face with Pancho Villa. The Argentine hero then tries to justify his

La justicia de Pancho Villa (1938) was the last film directed by Calles. He is seen here with cinematographer Ross Fisher and an unidentified staffer. To the left is Luis Álvarez as Pancho Villa (Rudy Calles Collection).

presence in the rebel army's territory. Suspicious of the foreigner, Villa orders his execution. At the last minute, the *gaucho* is declared innocent and set free.

The meager publicity campaign for the opening of *La justicia de Pancho Villa* affected its box office performance negatively. In view of this failure, Guz Águila retired from making movies. He continued his career as an author and scriptwriter, though. For Calles this turned out to be his last effort at directing. He went back to acting at the end of the decade, appearing in *Los de abajo*. Adapted from the famous novel written by Mariano Azuela, *Los de abajo* tells the story of a group of peasants forced by circumstances to join the Revolution. A colorful assortment of men and women are drawn to the chaos and looting engulfing the region. Calles appeared briefly in the role of a soldier chatting with comrades. He tells of his adventures with Pancho Villa and bursts out in praise of the revolutionary leader, whom he calls the Mexican Napoleon. Commenting on the airplanes used by Villa to fight the enemy, he says, "Just imagine a big bird, very big. Inside this bird, there is a gringo and he carries a bunch of grenades. When the time comes for fighting and as if feeding corn to the chicken, he throws lots and lots of grenades to the enemy." Calles makes this a memorable moment.

After participating in *Los de abajo*, Calles abandoned the film studios without giving any explanation. According to author Emilio García Riera, the filmmaker intended to shoot the political campaign of the presidential candidate Juan Andreu Almazán.[8] It is probable that Calles committed himself to follow General Almazán in his travels around the country, beginning in October of 1939 and ending in June of the following year. However, there is no proof of this involvement. Almazán's presidential campaign ran into many troubles. His most powerful opponents used every method to discredit him and put him out of the race. The general once said that certain federal authorities had paid the "communist newspapers" to publish defamatory articles against him. He complained bitterly that the government tried to silence all opposition by "preventing people from using the most efficient means of modern propaganda: the radio and the cinema, while the [official candidate] enjoyed free publicity from these resources."[9] Adding to this, Almazán was the object of several assassination attempts during his bid for the presidency.

The whereabouts of Willie Calles during a period of three and a half years are shrouded in mystery. A still from *Konga roja* (1943) (Agrasánchez Film Archive).

The whereabouts of Guillermo Calles during a period of three and a half years are shrouded in mystery. From his participation in *Los de abajo*, in September 1939, to his reappearance in the cast of *Konga roja*, in March 1943, his name was missing from the roster of actors for films shot in Mexico. It is not likely that he attempted to go back to Los Angeles, as he was no longer a U.S. resident. A note appearing in *La Prensa* of San Antonio, Texas, is the only clue we have of the artist's situation. At the end of March 1940, this newspaper mentioned that critics had pounded at Calles's *La justicia de Pancho Villa*. He therefore decided to take a break, relocating to the port of Acapulco, where he set up a business selling cold drinks. There is further indication of his presence there in the early 1940s. A Canadian Club Whisky ad in a magazine showed Calles posing as a native of "Mexico's gorgeous Acapulco." He has a smiling face and looks at a macaw on his shoulder. The full-page color ad recommends, "A pageant of bird and animal life, of warmth and color."

9

Confrontation with Labor Unions and Hunger Strike

Filmmaking in Mexico developed at a fast pace during the 1940s. What started out as a feeble entrepreneurial activity in the early sound period, evolved into a structured organization of great impact in the economy of the country. By some accounts, the motion picture industry came to occupy sixth place in national importance, after such manufacturing products as cotton textiles, iron metals, lamination, automobile assembly and beer production. A sure sign of the advance of moviemaking in the mid-forties was the creation of the Churubusco studios, the largest film facilities in Latin America. Also providing services to producers were the Azteca, Clasa, Tepeyac, and San Angel Inn studios. Because of this expansion, the turnout of movies soared to an unprecedented 108 films in 1949, reaching a record-breaking 123 pictures the following year. Mexico's cinema was exported to all the Spanish-speaking countries. In the United States, hundreds of theaters catering to Hispanics billed Mexican films on a daily basis, complemented them with Hollywood pictures.[1]

In this highly competitive entertainment industry, Calles carved himself a place as a character actor. After 1940, he worked in more than fifty films including some U.S. productions shot in Mexico. His specialty roles were Indians, peasants and witch doctors. Calles felt at ease interpreting any of these types, contributing an unobtrusive presence that complemented the work of other actors. Even though he possessed vast performing experience, none of the films of the period fully exploited it. Keeping a low profile thus seemed to confirm the proverbial modesty of this artist.

Besides his brief appearances on film, he was involved in the itinerant exhibition of movies, an activity that he enhanced with the staging of live shows. Calles spent a great deal of time traveling in Mexico hauling his mobile home, a 16mm projector, film prints and other props. These resources, coupled with his acting experience, allowed him to work anywhere he wanted. An assistant, Manuel Fuentes, and a few other artists usually accompanied him on these tours. Calles delighted in putting on sensational shows. One of his favorite tricks involved the display of a shrunken head, which he called "my inseparable friend." He recounted that he obtained it from a South American Jíbaro tribe. This macabre trophy previously belonged to an Indian prince who lived many years ago in Ecuador. Possessing exuberant black hair and child-like features, the bizarre cranium seemed to sweat when exposed to the sun. The stage recreation of Jíbaro rituals attracted curious people at

9. Confrontation with Labor Unions and Hunger Strike

Calles (right) had an itinerant show. One of his favorite tricks involved the display of a shrunken head. Ramón Sánchez Hernández (center) often participated as an Indian in these performances. The young man at right is an unidentified assistant (Rudy Calles Collection).

every stop. A tall and muscular actor, Ramón Sánchez Hernández often participated as an Indian in these performances. The bare-chested figure of Sánchez provided an imposing element to the show. A curious 1950s photograph shows him sharing the spotlight with his friend Calles and a young assistant, who are wearing safari outfits.

The list of movies in which Calles appeared at this time is long; he is at his best in three films starring Pedro Infante: *Los tres Huastecos*, *La mujer que yo perdí* and *El enamorado*. The first is an amusing rural comedy made in 1948 that tells the story of the triplets: Víctor is an army officer, Juan is a priest, and the fierce Lorenzo owns a local cantina. There is also a six-year-old tomboy called "Tucita" (played by María Eugenia Llamas). Looking after her is Bronco (Calles), Lorenzo's loyal servant, who balks at the girl's uncouth manners. An enjoyable film with pleasant songs, it stands out for its innovative optical effects that multiply Infante's image on the screen. Other actors performing in *Los tres Huastecos* were Blanca Estela Pavón and Fernando Soto "Mantequilla."

In the drama *La mujer que yo perdí* (1949), Calles played an Indian whose daughter (Blanca Estela Pavón) falls in love with the story's hero (Infante). Both father and daughter are killed during battles with federal soldiers. Calles made a frightening villain called "El Cuervo" in *El enamorado* (1951), a sequel to *Ahí viene Martín Corona*, both starring Pedro Infante and Sarita Montiel. One of the highlights of the film is the stealing of a baby by the villain. After a chase to the top of a mountain, "El Cuervo" uses the child as a shield, threatening to let him fall down a precipice. Infante saves the child, getting rid of the evildoer at the last minute.

Matilde Landeta, the only woman director in Mexico during this period, summoned Calles to perform in *Lola Casanova* (1948) and *La negra Angustias* (1949). *La negra Angustias* depicted the rise of a mulatto woman who becomes the leader of a rebel army during the Mexican Revolution. *Lola Casanova* dealt with the racial problems of the Seris, an Indian tribe of Sonora. In this "ethnographic melodrama," a white woman, Lola Casanova, falls in love with one of the chieftains of the tribe and gradually helps transform the lives of the Indians. They now begin to dress "in the impeccable white cottons of the working peasant," while establishing commercial relations with the Yoris (Mexicans). Calles played an old Seri Indian in this story.[2] While shooting *Lola Casanova* in July 1948, Calles received news of the death of his mother, Anatolia Guerrero. She passed away in Los Angeles at age ninety-five.

Another film that focused on the plight of Indians was *Tierra muerta*, which began production in January 1949. Scripted and directed by Vicente Oroná, it recounted the hardships of the Tarascan Indians. A half-breed called "El Renegado" (Carlos López Moctezuma) is as obsessed with obtaining the lands of peasants as he is with getting the young Indian

A dramatic moment in *La mujer que yo perdí* (1949): Pedro Infante (left) mourning the death of Calles' loyal Indian (Agrasánchez Film Archive).

María (Irma Torres) to love him. "El Renegado" sets the Indians' crops on fire and orders his henchmen to rape María. The Indian José de Jesús (Víctor Manuel Mendoza) loves María and seeks revenge but is obstructed by the locals. Siding with the villain, the mob plans to burn José de Jesús at the stake. María enters the church and calls upon a crucifix to save his life. A nearby volcano erupts, causing havoc. "El Renegado" is killed during a strong earthquake. After the tragedy, José de Jesús and María reunite and leave the deserted village in search of a better life.

Calles' appearance in *Tierra muerta*, as María's father, was not his only contribution to this film. Although the screenplay is attributed to Oroná, some of its central ideas came from Calles' *Dios y ley*. Oroná in all probability saw *Dios y ley* when it played in Los Angeles in 1929. The Uruguayan-born artist worked as a bit player in Hollywood at this time and it is likely that he knew Calles or his films. In Mexico, he continued performing in movies and wrote screenplays prior to becoming a director in the forties. *Tierra muerta* reflects an episode that took place in 1943 when a volcano destroyed the town of Paricutín, Michoacán. The cataclysm left only a ruined church surrounded by a huge mass of basalt rock. These events, still fresh in the memory of Mexicans, provided a dramatic background to Oroná's tale. Similarly, twenty years before, *Dios y ley* recounted another catastrophe: the eruption of the Colima Volcano in 1913. While such episodes suggest some correspondence in the narratives of Oroná and Calles, other details confirm an obvious connection between these two movies.

Dios y ley and *Tierra muerta* present as the central figure a heroic Indian: Daniel, interpreted by Calles in the first film, and José de Jesús, played by Víctor Manuel Mendoza in the second production. Carmen Guerrero plays the female character of *Dios y ley*. Although not really an Indian, she is a worthy descendant of Indians. *Tierra muerta* goes a step further: María (Irma Torres) represents the earth. Her faithful lover, José de Jesús, refers metaphorically to her as "mi buena tierra" (my good earth). Fire and flames are a recurring theme in these two movies. In *Dios y ley*, a sinister villain uses a burning stick to blind forever the unfortunate Indian Daniel. In like manner, at the end of *Tierra muerta* the villagers, consumed with anger, attempt to burn alive the Indian José de Jesús. Furthermore, these narratives establish the villain as a half-breed and *Tierra muerta* even calls him "El Renegado" (betrayer) because he despises his own Indian heritage. Lastly, the invocation of divine justice by the oppressed and the ensuing of a natural catastrophe are climactic moments in both stories. The presence of a crucifix in both narratives speaks of a deity who is merciful towards humanity.

Calles' name did not always appear in the on-screen credits of films. Examples are *Bajo el cielo de Sonora* (1947), *Pasión jarocha* (1949), *Sentencia* (1949), *Dos caras tiene el destino* (1951), *El bruto* (1952), *Espaldas mojadas* (1953), and *The Beast of Hollow Mountain* (1954). Calles's brief presence in these pictures is not mentioned in any filmography. In *Bajo el cielo de Sonora*, he played the role of a Yaqui Indian. Calles gave life to a vengeful Yaqui chief who tortures a white man by peeling the skin off his feet. The story has considerable depth for a fictional film, scrutinizing the real situation and conflicts between Mexicans (or "Yoris") and Indians. Calles again personified an old Indian in the historical melodrama *Sentencia*, which was set during the French Intervention in Mexico. When the movie opens, we hear his voice reading to other Indians an infamous Maximilian decree that condemned all enemies of the Empire to the death penalty. In *Espaldas mojadas*, Calles is a "wetback" eager to cross the Rio Grande swimming "de ranita," or frog style. The Mexican-U.S. co-production *The Beast of Hollow Mountain* is a cult film about a prehistoric creature that shows up in a remote region of Mexico. Through careful viewing, one might be able to discover Calles' presence in other movies.

Besides acting in local productions, Calles participated in many Hollywood films shot in Mexico. Some of the better known in this category are *The Treasure of Pancho Villa* (1954), *Seven Cities of Gold* (1954) and *The Last Frontier* (1955). Perhaps the most famous of all was John Farrow's *Hondo* (1953), a 3-D film featuring John Wayne and Geraldine Page, with the participation of the Mexican actors Rodolfo Acosta and Calles. In this Western, shot in Camargo, Tamaulipas, Calles played the role of a native sorcerer and Acosta appeared as a young Indian leader. In *The Treasure of Pancho Villa*, Calles made a brief appearance as a Yaqui Indian who helps a group of Mexican soldiers track down an American treasure-hunter. Directed by George Sherman, this RKO production featured Rory Calhoun, Shelley Winters, Gilbert Roland, and Joseph Calleia. Its Mexican cast was composed of Fanny Schiller, Tony Carbajal, Carlos Múzquiz, Pascual García Peña, and Calles.

Another movie of importance was *Seven Cities of Gold*, directed by Robert D. Webb and starring Richard Egan, Anthony Quinn, Michael Rennie, and Rita Moreno. Also taking part were the Mexicans Eduardo Noriega, Víctor Junco, Carlos Múzquiz, and Calles. A voice at the beginning of the movie announces, "This is a story of the Spanish conquest of California and the search for the legendary Seven Cities of Gold. A story of primitive Indians, an army of mercenaries and a man of God: his name was Junípero Serra." Rennie played Serra while Calles interpreted an old Indian chief who refuses to abandon his traditions. In an effort to win him over to Catholicism, the Franciscan priest offers a pair of scissors as a gift. Although amused by this mechanical novelty, the Indian keeps his sentiments to himself. It is true that Calles's role is a small one but his presence commands total attention for a few seconds; his eyes spark with a fiery liveliness and his voice reverberates like a far-flung surge. This sequence provided a breathing space in the lavish historical epic made by Twentieth Century-Fox.

In contrast to his effective interpretation in *Seven Cities of Gold*, Calles later accepted other roles that failed to utilize his talent. For example, he took part in *La guarida del Buitre* (1956), a Western in which he plays a small-town mayor who appears briefly and has almost no dialogue. There are times when his voice sounds slurred and his figure is murky. Even worse, other secondary actors who are more aggressive usually step in front of Calles, blocking him from view. Understandably, the pioneer filmmaker seemed tired and a lot less interested in acting by now.

In 1954, the devaluation of the Mexican currency affected everyone, but especially the working classes. The rate of exchange was fixed at 12.50 pesos to the U.S. dollar, a 44 percent depreciation of the legal tender. As a result, prices went up on products and services, distressing even further the underprivileged. Because current salaries were insufficient, the

Original one-sheet poster for *Tierra muerta* (1949). The film's director, Vicente Oroná, was probably influenced by Calles's *Dios y ley* when he wrote this story (Agrasánchez Film Archive).

The U.S.-Mexico co-production *The Beast of Hollow Mountain* (1954) starring Guy Madison (left) is a movie about a prehistoric creature that shows up in a remote village. Calles (center) plays a minor role in this film. Carlos Rivas is at right (Agrasánchez Film Archive).

country's powerful labor unions threatened to go on strike if their demands for pay raises went unheard. This crisis extended to the film industry; movie theater employees walked out of their jobs on over one thousand occasions throughout the year. Adding to this, the National Actors Union (ANDA) pushed for a 24 percent raise in salaries for its members. The Sindicato de Autores y Adaptadores, which involved the screenwriters, made similar demands.

As a consequence of high costs and inflation, the quality of films began to decline. Movie companies tried to save money, shrinking their budgets. In some cases, producers cut down shooting schedules to only two or three weeks. Such was the practice of Jesús Grovas who, aided by director Juan Bustillo Oro, turned out five movies in a period of only eight months.[3] Another producer, Edgardo Gazcón, came up with a formula to make three Westerns at the same time with the same cast. Adventure stories were in demand and one company shot a series of sci-fi movies featuring a masked wrestler hero: *La Sombra Vengadora* and *La Sombra Vengadora contra la Mano Negra*. This same company followed swiftly

9. Confrontation with Labor Unions and Hunger Strike

César Romero (center) as Cortés and Tyrone Power (right) as Pedro de Varga, in *Captain from Castile* (1947). Calles can be seen in the background playing an Indian chief (Agrasánchez Film Archive).

with two pictures that included the masked hero of the previous films, plus a most celebrated character: Pancho Villa. This formula of quick and simultaneous productions proved very effective, becoming an accepted practice in the industry. It inspired Raúl de Anda to film a triple Western featuring Fernando Casanova. The resulting footage, however, was not enough for three features so the average running time of each barely reached one hour.

The brothers Alfonso and Rodolfo Rosas Priego, descendants of pioneer filmmaker Enrique Rosas, announced in August 1954 the production of several movies. Rodolfo made plans for the immediate shooting of three Westerns: *La barranca de la muerte*, *La huella del Chacal* and *La guarida del Buitre*. Like Alfonso, who had contracted an old-timer to direct his movies, Rodolfo sought to bring Calles back to the director's chair. Problems ensued when the news reached the union of cinema directors, of which Calles had long ceased to be a member. A powerful branch of the STPC (Sindicato de Trabajadores de la Producción Cinematográfica), this union opposed the producer's plan to hire *El Indio* Calles. Like most labor unions, the Directors Guild was hermetically sealed to new members. Controlled by the elite of filmmakers, it effectively enforced a "closed door" policy.

Heading the Directors Guild were Alejandro Galindo (secretary general), Ernesto Cortázar (internal affairs), Carlos Toussaint (external affairs), Emilio Gómez Muriel (treasurer), Gilberto Martínez Solares (labor disputes), Marco Aurelio Galindo (cultural affairs), Matilde S. Landeta (propaganda) and Juan José Segura (minutes). Members of this organization blocked all competition from prospective filmmakers, in order to guard their employment and salary privileges.

This incident revealed the inner corruption of the Directors Guild, which would not allow one of its founders to direct a movie, while welcoming others with less experience to do so. For instance, Carlos Toussaint, who had only made two or three films, returned in 1954 to direct *El crucifijo de piedra*. Another case involved Humberto Gómez Landero, who had not directed a picture since 1949. He came back to shoot one movie and waited five more years to make another one. Journalist Carlos Bravo "Carl-Hillos" published an open letter to the Mexican president in which he complained about these irregularities; Carl-Hillos exposed the corruption of the film industry, blaming its leaders and bureaucrats who enjoyed a comfortable position thanks to the old practice of "compadrazgo,"

Gilbert Roland (left, holding baby), Paulette Goddard, Walter Reed, Willie Calles and an unidentified gentleman during a break while filming *The Torch* (1949) (courtesy of Dick Domínguez).

or nepotism. Notwithstanding, the Directors Guild persisted in rejecting new members. Benito Alazraki was banned from the STPC but he got an opportunity to direct a movie and joined a rival union of cinema workers, the STIC (Sindicato de Trabajadores de la Industria Cinematográfica). This union could only carry out the production of short features, though. Journalist Arturo Perucho wrote at this time a controversial article which said in part:

> In Mexico, as in any other country of liberal regime, monopolies are prohibited. Nevertheless, there is one such monopoly: that of the cinematographic directors. Like in all the liberal countries, in Mexico there is freedom to work in any legal activity. But there is one legal doing that is barred to the immense majority of citizens: that of directing pictures. Any person who has the talent or thinks that he has it, can make a sculpture, a painting, a book, a symphony; but cannot create a film work because the cinema directors that are grouped in an all-powerful monopoly, infamously called union, do not allow it.... This attitude of the Directors Guild has one explanation: approximately sixty members are part of it, and they shield their incompetence by virtue of this monopoly and prevent potential rivals from ruining them. In fact, many of them are so inept that they have not been able to direct a movie in many years; but they still belong to their union and persist in opposing others [who want] to direct.[4]

9. Confrontation with Labor Unions and Hunger Strike

After a wait of almost four months petitioning a place in the Directors Guild, and receiving no answer, Calles considered an extreme option: to protest publicly by means of a hunger strike. Obviously frustrated, on November 10, 1954, the Indian artist took to the streets wearing a dark suit, a tie and sunglasses. He walked from his home to the downtown Teatro de Bellas Artes, an imposing building of white marble dedicated to the performing arts. Here, *El Indio* Calles set up his chair and unfolded a sign with the inscription: "Guillermo Calles El Indio, actor and director of national cinema. By my own right, I put on a hunger strike appealing for justice. Mr. President of Mexico: I ask that I be allowed to practice my profession." The press in the capital immediately focused on this incident, publishing several photographs of the protestor:

> Surrounded by noisy sensationalism, Guillermo Calles, better known as *El Indio* and whose name is linked to the history of the Mexican movie industry since the distant days of the silent screen, crossed several downtown avenues until reaching the Palace of Fine Arts. He set up a sign that explained his resolution and sunk in his canvas chair ... starting a hunger strike that would last for over fifty hours. The method that Calles selected was not, however, the most appropriate in obtaining his admission to the Section of Directors of the S.T.P.C. of the R.M. But he was left with no other choice by the directors, who have imposed the absurd requisite to all persons engaged in artistic creation of belonging to their union. The entry to this union is practically impossible, because the rules that have been devised and approved by a greater part of inept people constitute a sure cover for this incompetent majority who is afraid to be deprived of working in a capacity for which it is not proficient.... It is a shame to the Mexican film industry that *El Indio* Calles would have picked such an unfortunate means to break the iron circle built around the Directors Guild.[5]

Some journalists condemned "the obvious discrimination" against Calles, yet other people condemned this artist's unorthodox style of protesting. The editor of *Cinema Reporter* expressed his disappointment saying that, "the sensational system used by our old friend Calles is not of our approval." *Cinema Reporter* added that some of the directors threatened to resign if Calles entered this union; among them were Rogelio A. González and Rafael Portillo.[6] The thirty-four-year-old González had already directed twelve movies, several of them starring the popular Pedro Infante. Portillo's only work had been the comedy *El fantasma se enamora* (1952). By contrast, people like Emilio Fernández, who was by now a recognized filmmaker, always decried the "closed door" policy of the Directors Guild. Fernández charged that this attitude of segregation had a negative effect on the advancement of filmmaking in Mexico.

Following a fifty-six-hour period of fasting in the middle of the downtown avenue, the physically weakened Calles was taken to a medical center. There arrived the actor Rodolfo Landa, leader of the Actors Union, and José Rodríguez Granada, head of the STPC labor union. They brought good news of the acceptance of Calles as a member of the Directors Guild. The convalescent only responded "I was never alone" in allusion to the crowds that cheered him during his protest. Putting on a smile, he said jokingly to Landa: "At last, I am going to have the opportunity of directing the Union's General Secretary in a movie, but be sure: you are going to have to walk very straight, or else...."[7]

Although the Sección de Directores granted membership to *El Indio* Calles, he was

In 1954, powerful labor unions prevented Calles from working as a director. To protest, he staged a hunger strike in downtown Mexico City (Rudy Calles Collection).

unable to direct a movie. Those opposing his admission simply made a symbolic concession to the beleaguered artist. The pressure of this labor union on producers like Rodolfo Rosas Priego was enormous, and the three Westerns to be directed by Calles were assigned instead to Jaime Salvador, a prolific Spanish-born filmmaker. Ironically, Calles appeared briefly in two of these movies, *La huella del Chacal* (1955) and *La guarida del Buitre* (1956).

The Sección de Directores was not the only entity in the film industry to deny Calles his rightful place as a director. Even the authors of the 1955 *Enciclopedia Cinematográfica Mexicana*, Ricardo Rangel and Rafael E. Portas, ignored Calles when listing the names of 117 current and past directors. Their impressive calculations missed *El Indio* Calles. At least they included him in a section dedicated to actors. There is one probable reason why this 1,322-page volume neglected to mention Calles as a director. Clearly, the only source consulted was the archives of the Directors Guild. When authors Rangel and Portas did their research, Calles's name had been removed from the files of this institution. Therefore, the much-publicized strike and efforts to become part of the STPC had accomplished nothing.

9. Confrontation with Labor Unions and Hunger Strike

Calles' hunger strike was legendary. In the mid-fifties, journalist Raúl Talán interviewed the Indian artist, who gave more details of his protest. He said that more than five thousand theater employees were ready to go on strike if Calles's demand was not heard. The physician who checked his health after fifty hours without water and food commented: "If this man stays another ten hours without eating he will die." Calles had words of gratitude for Rodolfo Landa, the leader of the Actors Association. Landa was supportive of Calles's decision to go on strike and defended the struggling actor at all times.

Although the industry produced about a hundred movies per year in the mid-fifties, the quality of most of them declined. Because more pictures were made on location to save money, the oldest studios began to close their doors. The film facilities of Tepeyac and Clasa disappeared in 1957. Azteca studios went out of business in 1958. To account for their demise were the new Estudios América, which offered an economic alternative to producers. The América specialized in short features but the producers came up with the idea of making serials that were later put together as feature films. The exclusive San Angel Inn and Churubusco studios continued providing services to the most affluent companies, including Hollywood producers.

Foreign pictures were usually shot at the Churubusco studios. Many Hollywood productions also took advantage of locations throughout the country. Calles appeared in some of these movies of the 1950s: *Sitting Bull*, *Run for the Sun*, and *The Brave One*. Besides employing professional Mexican actors for secondary roles, U.S. companies hired many extras to perform as Indians. Naturally, adventure films did not attempt to represent historical truth in any way. *Sitting Bull*, for example, took many liberties in its interpretation of Indian reality. When it played in North Dakota, Sioux audiences were critical of the attire and language. "The Indians talked and looked like Mexicans," observed Chief Ben American Horse after watching the film. Although *Sitting Bull* was filmed in Mexico, many of its locales very much resembled the Black Hills.[8]

Circa 1957, Calles also appeared in *Captain David Grief*, a movie series produced by Sidney T. Bruckner for television. He played the role of Kulai in the second-season episode called "Port of Rogues." He was third-billed behind Maxwell Reed and Yerye Beirute. Also acting in *Captain David Grief* were Federico Curiel and Elvira Quintana. Calles had previously worked in another Bruckner production, the Mexican comedy *Delirio tropical* (1951).

Yo el aventurero, a rural comedy featuring singer Antonio Aguilar, was Calles's final screen appearance. On February 28, 1958, while filming was still in progress at the Churubusco studios, the sixty-six-year-old actor died of a heart attack. He was living alone in his mobile home parked outside of the Hotel Juan Diego, on 1917 North Insurgentes Avenue. Just a day before, he had a casual conversation with a group of friends at the headquarters of the Actors Union (ANDA). Calles did not have any relatives in Mexico; therefore, the money from his life insurance would revert to the Actors Union. Very few people gathered for his funeral. Among the persons attending were directors Emilio *Indio* Fernández and Ramón Peón and actors Felipe de Flores, Gregorio Dante and Gustavo Aponte. The association of cinema extras showed its respects by sending a wreath. Similarly, members of the ANDA commissioned its leader, Rodolfo Landa, and the comedian José Ángel Espinoza

Ferrusquilla to offer a floral ornament. Obviously moved, Emilio Fernández conveyed his thoughts to the press: "We cannot pay back Willie's actions; in Hollywood, he helped us a lot, and in Mexico he was the first one to direct a movie. He became a pioneer of the cinema and I think it is only appropriate that a posthumous tribute be paid to him. He was very Mexican."9

Immediately after Calles died, the newspaper *Cine Mundial* dedicated several pages to his career and unique lifestyle. Many previously unseen photographs of the artist appeared in the pages of this daily on March 1 and 2, 1958. An article titled "Trophies and Relics that Surrounded Calles" revealed some interesting facts:

> Several trophies from Central America; others from the Mexican Cinema Reporters (PECIME); pictures of silent Mexican films; his mother's photograph; a small idol from Indonesia, plus other curious gadgets and relics make up the decoration of the "itinerant home," which was also an office, where the late *Indio* Calles lived and where he received people. All these [artifacts] were guarded by an image of the Christ in the supreme sacrifice of the cross. The young Manuel Fuentes was a secretary to the deceased; he helped Calles show films during itinerant sessions offered by the actor and film director. It was also this young man who witnessed the anguish of Guillermo Calles Guerrero when his heart refused to keep pumping, suffering a stroke that cost him his life. His young secretary took down the crucifix from the bedroom's wall and placed it on the chest of the ill-fated *Indio* Calles.10

This issue of *Cine Mundial* showed a photograph of a diploma given to Calles in 1949 by PECIME, an organization of cinema reporters. The occasion was the release of *Canciones y recuerdos*, a documentary produced and directed by Fernando A. Rivero portraying the history of local movies. PECIME awarded the diploma to several filmmakers and artists, including Calles. The inscription on this certificate read: "Homage to the National Cinema, upon the release of *Canciones y recuerdos*. PECIME is proud to pay a tribute to Guillermo Calles, for his hard work in the enhancement of the Mexican movie industry."

During the forties and fifties, Calles kept a low profile in the film industry. As happened to many actors before and after him, the final stage of his career went almost unnoticed. Still, he was in the spotlight during the much-publicized hunger strike of 1954. Although his plea did not restore him as a director, it exposed the prevailing elitism of the Directors Guild. Beginning when he was a child in Morenci, Arizona, Calles learned how to stand up for his rights. In 1903, he witnessed an imposing strike of Mexican miners that was suppressed by the federal army. The Morenci strike did not bring justice to the

During the last years of his life, *El Indio* Calles lived in a mobile home. Thus he was able to travel everywhere carrying a 16mm projector and films that he exhibited to audiences (Rudy Calles Collection).

9. Confrontation with Labor Unions and Hunger Strike

Mexican workers either, but in the end it showed the courage and determination of a people fighting for a cause. Fifty years later, in Mexico City, Guillermo was at the center of a storm, risking his own life for the realization of a professional ideal.

A pioneer of Hollywood movies since 1912, Calles had an extraordinary career that covered forty-seven years. There were many highlights. One of the first studios, the Lubin Company, put him in the cast of *A Mexican Tragedy*. Afterwards, he worked as a stuntman and landed some important roles in the popular Vitagraph serials. But his vision was to produce movies, a challenge that he tackled with limited resources but enormous faith. This dynamic artist launched the first Mexican film with synchronized sound, *Dios y ley*. Calles arrived in Mexico City in the early 1930s to collaborate in the birth of local talkies as an actor and director. During the following decades, he was seen playing bit parts in numerous Mexican and Hollywood productions. Next to his impressive career in front and behind the camera, the actor lived the life of an itinerant exhibitor, bringing films and live spectacle to a varied public. *El Indio* Calles always felt proud of his racial background and valued a life of simplicity. When he died, the press universally acknowledged him as "el último bohemio del cine mexicano": the last bohemian of Mexican cinema.

Epilogue: The Calles Family

The story of Guillermo Calles cannot be complete without mentioning the lives of others around him. Even though he treasured his independence and lived a wandering life, relatives and friends were always important to him. Guillermo came from a large family; his father married three times and had fifteen children. Nepomuceno's first wife was Francisca González, with whom he had four children. After becoming a widower, he married Dolores Tena and had one more child. Nepomuceno was widowed again and remarried, this time to Anatolia Guerrero, with whom he had ten children, the youngest of whom was Guillermo. Nepomuceno died in 1893, two years after fathering Guillermo.

As a child, Guillermo always lived with his mother, who was of Tarahumara origin. Physically, Guillermo strongly resembled her. Anatolia passed on to her youngest son many of her Indian traits, including a fiercely independent character. Of all the children of doña Anatolia, Guillermo was the most radical in clinging to his Indian past. The rest of the family did not share in this obsession, taking for granted their racial condition of *mestizos*, or mixed blood Mexicans. In fact, subsequent generations were raised unaware of any connection to a Tarahumaran ancestor. For example, Rudy Calles, Guillermo's nephew, never mentioned that his paternal grandmother was an Indian. Even the intricate genealogies of the Calles family that were written by Pascual Calles, Daniel M. Santa Ana, and Emil C. Espinosa, Jr., lack all reference to an Indian past.

It is possible to get a glimpse of Guillermo's intimate connections with his folks by looking at family memorabilia. Nepomuceno's eldest son, Mariano, appears to have been close to doña Anatolia and her offspring. A 1902 family photograph taken in Morenci, Arizona, shows the forty-eight-year-old Mariano surrounded by Anatolia and several of her children and grandchildren. He looks very much like a paternal figure; his face strongly resembles that of eleven-year-old Guillermo. In the early twenties, when Mariano lived in El Paso, Guillermo used to visit him regularly. Other relatives whom he saw frequently in the El Paso–Ciudad Juárez area at this time were his sister, María de Jesús Calles de Calvillo, and her son José María Calvillo. María de Jesús was perhaps Guillermo's closest sister. A son from her first marriage, José "Pepe" Domínguez, became a bit player in Hollywood films. Naturally, Guillermo had much in common with his nephew Pepe. But he also became close to José María Calvillo, who visited his uncle Willie in Mexico on several occasions.

The images and handwritten inscriptions on photos of the family reveal a desire for sharing. Publicity and snapshots of the artist were a favorite gift to relatives. A 1920s stu-

Epilogue: The Calles Family

dio portrait showing Calles in Indian fashion bears a simple dedication to his sister: "A mi hermana Jesús C. de Calvillo, de Willie Calles." Several 8 × 10 signed photographs were presented to his brother Pascual and his nephew Rodolfo "Rudy" Calles. The inscription on one of them reads, "Con todo cariño para mi ahijado y sobrino Rodolfo Calles. Wm. Calles" ("With all my love to my godson and nephew, Rodolfo Calles. Wm. Calles"). In 1916, Pascual chose his brother Guillermo to be a "padrino," or godfather, for his newborn son Rudy. Traditionally, having a relative as a "compadre" reinforced family ties in the Hispanic culture. Uncle Willie enjoyed being a "padrino" and cultivated this relationship over the years, sometimes exchanging personal photographs with Pascual and his son. Rudy carefully kept these objects all of his life, believing that Willie's cinematic career was something the family should take pride in. After Rudy died in 2001, these photos passed on to his stepdaughter Gloria Ortega, who made them available to illustrate this book.

María de Jesús Calles de Calvillo and Anatolia Guerrero, sister and mother of Guillermo Calles, in the early 1940s (courtesy of Ernie Domínguez).

Epilogue: The Calles Family

Rudy's parents were Pascual Calles and Justina Hernández. The couple married in Chihuahua in 1900 and lived for a while in Clifton-Morenci, Arizona. Subsequently they moved to Ciudad Juárez, Chihuahua, and El Paso, Texas, before settling in Pasadena, California. Their children were Belén, Raymundo, Arturo, Dora, Pascual Jr., Rodolfo (Rudy), Beatrice, and Elena. Before marrying, Pascual traveled in Mexico as an amateur actor in a stage company. His love for the performing arts and a predilection for the itinerant life surely influenced his brother Guillermo, who was eleven years his junior.

Pascual enthusiastically supported civic organizations in the 1920s. His name was mentioned several times by the Los Angeles's Spanish-language newspapers, establishing him as a member of the "Liga Protectora Latina" in Pasadena. A publication refers to him as a "Venerable Maestro" of a Masonic lodge, "La Logia Masónica Minerva del Rito Nacional Mexicano." It seems that he was also good at writing, as he often read poems at public gatherings sponsored by his lodge. During the 1930s, Pascual took on the job of a gardener at the Busch Gardens, near Pasadena. He witnessed the filming of a scene from the movie *Gone with the Wind* at this location. Pascual boasted of having a sharp memory, quoting the names and birthdates of many of his ancestors. Emil C. Espinosa, Jr., son of Belén Calles, compiled a genealogy of the Calles family based in part on information provided by Pascual. In 1944, the sixty-four-year-old Pascual died in San Diego, California, leaving Justina a widow for thirty-four years.

Pascual's sixth child, Rudy, also inherited artistic talents. At an early age, he took up acting lessons in Pasadena. In addition, while attending school he held an assortment of garden-related jobs. Eventually, he became a hairdresser. During World War II, Rudy joined the U.S. Navy and worked as an aircraft mechanic, cook and baker. Subsequently, he took up cosmetology and won five trophies in hairstyling. His hobbies included swimming, dancing and going to the movies. Rudy liked old films and was a fan of Rudolph Valentino. He also enjoyed writing and reading. On one occasion, activist César Chávez requested his poem "Chicano Land of Opportunity" for a publication. Rudy took pride in being a Mexican American; his involvement during the 1960s with various college magazines like *El Grito* and *El Excéntrico* is proof of this.

A penchant for the performing arts seemed to be recurrent in the family. Patriarch Nepomuceno made a living from his musical aptitudes. A late nineteenth-century document states that he was a "filarmónico." It is probable that he played several instruments including the organ, as he spent much time in the local church in Ciudad Guerrero, Chihuahua. His sons Pascual and Guillermo picked up a desire for acting. Pascual's daughter, Belén Calles, also seemed to have enjoyed acting; at the age of seventeen, she was already a good singer. Guillermo's sister María de Jesús performed in several movies directed by Calles. In the same manner, José Domínguez, the son of María de Jesús, dedicated his life to acting. Even Juan V. Calles, who was an Italian orphan adopted by the family, became a cinema actor at a very young age. He took the name of Guillermo's eldest brother. After his relevant role in *El indio yaqui*, Juan seemed to have vanished; there are no more traces of his activities in films or elsewhere.

From 1920 to 1968, José "Pepe" Domínguez appeared in supporting roles in over one hundred films. Although José did not direct films, he established himself as a forerunner among Mexican actors in Hollywood. Besides, he was one of the first Mexicans in Hollywood to organize a Latin Motion Pictures Extras Association in the mid–1920s. José married Francisca (Panchita) Almaraz in 1919 and had ten children: José (Sonny), Eugenio (Buddy), Ricardo (Dick), Francisco (Father Frank), Gilberto, Ernesto, Federico, Roberto, Guillermo, and Jimmy. (Eugenio joined the Marine Corps and fought in the Second World War. He was killed in combat at Saipan Island in 1944.) José brought his wife and sons along to work as actors in the movie studios.

Though they shared a common background and vocation, José and Guillermo possessed different personalities. Certainly, they both loved performing in movies but their lifestyles diverged significantly. José, for instance, settled for a job at the movie studios and dedicated his energy to raising a family in the company of his wife. *El Indio* Calles, on the other hand, constantly sought new adventures. He liked challenge; not only was he a stuntman and an actor but also worked hard at producing and directing his own films. Calles too married a Mexican woman, María Ángela Salcedo. But unlike his nephew José, he had no children and eventually divorced Angelita. Calles never again married. In contrast to José Domínguez, who stayed in Los Angeles the remainder of his life, Guillermo moved regularly between the U.S. and Mexico promoting his films and making personal appearances in theaters. Wherever he went, he brought along his dog Águila, a gift he received from the famous actor Rudolph Valentino.

There is scant information on Calles' wife. Angelita Salcedo was born in El Dorado, Sinaloa, around 1910, and lived in an orphanage just before meeting her future husband. According to a family member, Calles's mother set up their encounter and arranged for the

Rudy Calles, ca. 1943. During World War II, he joined the U.S. Navy and worked as an aircraft mechanic, cook and baker (Rudy Calles Collection).

Epilogue: The Calles Family

José Domínguez in charro costume, early 1920s. A pioneer film actor, he appeared in scores of Hollywood productions (Rudy Calles Collection).

marriage. Because her bachelor son was already thirty-six years old, doña Anatolia recommended that he settle down and start a family. By June 1927, Angelita was living with Guillermo at 714 South Fresno Street in Los Angeles. They gave that address to immigration officers whenever they crossed the U.S.–Mexico border (it is the same address as José Domínguez' family). Angelita Salcedo acted in several movies directed by her husband, including *El charro* and *Regeneración*, both made in 1930. She was also one of the participants in *Pro-Patria*. This documentary includes a scene that shows Angelita and Guillermo meeting President Pascual Ortiz Rubio at the Chapultepec castle.

When Calles began to direct films in the Mexico City studios, he planned to bring his wife along. However, it seems that Angelita did not like the idea. Ultimately, she remained in California and continued working in the entertainment business, sometimes participating in films as an extra and performing for live shows. In 1934, she was part of the thrilling spectacle of Steve Clemente, a famous knife thrower. There is a newspaper photograph showing Clemente dressed as a charro and two fearless girls wearing swimsuits. The caption explains: "Eva Ontiveros and Angela Calles earn their living by standing shoulder-to-shoulder against a two-inch backstop while Steve Clemente outlines their figures with miners' picks, which he hurls from a distance of 40 feet." There are no clues about Angelita after this date. The Calles couple separated in the 1930s and got a divorce sometime in the late 1940s.

Although Guillermo left California for Mexico, he always kept in touch with family members in the United States, sending letters and photographs; at times, he took trips to Los Angeles. A photo in an old scrapbook shows Guillermo visiting José Domínguez, who lived in East Los Angeles. This reunion with José's family probably took place in the early 1940s. There are also snapshots of trips to Mexico made by doña Anatolia Guerrero and her daughter María de Jesús Calles de Calvillo. In 1957, Guillermo's niece Beatrice Calles de Roiz and her daughter Marianne flew to Mexico City on their way to Acapulco. Marianne still recalls that she and her mother enjoyed dining with Uncle Willie at a downtown restaurant.

Other relatives who spent a great deal of time with Guillermo were his sister María de Jesús and sons. She played the mother of Guillermo in *Sol de gloria* (1928) and appeared as one of the nuns in *Dios y ley* (1929). Her son, José Domínguez, became famous by playing the role of a villain in both pictures. María de Jesús's second son, José María Calvillo, went to Mexico City in the 1930s and spent some time with his uncle Willie. José María later married Anita Silva, a young woman from Mexico City. According to some records, he and his wife traveled by boat from Acapulco to Los Angeles in 1937. Upon the death of Calles in 1958, José María traveled once again to the capital of Mexico to take care of legal matters concerning the estate of his uncle.

Calles visiting his relatives at the Domínguez residence on 714 South Fresno Street, Los Angeles, California. From left: unidentified, unidentified, María de Jesús Calles de Calvillo, Guillermo Calles, Angelita Solcedo de Calles, Parchita Almaraz de Domínguez and José Domínguez. The young boy in front is Bobby Domínguez (courtesy of Ernie Domínguez).

One of José Domínguez's several sons is Richard "Dick" Domínguez. Like his parents, Dick also appeared in movies. In fact, he stated that he acted in *Raza de bronce* when he was only a baby. Married to Norma Rafaela Romero, he later followed a career in public safety. A widower, Dick resides in Whittier, California, staying busy around the clock visiting his eight children and nineteen grandchildren. His appreciation of the family's history prompted him to write a tribute to the family's cinema pioneers:

> From our barrio of La Purísima came two gentlemen who entered the movie industry at almost its inception, the era of the silent movies. They continued in this business until the time of their retirement. Guillermo Calles Guerrero and José Domínguez ... were born in Chihuahua, Mexico. In early 1900, their families immigrated to Clifton, Arizona, where work was plentiful in the copper mines. After a few years there, Mr. Calles left Arizona and came to Los Angeles to seek his fortune. Soon after arrival, he worked his way into the industry starting as a sweeper and "gofer." Before long, he was doing bit parts. Since many of the movies were Westerns he had plenty of work, as his specialty was playing Indian roles. He urged his nephew, José Domínguez, to join him, which he did. And because of Mr. Calles's connections, José started his movie career. Mr. Calles's astuteness served him well. Having had only a primary education, he learned the trade and before long, he was directing films. They were *El indio yaqui*, *Raza de bronce*, and the most noteworthy, *Dios y ley*. These were silent movies and they were shown in the U.S. and outside in other countries. Mr. Calles is credited as being the first Mexican actor to appear in a film. Another first for him was being the foremost Mexican director to film a talkie. The movie *Dios y ley* (*God and Law*) was filmed in Hollywood but many

Epilogue: The Calles Family

Family memories: José Domínguez with sons Eugene and Joe, Jr. Eugene was killed in action during World War II (courtesy of Ernie Domínguez).

of the outdoor scenes were shot in the Mexican State of Sonora. Later in years, on one of his visits to Mexico, Mr. Calles was denied re-entry and he spent the remainder of his years in Mexico continuing to work in the cinema industry.

Meanwhile, back at the ranch, José Domínguez was starting his career in Hollywood. Shortly after his arrival in Los Angeles, he met and married Frances "Panchita" Almaraz. They were married at La Placita Church, by Olvera Street, and settled down in Boyle Heights in the Barrio of La Purísima Church, where they lived for almost fifty years while raising a family of ten boys. José started out as an extra, doing silent films, and through the years, he established himself as a character actor doing bit parts until his retirement in 1968. He has more than 100 films to his credit including many TV appearances. His wife, Panchita, also worked in the movies now and then, doing a few films where she had minor roles. When José's sons were old enough, seven or eight years old, they received their work permits and, of course, what they earned helped to supplement the household income. Finally, Mr. Domínguez used his talents elsewhere. He encouraged fellow parishioners of La Purísima Church to play roles in stage dramas and comedies that he directed. These plays were in Spanish and were put on as fundraisers for La Purísima Church. Usually after playing at La Purísima, they would be asked to perform at neighboring churches, which they willingly did in order to help that particular church to raise funds....

Epilogue: The Calles Family

Every other year, the large progeny of Nepomuceno Calles has a chance to meet during a family reunion. In 2008, this gathering of relatives took place in San Diego, California. Marianne Roiz and Justina White, daughter and granddaughter of Beatrice Calles de Roiz, respectively, organized it. Beatrice, who goes by her nickname "Nena," is one of two surviving children of Pascual Calles and Justina Hernández (the other is her younger sister Elena or Helen). In spite of a hearing impairment, the eighty-eight-year-old lady still drives her automobile. She is also the keeper of tradition and has many memories to describe.

Today, the size of the Calles family has grown enormously. Most members have settled in California, with a few residing in Texas, Washington, and other states. Beatrice Calles, Gloria Ortega, and retired police officer Richard "Dick" Domínguez live in California. Following the example of their father, Richard Jr., Phillip, and David Domínguez have been involved in their community's public safety institutions. Captain Richard and fireman Phillip work for the Los Angeles County Fire Department. David Domínguez has served thirty years as a law enforcement officer. In 2008, he was sworn in as Palm Springs Police Chief. An article in San Bernardino's *Hispanic News* (February 20, 2008) noted that

Richard "Dick" Domínguez (armed with crossbow) appeared in Tarzan movies; this shot is from *Tarzan's Magic Fountain* (1949). When he was a toddler, he came out in *Raza de bronce* (1927). Standing just behind Domínguez are Lex Barker, Evelyn Ankers and Alan Napier (courtesy of Dick Domínguez).

Epilogue: The Calles Family

Mother's Day, 1946, Los Angeles. The Domínguez family surrounding María de Jesús Calles, José Domínguez's mother. She can be seen standing between the two men at the palm tree (courtesy of Ernie Domínguez).

he was "raised in a close-knit family of eight children with traditional family values: religious faith, work ethics, integrity, community involvement and emphasis on education."

The chronicle of the Calles and Domínguez families is paradigmatic. It is the story of a Mexican immigrant family that crossed the border into Arizona more than a hundred years ago. As many Mexican expatriates, the offspring of Nepomuceno Calles and Anatolia Guerrero rose from humble beginnings and went through difficult times. Two members of the family, Guillermo Calles and José Domínguez, fought hard for the realization of an ideal. Their childhood dreams of becoming actors took them on a journey of unexpected twists and turns.

Guillermo's creative energy and nationalistic ardor found expression in the production of movies. After being a pioneer actor in Hollywood he decided to make his own films, a task that very few Mexicans dared to undertake. He will be remembered for his love of Mexico and his staunch defense of "la raza de bronce."

Appendix 1: Filmography

Films Directed by Guillermo Calles

1921: *De raza azteca*. Co-director and producer: Miguel Contreras Torres. Story: Guillermo Calles and Miguel Contreras Torres. Cinematographer: Julio Lamadrid. Cast: Miguel Contreras Torres, Guillermo Calles, Carlota Santuggini, Irma Domínguez, Enrique Cantalaúba, Everardo Montoya, Irineo Martínez, Víctor Herrera, Felipe Montoya.

1926: *El indio yaqui*. Story and special effects: Guillermo Calles. Cast: Guillermo Calles, Agustina López, José Duarte, Neal Hart, Betty Brown, José Domínguez, Juan V. Calles, Walter Shumway, the dog Águila.

1927: *Raza de bronce*. Story: Alfonso Tovar. Cast: Guillermo Calles, Esther García, José Domínguez, Alfonso Tovar, Eduardo Gastine, Manuel J. Millán.

1928: *Sol de gloria*. Story: Guillermo Calles. Cast: Guillermo Calles, Carmen La Roux, José Domínguez, María de Jesús Calles, Carlos Molina, Belén Espinosa, the dog Águila.

1929: *Dios y ley*. Story: Guillermo Calles. Cast: Guillermo Calles, Carmen Guerrero, José Domínguez, Juan Martínez, Plácido Siqueiros, Anatolia Guerrero, María de Jesús Calles de Calvillo, Margarita Calles, the dog Águila.

1930: *El charro*. Story: Guillermo Calles. Cast: Guillermo Calles, Angelita Salcedo, Margarita Calles. *Regeneración (La mujer que supo amar)*. Story: Areu brothers. Cast: Dorita Seprano, Enrique Areu, José Areu, Roberto Areu, Oscar Guisado, Juan Aristi, Ramón Muñoz, Angelita Salcedo. *La venganza del indio* (no information available).

1932: *Pro-Patria*. Cinematographer: Ernie Smith. Appearing in this documentary: Guillermo Calles, Angelita Salcedo, *et al.*

1933: *La Chillona*. Cinematographer: Ezequiel Carrasco. Sound: B.J. Kroger. Cast: José Duarte, Carmina de la Llata, Flora Martínez, Jesús Graña. *El héroe de Nacozari*. Story: Guillermo Calles and Gustavo Sáenz de Sicilia. Cinematographer: Antonio Fernández. Sound: Rodríguez brothers. Cast: Ramón Pereda, Lucha Díaz, Antonio R. Frausto, Conchita Banuet, Luciano Rueda, Consuelo Segarra. *El pulpo humano*. Co-director and story: Jorge Bell. Cinematographer: Antonio Fernández. Sound: B.J. Kroger. Cast: Margot Erbeya, Arturo Campoamor, Elena San Martín, Pepe Martínez. *El vuelo de la muerte*. Story: Guz Águila. Cinematographer: Ezequiel Carrasco. Sound: Rodríguez brothers. Cast: Ramón Pereda, Adriana Lamar, Jorge del Moral, Sara García, Julio Villarreal, Luis G. Barreiro.

1938: *Pescadores de perlas*. Story: Guillermo Calles. Dialogue: Alfonso Patiño Gómez. Cinematographer: Víctor Herrera. Sound: José B. Carles. Cast: Víctor Manuel Mendoza, Victoria Blanco, Ángel T. Sala, Carlos Villatoro, Efrén Buchelli, Sara García, Alfonso Bedoya, Eufrosina García. *La virgen de la sierra*. Story: María Luisa Alvaradejo. Cinematographer:

Raúl Martínez Solares. Sound: Rodríguez brothers. Cast: Anita Campillo, Carlos Villatoro, Raúl de Anda, José Eduardo Pérez, Armando Soto la Marina, Carmen Rivas Cacho, Pepe Martínez, Antonio Díaz, Victoria Argota, César Rendón, Jesús Navarro, Carolina Barrett. *La justicia de Pancho Villa.* Co-director and story: Guz Águila. Cinematographer: Ross Fisher. Sound: Joselito Rodríguez. Cast: Vicente Padula, Stella Inda, Amparo Arozamena, Loló Trillo, Luis Álvarez.

Films in Which Guillermo Calles (a.k.a. Willie Calles and William Calles) Participated as an Actor

1912: *A Mexican Tragedy* (Lubin). Cast: Ray Gallagher, Henry King, William Ryno, Velma Whitman.

1913: *The Squaw Man* (Jesse L. Lasky). Director: Cecil B. DeMille. Cast: Dustin Farnum, Princess Red Wing, Art Acord, William Elmer.

1914: *The Virginian* (Jesse L. Lasky). Director: Cecil B. DeMille. Cast: Dustin Farnum, William Elmer, Jack W. Johnston, Winfred Kingston. *The Girl of the Golden West* (Lasky-Belasco). Director: Cecil B. DeMille and David Belasco. Cast: Mabel Van Buren, Theodore Roberts, House Peters, Anita King, William Elmer.

1915: *The Arab* (Lasky). Director: Cecil B. DeMille. Cast: Edgar Selwyn, Horace B. Carpenter.

1917: *Joan the Woman* (Cecil B. DeMille). Director: Cecil B. DeMille. Cast: Geraldine Farrar, Wallace Reid, Raymond Hatton, Hobart Bosworth, Theodore Roberts. *The Captain of the Grey Horse Troop* (Vitagraph). Director: William Wolbert. Cast: Antonio Moreno. *The Fighting Trail* (Vitagraph). Serial. 15 episodes. Director: William Duncan. Cast: William Duncan, Carol Holloway, George Holt, Joe Ryan, Fred Burns, Walter Rodgers, H. Ducrow, Jack Pierce, Al Jennings, Alfred Paget. *Vengeance and the Woman* (Vitagraph). Serial. 15 episodes. Director: William Duncan. Cast: William Duncan, Carol Holloway, George Holt, Tex Allen, Vincente Howard, Fred Burns, S.E. Jennings, Walter Rodgers.

1918: *A Fight for Millions* (Vitagraph). Serial. 15 episodes. Director: William Duncan. Cast: William Duncan, Edith Johnson, Joe Ryan, Walter Rodgers.

1919: *The Man of Might* (Vitagraph). Serial. 15 episodes. Director: William Duncan. Cast: William Duncan, Edith Johnson, Joe Ryan, Walter Rodgers, Del Harris, Frank Tokanaga, Otto Lederer. *Smashing Barriers* (Vitagraph). Serial. 15 episodes. Director: William Duncan. Cast: William Duncan, Edith Johnson, Walter Rodgers, George Stanley, Fred Darnton, Slim Cole, William McCall.

1920: *The Silent Avenger* (Vitagraph). Serial. 15 episodes. Director: William Duncan. Cast: William Duncan, Edith Johnson, Jack Richardson, Virginia Nightingale, Ernest Shields, Willis L. Robards, William S. Smith.

1921: *The Fighting Fate* (Vitagraph). Serial. 15 episodes. Director: William Duncan. Cast: William Duncan, Edith Johnson, Ford West, Frank Weed, William McCall, George Stanley, C.L. Davidson, Burwell Hamrick. *De raza azteca* (Contreras Torres). Director: Guillermo Calles and Miguel Contreras Torres. Cast: Miguel Contreras Torres, Carlota Santuggini, Irma Domínguez, Enrique Cantalaúba, Everardo Montoya, Irineo Martínez, Víctor Herrera, Felipe Montoya.

1922: *El sueño del caporal* (Contreras Torres). Director: Miguel Contreras Torres. Cast: Miguel Contreras Torres, Irma Domínguez, Julio Navarrete, Víctor Herrera. *The Silent Vow* (Vitagraph). Director: William Duncan. Cast: William Duncan, Edith Johnson, Dorothy Dwan, Maud Emery, J. Morris Foster, Henry Hebert, Fred Burley, Jack Curtis, Charles Dudley.

1923: *The Fighting Strain* (Neal Hart Productions). Director: Neal Hart. Cast: Neal Hart, Beth Mitchell, William Quinn, Bert Wilson, Gladys Gilland, James McLaughlin.

1924: *Branded a Thief* (William Steiner). Director: Neal hart. Cast: Neal Hart, Joan Lowell. *The Left Hand Brand* (William Steiner). Director: Neal Hart. Cast: Neal Hart, Fred Burnworth, Betty Davies, Buck Moulton. *The Dirty Little Half-Breed* (National Film Corporation of America). Short feature. *Behind Two Guns* (Anthony J. Xydias). Director: Robert N. Bradbury. Cast: J.B. Warner, Hazel Newman, Jim Welch, Otto Lederer, Marin Sais, Jay Morley, Jack Waltemeyer, Emily Gerdes, Bartlett A. Carre.

1925: *Kit Carson Over the Great Divide* (Sunset Productions). Director: Frank S. Mattison. Cast: Roy Stewart, Henry B. Walthall, Marguerite Snow, Sheldon Lewis, Earl Metcalfe, Charlotte Stevens, Jack Mower, Arthur Hotaling. *The Verdict of the Desert* (William Steiner Productions). Director: Neal Hart. Cast: Neal Hart, Jane Tallent, Harry Demere, Thais Valdemar, Chet Ryan, Chas Chambers, Adela Zambrano, Mike Brahm.

1926: *Davy Crockett at the Fall of the Alamo* (Anthony J. Xydias). Director: Robert N. Bradbury. Cast: Cullen Landis, Kathrin McGuire, Joe Rickson, Bob Fleming, Ralph McCullough, Fletcher Norton, Jay Morley, Betty Brown, Bob Steele, Steve Clemente. *Daniel Boone Thru the Wilderness* (Anthony J. Xydias). Director: Robert N. Bradbury. Cast: Roy Stewart, Kathleen Collins, Bob Steele, Jay Morley, Jim O'Neil, Frank Rice, Emily Gerdes. *El indio yaqui* (Guillermo Calles and José Duarte). Director: Guillermo Calles. Cast: Agustina López, Betty Brown, Manuel F. Rodríguez, Walter Shumway, Neal Hart, Joe Ryan, Roy Stewart, José Duarte, Juan V. Calles, José Domínguez, Enrique Acosta, Margarita Calles, the dog Águila. *The Scarlet Brand* (New-Cal Productions). Director: Neal Hart. Cast: Neal Hart, William Quinn, Lucille Irwin, Carmen La Roux, Henry Britt, Tom Wortham.

1927: *Raza de bronce* (Rafael Corella). Director: Guillermo Calles. Cast: Esther García, José Domínguez, Sara C. Villaseñor, Alfonso Villaseñor, Alfonso Tovar, Eduardo Gastini, Saúl Sanabria, Manuel J. Millán, Captain Fausto Morlett.

1928: *Sol de Gloria* (Independencia Productions). Director: Guillermo Calles. Cast: Carmen La Roux, José Domínguez, Carlos Molina, María de Jesús Calles, Belén Espinosa, the dog "Águila."

1929: *Dios y ley* (Guillermo Calles). Director: Guillermo Calles. Cast: Guillermo Calles, Carmen Guerrero, José Domínguez, Juan Martínez, Plácido Siqueiros, Anatolia Guerrero, María de Jesús Calles, Margarita Calles, the dog Águila.

1930: *El charro* (Guillermo Calles). Director: Guillermo Calles. Cast: Angelita Salcedo, Margarita Calles.

1932: *Pro-Patria* (Guillermo Calles, Ernie Smith). Travelogue. Director: Guillermo Calles. Appearances by Calles and Angelita Salcedo.

1934: *Corazón bandolero* (México Films). Director: Raphael J. Sevilla. Cast: Juan José Martínez Casado, Victoria Blanco, Domingo Soler, Joaquín Busquets, Julio Villarreal, Carlos López "Chaflán," Emma Roldán, Emilio Fernández. *Tribu* (Miguel Contreras Torres). Director: Miguel Contreras Torres. Cast: Miguel Contreras Torres, Medea de Novara, Alfredo del Diestro, Carlos Villatoro, Julio Villarreal, Emilio Fernández, Manuel R. Ojeda.

1935: *Martín Garatuza* (Águila Films). Director: Gabriel Soria. Cast: Leopoldo Ortín, Juan José Martínez Casado, Josefina Escobedo, Sofía Álvarez, Mimí Derba, Alberto Martí. *María*

Appendix 1

Elena (Impulsora Mex-Art). Director: Raphael J. Sevilla. Cast: Carmen Guerrero, Juan José Martínez Casado, Adolfo Girón, Beatriz Ramos, Lucy Delgado, Pedro Armendáriz, the dog Águila. *El tesoro de Pancho Villa* (San Vicente y Mier). Director: Arcady Boytler. Cast: Antonio R. Frausto, Victoria Blanco, Raúl de Anda, A.M. Williams, Juan F. Triana, Carlos López "Chaflán," the dog Águila.

1937: *Almas rebeldes* (Raúl de Anda). Director: Alejandro Galindo. Cast: Nancy Torres, Raúl de Anda, Eduardo Arozamena, Emilio Fernández, Arturo Manrique "Panseco," Ramón Vallarino, Jorge Treviño, Pedro Galindo, Gilberto González, Max Langler, Alfonso Bedoya. *A la orilla de un palmar* (Rex Films). Director: Raphael J. Sevilla. Cast: Vicente Oroná, Marina Tamayo, Alberto Martí. Carlos Villatoro, Aurora Walker, Saúl Zamora. *Así es mi tierra* (Felipe Mier). Director: Arcady Boytler. Cast: Mario Moreno "Cantinflas," Manuel Medel, Antonio R. Frausto, Mercedes Soler, Juan José Martínez Casado, Margarita Cortés, Luis G. Barreiro.

1939: *Los de abajo* (Luis Manrique). Director: Chano Urueta. Cast: Miguel Ángel Ferriz, Esther Fernández, Isabela Corona, Carlos López Moctezuma, Beatriz Ramos, Domingo Soler, Alfredo del Diestro, Emilio Fernández.

1943: *Konga roja* (Raúl de Anda). Director: Alejandro Galindo. Cast: Pedro Armendáriz, María Antonieta Pons, Carlos López Moctezuma, Tito Junco, Clifford Carr, Toña la Negra, Luis G. Barreiro. *Balajú* (Excélsior). Director: Rolando Aguilar. Cast: María Antonieta Pons, David Silva, Mario Tenorio, Katy Jurado, Mimí Derba, Armando Soto La Marina, Manuel Dondé.

1944: *Rosalinda* (Raúl de Anda). Director: Rolando Aguilar. Cast: María Antonieta Pons, Rafael Baledón, Tito Junco, Agustín Isunza, Miguel Ángel Ferriz, Luis G. Barreiro, Max Langler, Gilberto González, Roberto Corell.

1945: *La perla* (Águila). Director: Emilio Fernández. Cast: Pedro Armendáriz, María Elena Marqués, Fernando Wagner, Gilberto González, Charles Rooner, Juan García, Alfonso Bedoya, Max Langler.

1946: *Enamorada* (Panamerican). Director: Emilio Fernández. Cast: María Félix, Pedro Armendáriz, Fernando Fernández, José Morcillo, Eduardo Arozamena, Miguel Inclán. *A la sombra del puente* (Ramex). Director: Roberto Gavaldón. Cast: Esther Fernández, David Silva, Rodolfo Landa, Andrés Soler, Agustín Irusta, Carlos López Moctezuma. *Captain from Castile* (20th Century–Fox). Director: Henry King. Cast: Tyrone Power, Jean Peters, Cesar Romero, Lee J. Cobb, John Sutton, Antonio Moreno, Thomas Gomez, Barbara Lawrence.

1947: *La casa colorada* (José Elvira). Director: Miguel Morayta. Cast: Pedro Armendáriz, Amanda del Llano, Bernardo Sancristóbal, Rita Macedo, Gilberto González, José Eduardo Pérez. *Pito Pérez se va de bracero* (Clasa-Mundiales). Director: Alfonso Patiño Gómez. Cast: Manuel Medel, Joan Page, René Cardona, Julián de Meriche, Charles Rooner, Rafael Icardo, Clifford Carr, Edmundo Espino. *La hermana impura* (Clasa-Mundiales). Director: Miguel Morayta. Cast: Sofía Álvarez, Domingo Soler, José María Linares Rivas, Gilberto González, Fanny Schiller, Elena Contla, Hernán Vera. *Bajo el cielo de Sonora* (Raúl de Anda). Director: Rolando Aguilar. Cast: Leonora Amar, Carlos López Moctezuma, Domingo Soler, Raúl de Anda, José Elías Moreno, Roberto Meyer. *The Treasure of the Sierra Madre* (Warner Brothers). Director: John Huston. Cast: Humphrey Bogart, Walter Huston, Tim Holt, Bruce Bennett, Alfonso Bedoya, Barton MacLane. Arturo Soto Rangel, Manuel Dondé, José Torvay, Margarito Luna. *Canciones y recuerdos* (Rivero). Documentary. Director: Fernando A. Rivero.

Filmography

1948: *Los tres huastecos* (Rodríguez Hermanos). Director: Ismael Rodríguez. Cast: Pedro Infante, Blanca Estela Pavón, Fernando Soto "Mantequilla," María Eugenia Llamas "Tucita," Alejandro Ciangherotti, Antonio R. Frausto. *Lola Casanova* (Tacma). Director: Matilde Landeta. Cast: Meche Barba, Isabela Corona, Enrique Cansido, Armando Silvestre, José Baviera, Carlos Martínez Baena, Ernesto Vilches, Ramón Gay, Enriqueta Reza. *El mago* (Posa Films). Director: Miguel M. Delgado. Cast: Mario Moreno "Cantinflas," Leonora Amar, José Baviera, Ernesto Finance, Alejandro Cobo, Pepe Martínez, Roberto Corell, Miguel Manzano, Oscar Pulido. *Al caer la tarde* (César Santos Galindo/Rodríguez Hermanos). Director: Rafael E. Portas. Cast: Pedro Armendáriz, Carmen Montejo, Queta Lavat, Rodolfo Landa, José Baviera, José Muñoz. *Ahí viene Vidal Tenorio* (Luis Manrique). Director: René Cardona. Cast: Tito Guízar, Alicia Caro, Tito Junco, Manuel Dondé, Alfredo del Diestro, Aurora Cortés, Alejandro Cobo.

1949: *Tierra muerta* (Productores Unidos). Director: Vicente Oroná. Cast: Víctor Manuel Mendoza, Irma Torres, Carlos López Moctezuma, Beatriz Aguirre, Agustín Isunza, Miguel Inclán, Eduardo Arozamena, Enriqueta Reza, Arturo Soto Rangel. *Rayito de luna* (Filmadora Chapultepec). Director: Chano Urueta. Cast: David Silva, Brenda Conde, Arturo Martínez, Miguel Inclán, Manuel Dondé, Guillermo Bravo Sosa, Victorio Blanco. *La mujer del Puerto* (Oscar J. Brooks). Director: Emilio Gómez Muriel. Cast: María Antonieta Pons, Víctor Junco, Eduardo Noriega, Arturo Martínez, Arturo Soto Rangel, Miguel Manzano. *La mujer que yo predí* (Rodríguez Hermanos). Director: Roberto Rodríguez. Cast: Pedro Infante, Blanca Estela Pavón, Manuel R. Ojeda, Eduardo Arozamena, Silvia Pinal, José Luis Jiménez, Aurora Walker. *La negra Angustias* (Tacma). Director: Matilde Landeta. Cast: María Elena Marqués, Agustín Isunza, Eduardo Arozamena, Gilberto González, Enriqueta Reza, Fanny Schiller, Ramón Gay. *Pancho Villa vuelve* (Hispano Continental). Director: Miguel Contreras Torres. Cast: Pedro Armendáriz, Esther Fernández, Rodolfo Acosta, Rafael Alcaide, Gilberto González, Lucy del Campo. *Amor con amor se paga* (Rosas Priego). Director: Ernesto Cortázar. Cast: Marga López, Antonio Badú, Víctor Junco, Lilia Prado, Alfredo Varela, Arturo Soto Rangel. *Ventarrón* (Filmadora Chapultepec). Director: Chano Urueta. Cast: David Silva, Martha Roth, Alberto Mariscal, Isabel del Puerto, Tana Lynn, Gustavo Rivero, Juan García, Manuel Trejo Morales, José Luis Rojas. *The Torch* (Eagle Lion, Bert Granet). Director: Emilio Fernández. Cast: Paulette Goddard, Pedro Armendáriz, Gilbert Roland, Walter Reed, Julio Villarreal, Carlos Múzquiz, Margarito Luna, José Torvay, Pascual García Peña. *Pasión jarocha* (Véjar). Director: Carlos Véjar. Cast: Víctor Manuel Mendoza, Irma Torres, Rafael Lanzetta, Bertha Lomelí, Nora Veryán, Salvador Quiroz, María Gentil Arcos, Edmundo Espino. *La fe en Dios* (Cinematográfica Internacional). Director: Raúl de Anda. Cast: Domingo Soler, Víctor Parra, Lilia del Valle, Agustín Isunza, Eduardo Arozamena, Raúl de Anda Jr., Aurora Segura, Arturo Soto Rangel. *Sentencia* (Clasa). Director: Emilio Gómez Muriel. Cast: Emilio Tuero, Gloria Lozano, Carlos López Moctezuma, Carlos Navarro, José Pulido, Antonio Bravo, Juan Orraca, Roberto Meyer, Paco Astol.

1950: *El cristo de mi cabecera* (Rubén C. Navarro). Director: Ernesto Cortázar. Cast: Roberto Cañedo, Lilia del Valle, Evita Muñoz "Chachita," Manuel Dondé, José Torvay, Arturo Soto Rangel, José Loza. *Una viuda sin sostén* (Alameda Films). Director: René Cardona. Cast: Abel Salazar, Emilia Guiú, Oscar Pulido, Consuelo Múgica, Paco Martínez, Rogelio Fernández.

1951: *Todos son mis hijos* (Rodríguez Hermanos). Director: Roberto Rodríguez. Cast: Blanca de

Castejón, Carmen Montejo, Miguel Ángel Ferriz, Joaquín Cordero, Luis Beristáin, Emma Rodríguez. *Cuatro noches contigo* (Raúl de Anda). Director: Raúl de Anda. Cast: Elsa Aguirre, Luis Aguilar, Domingo Soler, José Torvay, Jorge Treviño, Charles Rooner, Gregorio Acosta, Antonio R. Frausto. *¡Mátenme porque me muero!* (Rodríguez Hermanos). Director: Ismael Rodríguez. Cast: Germán Valdés "Tin Tan," Oscar Pulido, Yolanda Montez "Tongolele," Marcelo Chávez, José René Ruiz "Tun Tun," Emma Rodríguez, Tito Novaro. *Delirio tropical* (Prod. Espada). Director: Miguel Morayta. Cast: Amalia Aguilar, Carlos Valadez, Lupe Llaca, Víctor Alcocer, Bertha Lomelí, Beatriz Ramos, Conchita Gentil Arcos. *La justicia del Lobo* (Cinematográfica Jalisco). Director: Vicente Oroná. Cast: Dagoberto Rodríguez, Flor Silvestre, José María Linares Rivas, Rosa de Castilla, Federico Curiel, Lupe Carriles, Ana Bertha Lepe. *Dos caras tiene el destino* (Noriega). Director: Agustín P. Delgado. Cast: Miroslava Stern, Eduardo Noriega, Carlos López Moctezuma, Andrés Soler, Prudencia Griffel, José Baviera, Angélica María, Gilberto González, Arturo Soto Rangel. *Ahí viene Martín Corona* (Zacarías). Director: Miguel Zacarías. Cast: Pedro Infante, Sarita Montiel, Eulalio González "Piporro," Armando Silvestre, Florencio Castelló, Ángel Infante, José Pulido, Irma Dorantes, José Torvay. *El enamorado* (Zacarías). Director: Miguel Zacarías. Cast: Pedro Infante, Sarita Montiel, Eulalio González "Piporro," Armando Silvestre, Florencio Castelló, Ángel Infante, José Pulido, Irma Dorantes, José Torvay. *My Outlaw Brother* (Eagle Lion). Director: Elliott Nugent. Cast: Mickey Rooney, Wanda Hendrix, Robert Preston, Robert Stack, Carlos Múzquiz, José Torvay, Felipe de Flores, Hilda Moreno, Margarito Luna, Chel López.

1952: *El bruto* (Internacional Cinematográfica). Director: Luis Buñuel. Cast: Pedro Armendáriz, Katy Jurado, Rosita Arenas, Andrés Soler, Beatriz Ramos, Paco Martínez, Roberto Meyer, Gloria Mestre, Diana Ochoa. *El rebozo de Soledad* (STPC, Televoz). Director: Roberto Gavaldón. Cast: Arturo de Córdova, Pedro Armendáriz, Stella Inda, Domingo Soler, Carlos López Moctezuma, Rosaura Revueltas, José Baviera, Gilberto González, Jaime Fernández. *La diosa de Tahití* (España Sono Films). Director: Juan Orol. Cast: Rosa Carmina, Arturo Martínez, Marco de Carlo, Salvador Lozano, Acela Vidaurri, Gilberto González, Mario Sevilla.

1953: *Espaldas mojadas* (Ata Films). Director: Alejandro Galindo. Cast: David Silva, Víctor Parra, Martha Valdés, Oscar Pulido, José Elías Moreno, Pedro Vargas, Carolina Barret. *La Rosa Blanca* (Mex-Cuba). Director: Emilio Fernández. Cast: Roberto Cañedo, Gina Cabrera, Julio Capote, Dalia Íñiguez, Julio Villarreal, Raquel Revuelta, Andrés Soler, Rebeca Iturbide. *El Águila Negra en el tesoro de la muerte* (Rosas Priego). Director: Ramón Peón. Cast: Fernando Casanova, Gloria Lozano, Eulalio González "Piporro," Oscar Pulido, Fernando Soto "Mantequilla," Joaquín García "Borolas," Armando Velasco. *The Littlest Outlaw* (Walt Disney). Director: Roberto Gavaldón. Cast: Pedro Armendáriz, Joseph Calleia. Rodolfo Acosta, Andrés Velázquez, Pepe Ortiz, Laila Maley, Gilberto González, José Torvay. *Hondo* (Warner Brothers). Director: John Farrow. Cast: John Wayne, Geraldine Page, Rodolfo Acosta, Pascual García Peña. *Sitting Bull* (United Artists–W.R. Frank Productions). Director: Sidney Salkow. Cast: Dale Robertson, Mary Murphy, Félix González, J. Carrol Naish, Ana Robinson Calles.

1954: *The Treasure of Pancho Villa* (RKO). Director: George Sherman. Cast: Rory Calhoun, Shelley Winters, Gilbert Roland, Joseph Calleia, Fanny Schiller, Tony Carbajal, Carlos Múzquiz, Pascual García Peña. *The Beast of Hollow Mountain* (United Artists–Edward Nassour/Películas Rodríguez). Director: Edward Nassour and Ismael Rodríguez. Cast: Guy

Filmography

Madison, Patricia Medina, Eduardo Noriega, Carlos Rivas, Mario Navarro, Pascual García Peña, Julio Villarreal, Lupe Carriles, Manuel Arvide, José Chávez, Margarito Luna.

1955: *Seven Cities of Gold* (20th Century–Fox). Director: Robert D. Webb. Cast: Richard Egan, Anthony Quinn, Michael Rennie, Rita Moreno, Jeffrey Hunter, Eduardo Noriega, Víctor Junco, Julio Villarreal. *The Last Frontier* (Columbia Pictures). Director: Anthony Mann. Cast: Victor Mature, Guy Madison, Robert Preston, James Whitmore, Anne Bancroft, Russell Collins, Peter Whitney, Pat Hogan. *La huella del Chacal* (Rosas Priego). Director: Jaime Salvador. Cast: Tony Aguilar, Agustín Isunza, Marina Camacho, Flor Silvestre, Víctor Alcocer, Joaquín García "Borolas," José Eduardo Pérez, Manuel Dondé.

1956: *Una cita de amor* (Latinoamericana/Unipromex). Director: Emilio Fernández. Cast: Silvia Pinal, Carlos López Moctezuma, Jaime Fernández, Amalia Mendoza "La Tariacuri," José Elías Moreno, Agustín Fernández. *La guarida del Buitre* (Rosas Priego). Director: Jaime Salvador. Cast: Tony Aguilar, Sara Montes, Lola Casanova, Esther Luquín, Agustín Isunza, Ignacio Navarro, Lupe Carriles, Miguel Arenas, Ángel Infante, José Eduardo Pérez. *The Brave One* (RKO). Director: Irving Rapper. Cast: Michel Ray, Rodolfo Hoyos, Elsa Cárdenas, Carlos Navarro, Fermín Rivera, Jorge Treviño, Carlos Fernández. *Run for the Sun* (United Artists–Harry Tatelman). Director: Roy Boulting. Cast: Richard Windmark, Trevor Howard, Jane Greer, Peter van Eyck, Juan García, José Antonio Carvajal, José Chávez, Margarito Luna.

1957: *El misterio del Látigo Negro* (G. Yévenes/Vergara). Director: Vicente Oroná. Cast: Luis Aguilar, Rosita Arenas, Federico Curiel, Rosa Elena Durgel, José Eduardo Pérez, Consuelo Frank, Paz Villegas, Victorio Blanco. *El Látigo Negro contra el anima del ahorcado* (Rodríguez/García Yévenes). Director: Vicente Oroná. Cast: Luis Aguilar, Rosita Arenas, Federico Curiel, Rosa Elena Durgel, José Eduardo Pérez, Consuelo Frank, Paz Villegas, Victorio Blanco. *Captain David Grief* (Sidney T. Bruckner). TV series. Episode: "Port of Rogues." Cast: Maxwell Reed, Elvira Quintana, Yerye Beirute, Federico Curiel.

1958: *Yo, el aventurero* (Rosas Priego). Director: Jaime Salvador. Cast: Tony Aguilar, Rosa de Castilla, Ángel Infante, Amalia Mendoza "La Tariacuri," Andrés Soler, Domingo Soler, Paco Michel, Agustín Isunza, Joaquín García "Borolas," Armando Soto La Marina.

Appendix 2: Exhibition of Films

A record of the exhibition of the films directed by Guillermo Calles.
The date indicates the first showing at the theater.

De raza azteca

Mexico City	February 5	1922	(shown at 10 theaters)
El Paso, Texas	May 21	1922	Teatro Colón
Ciudad Juárez, Chihuahua	June	1922	Bullfighting Arena
Los Angeles, California	June 24	1922	Hidalgo Theater
Los Angeles, California	September 15	1930	Estella Theater

El indio yaqui

Los Angeles, California	June 3	1926	Hidalgo Theater
El Centro, California	July	1926	?
Nogales, Sonora	July	1926	?
Mexico City	March 31	1927	(shown at 6 theaters)
Veracruz, Veracruz	June 3	1927	Teatro Eslava
Guadalajara, Jalisco	June 18	1927	(shown at 3 theaters)
Mérida, Yucatán	July 30	1927	Pathé and Esmeralda Theaters
Los Angeles, California	October 20	1928	México Theater
San Antonio, Texas	January 28	1929	Nacional Theater
Galveston, Texas	February	1929	?
Corpus Christi, Texas	February	1929	Azteca Theater
Cotulla, Texas	February 24	1929	Teatro Junco de la Vega
Albuquerque, New Mexico	February 28	1930	Pastime Theater
Edinburg, Texas	April 25	1930	Grande Theater
Los Angeles, California	August 23	1930	Hidalgo Theater
Los Angeles, California	September 17	1930	Estella Theater

Raza de bronce

Mexicali, Baja California	February 5	1927	Iris Theater
Los Angeles, California	April 4	1927	Hidalgo Theater
Mexico City	June 22	1927	(shown at 13 theaters)
Oakland, California	July 26	1927	Broadway Theater
Hayward, California	August 23	1927	Hayward Theater
Los Angeles, California	October 12	1927	México Theater

Exhibition of Films

Los Angeles, California	October 14	1928	México Theater
Los Angeles, California	September 16	1930	Estella Theater

Sol de Gloria

Los Angeles, California	March 21	1928	México Theater
Los Angeles, California	April 12	1928	México Theater
Ensenada, Baja California	May	1928	?
Fresno, California	August 29	1928	Lyceum Theater
Delano, California	September 15	1928	Star Theater
Los Angeles, California	October 6	1928	México Theater
Los Angeles, California	October 23	1928	Principal Theater
Mexico City	November 14	1928	Teatro Palacio
Houston, Texas	January	1929	?
San Antonio, Texas	January 21	1929	Nacional Theater
Galveston, Texas	January 26	1929	Azteca Theater
Corpus Christi, Texas	February	1929	Azteca Theater
San Antonio, Texas	February 25	1929	Nacional Theater
Cotulla, Texas	March 1	1929	Teatro Junco de la Vega
Nuevo Laredo, Tamaulipas	April 28	1929	Teatro Independencia
Los Angeles, California	May 3	1929	México Theater
San Diego, California	May	1929	U.S. Theater

Dios y ley

Los Angeles, California	August 30	1929	México Theater
San Diego, California	September 15	1929	Spreckles Theater
Phoenix, Arizona	January	1930	Plaza Theater
Guadalajara, Jalisco	February 4	1930	(shown at 3 theaters)
Mexico City	March 8	1930	(shown at 6 theaters)
San Antonio, Texas	March 24	1930	Nacional Theater
Los Angeles, California	July 18	1930	México Theater
Los Angeles, California	August 16	1930	Hidalgo Theater
San Antonio, Texas	October 4	1930	Nacional Theater

El charro

Los Angeles, California	October 17	1930	México Theater
Los Angeles, California	December 28	1930	México Theater

Regeneración

Los Angeles, California	December 23	1930	California International
Mexico City	April 2	1931	?
New York City	June 17	1931	?
Nuevo Laredo, Tamaulipas	December	1931	Teatro Concordia
Albuquerque, New Mexico	March 28	1932	Past Time Theater
Brownsville, Texas	April 10	1932	Dittmann Theater
Los Angeles, California	June 3	1932	California Theater
Key West, Florida	October 31	1932	Palace Theater

Appendix 2

San Antonio, Texas	August 29	1933	Nacional Theater
Brownsville, Texas	January 5	1940	Dittmann Theater

Pro-Patria

Los Angeles, California	July 22	1932	México Theater
Los Angeles, California	August	1932	Hidalgo Theater
El Paso, Texas	September 16	1932	Teatro Colón
Guadalajara, Jalisco	October 13	1932	(shown at 8 theaters)
Los Angeles, California	February	1933	Electric Theater

La Chillona

San Antonio, Texas	August	1934	Nacional Theater

El héroe de Nacozari

Mexico City	May 5	1934	(shown at 4 theaters)
Los Angeles, California	May	1934	California Theater
New York City	September 23	1935	Campoamor Theater

El pulpo humano

Mexico City	June 23	1934	Cine Mundial
New York City	May	1935	Campoamor Theater
San Antonio, Texas	October 21	1935	Nacional Theater

El vuelo de la muerte

Mexico City	June 13	1934	Cine Regis
Madrid (Spain)	December 17	1934	?
New York City	April 16	1935	Campoamor Theater
San Antonio, Texas	August 25	1935	Strand Theater
Albuquerque, New Mexico	May 15	1939	Mission Theater

Pescadores de perlas

Chino, California	December 16	1938	Woods Theater
Corpus Christi, Texas	March 9	1939	Melba Theater
San Antonio, Texas	May 28	1939	Nacional Theater
San Antonio, Texas	November 4	1939	Zaragoza Theater
San Antonio, Texas	December 16	1939	Nacional Theater

La virgen de la sierra

Mexico City	February 17	1939	Teatro Balmori
New York City	March 6	1939	Latino Theater
Chino, California	June 9	1939	Woods Theater
San Antonio, Texas	January 13	1940	Nacional Theater
Albuquerque, New Mexico	December 19	1940	Mesa Theater

La justicia de Pancho Villa

Chino, California	September 1	1939	Woods Theater
Brownsville, Texas	December 31	1939	Teatro El Tiro
Mexico City	February 8	1940	Cine Olimpia
San Antonio, Texas	March 25	1940	Nacional Theater

Appendix 3: Pro-Patria

This is an itinerary of the making of Calles' feature–length documentary *Pro-Patria*. Calles wrote the following letters en route from Los Angeles to Mexico City. Journalist Gabriel Navarro edited and published them in Los Angeles's *La Opinión* prior to the movie's release in 1932. This document has considerable historical value; it not only describes a geographical region that was basically unknown in those days but it provides excellent information on a film that has been missing ever since. Accompanying Calles in his excursion were his wife Angelita Salcedo, his dog Águila, and photographer Ernie Smith.

Published on March 13, 1932:

Guillermo Calles recounts his adventures along the West coast of our country.
A colorful letter that talks about the movie that is being made while on the road, the object of which is to show Mexico to the people of the United States.

Our mail this week has brought us a letter signed by the enthusiastic film director Guillermo Calles. We are having it as a feature now and will print it without major changes. Calles is doing a tour of the West coast of Mexico, capturing scenes for a sound movie that will later be exhibited in the United States. This letter of Calles reads as follows:

Tepic, Nayarit, February 1932.—Señor Gabriel Navarro, Los Angeles, California. Dear and fine friend: I have been very worried for not being able to write you since I left that city. But believe me, besides the normal responsibility of my work it has been necessary to gather information and to prepare all the things for the continuation of the trip. This has prevented me from taking a few minutes to communicate to you in general terms our impression of the journey. As you might remember, on January 13 we filmed the initial scenes outside the City Hall, saying goodbye to the mayor, Mr. Porter, and to Señor De la Colina, our consul in that city. This turned out to be my first contentment, for it is well known that both of these officers have on their shoulders a great volume of things to carry out daily. Notwithstanding, they were so generous by agreeing to be included in the initial scenes of this film. To them goes my acknowledgment...

Our arrival in Nogales was at 5 p.m., January 15, when the effects of the cold front were still being felt. If in Los Angeles it caused quite a stir, in Arizona it is something normal during the winter.

The following day we crossed the border, having all kinds of considerations from the authorities of both Nogales. Señor Eduardo L. Soto, mayor of Nogales, Sonora, assisted us and we were able to film the most important aspects of that place, including our passage where the tourists are required to fill out immigration paperwork. Five days we spent in Nogales. We had time to read the newspaper *La Opinión* and the notes you published about our trip. Your opinion has stimulated our endeavor and we sincerely appreciate it. Wearing heavy coats early in the morning of the 21st, we filmed our departure heading south.

During the journey to Hermosillo, and driving on a highway in excellent condition, we photographed the most beautiful spots. The change of scenery is notable, becoming more pleasant as the tourist approaches Magdalena, a place justly called the Eden of Sonora. It is the home of numerous orchards where delicious and varied fruits are grown; these are sold in the southern part of our country as product of the United States. Also worth seeing is the local church, which was built in colonial times by the same Franciscan friars who endowed California with an abundance of missions. Without delay, we continued driving to Hermosillo, the "Sultana" of Sonora, famous for its intoxicating aroma of thousands of orange trees in bloom, which is capable of driving more than a couple of newlyweds mad. There are splendid hotels and lots of automobiles. In spite of the Depression, the South Pacific railroad station presents a very animated aspect because of the constant movement of small engines and cargo trains that transport loads of merchandise and local produce everyday. Also very active and numerous are the people working at beer, soda, and cracker factories, and at the flour mills.

Because the state governor, Señor don Rodolfo Calles, was away in the capital of the Republic, I did not have the opportunity to personally express to him my gratitude; he was very kind and gave his moral support to our task. But it must be recognized that the engineer Señor Ramón Ramos, who was interim governor of the state, provided us with many exemptions. For we did not encounter any obstacles and Ernie Smith was able to photograph gorgeous and very interesting aspects of regional life. Among the many images recorded on the 24th, appear engineer Ramos, the State Treasurer Señor Rodolfo Tapia, and the Justice Chief Licenciado José Rojas. Also appearing were other prominent personalities of the current administration, of commerce and the industries.

We stayed in Hermosillo until the 26th and the next day we arrived in the port of Guaymas, being extremely pleased about the good condition of the road; of the absolute security for travelers and of the legendary candor and graciousness of the people of Sonora. We worked there on the 28th and found out that the maritime activities of the port have diminished since the refurbishing of the port of Yabaros, which has better topographical conditions and a great commercial advantage over Guaymas. The quiet bay of Guaymas, however, is something truly convenient for vessels because it offers a natural protection by way of its surrounding hills. Several shots of the port and bay were taken; also the settlement of Empalme, which is about ten kilometers away from Guaymas and is separated by a sea arm and several low hills called Batuecas. At this time of the year, people in Guaymas enjoy nice temperatures. From April to September, however, Empalme becomes a favorite spot for those who like to breathe fresh air, saturated with the breeze of the Gulf of California. Upon returning to the hotel, I found copies of *La Opinión*, which people like to read here just as much as Mexicans in Los Angeles.

We got back on the road and headed toward the Yaqui region, enjoying nice and secure roads. South of Cruz de Piedra, we made a stop to photograph the plains at the end of which rises the Sierra of Bacatete. This is where the principal groups of the untamed Yaqui tribe have settled. A few minutes after we had resumed driving, we noticed with alarm that Águila was missing. Águila is a beloved dog that has accompanied me during many years of my life. We went back to try to find her but were almost sure that we had lost her. The country is filled with cactus of all sizes and the "chamisos" are shrubs that are abundant and do not let the eye see further.

There, in the distance, we saw a group of Yaquis and we approached them. Our surprise was great when we noticed that Águila was part of the group. One of them knew Spanish and he told us that they had held the dog so that she wouldn't get lost. We thanked them and offered a tip that they refused to accept. We continued to Pitahaya and came across a fraction of the 46th Regiment under the command of Lt. Enrique Z. Araujo. This brigade exercises strict vigilance on the zone, maintaining the security of the road. General Jesús Gutiérrez Cázares, head of the 46th, lives in Esperanza station, a place on the South Pacific railroad where there is a short trail that leads to Cócorit, an important town of the Yaqui region. The members of this regiment are very attentive to foreigners.

We went to Ciudad Obregón, always filming things of interest; later we passed through Navojoa, where the remains of the martyr of La Bombilla, Álvaro Obregón, are buried. The camera recorded views of the austere monument erected to his memory. We continued through the province of the Mayo Indians, and took note of the conveniences that the traveler can enjoy in this fertile region. For example, there is an excellent service of "pangas," or ferryboats, for the transportation of automobiles across the Yaqui and Mayo rivers. We entered the State of Sonora, passing through Los Mochis and Guamúchil until we reached Culiacán, which is the seat of the state powers. In Culiacán we stayed for three days and then went on to Mazatlán....

Even before entering Mazatlán, the traveler on the highway perceives the fresh breeze of the Pacific. The nearness of the coast is made more appealing by the numerous coconut palms and the continuous squealing of "Cacalotes," parrots and other birds of rare and beautiful feathers that the traveler runs into frequently. We took very nice shots of several places in this delightful port. One of them shows an important hotel where a banquet was offered to Generals Venecio López, Manuel F. de Escobar, and other officers of the 12th Battalion. We found out that the people of Mazatlán were getting ready and putting the finishing touches for the Carnaval fiestas. This is one of the events that has made the locality famous, as it is also known as the "Perla del Pacífico." We took a ride on Paseo Claussen, an avenue with traffic circles built around rocks and dangerously near the sea. This road has become an attraction for drivers, being crowded every day.

The jetty of Olas Altas is situated between the hills of Nevería and La Cruz, to the west of Mazatlán. It substituted the old stockade built in that place to protect the properties facing the cove and which was destroyed by the waves some time ago. A person told me that the present jetty cost one hundred thousand pesos to make; its construction lasted from April 20, 1896, to April 14, 1908. A heavy wall of about five hundred meters long and four meters wide forms it... The Hotel Belmar occupies a prominent site in that area, facing the sea, with its dancing halls taking up the first floor.

Continuation published on March 14, 1932:

We stayed in that port four days, not being able to accept the invitation to attend the approaching Carnaval celebration, unfortunately. We appreciated very much the courtesy shown to us by the people of Mazatlán. With a little sadness, we departed and headed towards Rosario. This is a mining town that had its splendor many years ago. Today, its buildings rest above an extensive labyrinth of caves. It is common for the people who go to church for Mass to hear the exploding dynamite at the mines, exactly below their feet and only a few meters under the floor.

Acaponeta was our next destination, the first major spot entering the State of Nayarit from the North. The atmosphere of the place is cheerful and one does not notice here any indication of the actual crisis. There is a very colorful road of palm trees that is in excellent condition. Moreover, the wildlife along the mountainous road adds a touch of emotion to the traveler's experience. It seems that hunting is abundant and varied; we found deer, quail, wild turkey, hare, armadillo, squirrel, etc. From Acaponeta we drove down to Tuxpam, another attractive site because of its exuberant vegetation. Further down we reached Santiago Ixcuintla, located on the right bank of the Rio Grande, or Rio de Santiago. This river is born in the Central Plateau and passes through several states of the Republic, flowing into the Pacific, near the Port of San Blas and not too far away from Santiago Ixcuintla. Here the town's mayor, Señor Francisco Parra, treated us very courteously. The governor of Nayarit, General Juventino Espinosa, had previously given him instructions to welcome us, as he had done with the authorities of Acaponeta.

A marked hospitality to foreigners is clearly visible in Nayarit. This is not a unique virtue of those in government posts but it is a common trait of all inhabitants, who by being highly attentive and courteous stand out from other people in the Republic. They possess an instinctive sense of politeness that cannot be overlooked by even the least perceptive person. In Tepic, the capital of the state, this characteristic is more pronounced. The humble city dweller is never licentious when speaking in the streets, a moral vice of our people frequently observed in other places. When I arrived here, on February 6, a group of people from the Carnaval's committee welcomed us. Chano Ruvalcaba, a popular fellow who worked in show business in Los Angeles for nearly six years and who became quite estimable, headed this commission. Our vehicle crossed the old and sturdy colonial bridge that separates Tepic from the Heriberto Casas farming neighborhood. A great multitude, made mostly of happy children, came to give us a warm welcome and surrounded our automobile. These people awaited us just outside the tree-lined avenue, and when they approached us many started shouting "¡Viva Calles!" Obviously alarmed, Ernie feared that it would turn into a riot, and my dog Águila, annoyed, answered with a lot of barking. Some of these people accompanied us to the Hotel Palacio, where we stayed.

Tepic launched that day the festivities of Carnaval with a burning of "Bad Humor," which was represented by a dummy stuffed with firecrackers and made to symbolize the crisis. I met the gentleman Colonel Francisco Cortés Figueroa. He is sub–chief of staff of military maneuvers in the state. The following morning, the Carnaval beauty queens entered the city in gorgeous cars that were artistically adorned. We filmed this brilliant ceremony. The Princess of the State Institute powerfully grabbed the attention of everyone. She was a dark-skinned woman of big brown eyes, who wore an authentic Huichol dress and was being carried on an ornamented litter by a dozen muscular Indians clad in Cora costumes.

In the evening, we attended a clownish rodeo that was filled with hilarious incidents. The next day we went to the nearby Hacienda de San Cayetano, owned by Señor Carlos Rivas Varela. A young farmer, he is highly respected in the region. A *charreada*, or rodeo, took place in his hacienda and was dedicated to General Evaristo Pérez. The property's land, which extends to the slope of the defunct Sanguangüey volcano, has rich and fertile soil, producing sugar cane, rice, coffee, and mezcal. This is a liquor similar to tequila but of superior quality. Ernie Smith drank more than one glass with delight and in amends for the torture of Prohibition. During the rodeo, several young bulls were available for bullfighting. I couldn't resist the temptation to refurbish my aptitudes at this difficult art. After attempting to spear the bull, I was thrown to the ground and knocked about pretty good. I did learn why bullfighters don't wear boots.

At night, and upon returning to Tepic, we attended a dance at the casino and were graciously entertained by the upper crust of society. We came back to the hotel in the early hours of the next day. Arturo García Formenti, an orator who won the championship title in Washington, was also with us. During an incident he demonstrated his good humor, a typical characteristic of our modern and restless youth. The caretaker of the hotel, who at night sleeps in the corridor, refused to let my automobile into the patio, even when the owner of the hotel, Señor Yenny, had agreed to it. García Formenti thought it useless to exploit his brilliant rhetoric to convince the employee. Instead, he started by kicking a chair and throwing the makeshift bed, the pillows, the blankets, etc. In an instant, the servant hurried to the center of the patio holding his large underwear with both hands. The patio of the Hotel Palacio showed the signs of a battleground after a combat. By this indisputable logic, which served as a magic word, the door was opened. I had difficulty driving the car inside, for I had laughed so much that my eyes were filled with tears. I don't think I will ever again laugh as I did on that occasion.

In that same patio of the hotel, a special banquet took place the following night. It was given in honor of General Evaristo Pérez and his distinguished wife, Señora Delfina Pérez de Pérez, who belongs to a family of the educated society of Tepic. They had just been married in a ceremony at the main meeting room of the City Hall. Attending were the state governor General Juventino Espinosa and Pablo S. Rodríguez, chief of military operations. Both acted as witnesses on the part of the groom. The bride's brother-in-law, Señor Abraham D. Ortiz, and Señor Ramón J. Menchaca were witnesses for Señora Delfina.

During our stay in Nayarit State, we also visited the Port of San Blas and the Bay of Mexcaltitlán, which turned out to be very interesting places. San Blas is a seaport that has been abandoned but it would pay off to return it to its former glory. In order to travel to these locations, Governor Espinosa kindly provided us with the assistance of a major who is stationed in the Hacienda de Navarrete and who drove back with us to Tepic. San Blas has many resources awaiting the investment of capital. Coconut oil is plentiful in this extensive forest. There are all kinds of woods for construction, the most important of which is cedar. In Mexcaltitlán, where there are many lizards, we were welcomed with music. It was obvious that those people, whose livelihood is fishing, lead an uncomplicated life. The locally caught shrimp is first class and very large. Everyone in Mexcaltitlán is related to each other and those who are not have eventually become so by reason of being compadres, or godparents. The total population is about eight to nine hundred. We returned from this excursion in very good spirits.

In [Tepic], people gave us several presents: splendid works of art of the Cora and Huichol Indians, some samples of ceramic and even steamed bananas, which is a typical recipe of this region and has a pleasant taste. From all the social classes we have received many demonstrations of sympathy, in particular from the mayor, Señor Narváez, and from officers and the person in command of military operations at the local garrison. They were filmed in very interesting scenes taken at Loma de la Cruz, where the members of the Army have erected a stadium called Coso Estadio Marte, a polo field and a training track for horse riding. They also built a pelota court and a stand for target shooting. I was told that they are planning to construct an outdoor theater in the same place, which is a poplar grove.

The state of Nayarit is currently undergoing a nice transformation. Governor Espinosa is mainly dedicated to the improvement of highways; even in the city, he has ordered some streets paved with a mixture of soil and limestone that makes the automobile ride nice and smooth. This young governor, energetic and dynamic, represents a reassurance to the inhabitants of the state. In addition to the many attentions for which I will always thank him, the governor presented me with a very meaningful gift which I will treasure at all times. It was a detailed graphic of the main Yaqui tribes of Sonora, featuring aboriginal dances that are very emotive, like "Pascola" and "El Venado." This graphic includes several photographs with autographs of the tribal chiefs with an affectionate dedication to General Espinosa. To these inscriptions, he added moving phrases bestowed upon my humble self, for which I thank him with all my heart. As far as I know, there are only two of these graphics, the one given to me by General Juventino Espinosa and another one presented to General Álvaro Obregón. As I said publicly, before coming here the newspaper accounts of this beautiful land, which is the birthplace of poet Amado Nervo, positively impressed me. This impression has been corroborated now with the founding of new friendships to which I will reciprocate devotedly.

Tomorrow, when circumstances allow me to make not one but many films of national interest, I will come to Nayarit so as to provide these cinematographic works with the value and advantages found here; a film that would reproduce all the charm, all the beauty and majesty of Nayarit, with its forest, rivers, transparent skies, and its attractive and virtuous women.

You will have to forgive me, my lenient friend, if this time I have extended myself too much. But I could not help it in any way. Please acknowledge me as your attentive and loyal friend.

Guillermo Calles.

PS: I will write to you my new experiences when I arrive in Mexico City.

Continuation published on April 15, 1932:

Mexico City, April 1932.
Señor Gabriel Navarro (Los Angeles, California).

Dear and fine friend:

Hoping that you are in good health, I send to you warm greetings. Upon my arrival in this capital, I found a few copies of *La Opinión*; in the cinema section of March 13 and 14, I read the letter that I sent you from Tepic and which you kindly published. Let me express my gratitude for this new compliment granted to me by your prestigious publication. On purpose I delayed this second letter, because I wanted to inform you of the last and most important phase of my trip, which has been an expedition to film aspects of the International Highway between Los Angeles and Mexico City.

Before going into any detail, it is necessary to tell you that I am pretty sure that in this film I have gathered a wealth of features; illustrating the beautiful and romantic Mexico, of enormous natural resources, of unrivaled climate, and of a great variety of charming landscapes, which continues to be unknown among thousands of citizens of this country and that in the near future will become the hub of world tourism.

It was the crack of dawn on Wednesday, February 17, when we abandoned Tepic, a city so gracious and hospitable where we received countless considerations. Our automobile passed by the neighborhoods of the south side, which included vegetable gardens and numerous trees that produced mangos and other fruits. We enjoyed breathing fresh, pure air, saturated by the aroma of early morning flowers typical of the spring. We took the highway that leads to a nearby town in the state of Jalisco, about twenty-five kilometers away, and which seems to be in decline. However, in the near future it will recapture its former glory as a summer spot for the residents of Tepic. It is situated in an archaeological zone where there have been important discoveries of aboriginal objects. Between this place and Compostela we bumped into a herd of wild boars that we tried to chase; unfortunately we only caught one of them. In Compostela we had breakfast and toured the city. Compostela was the capital of Nueva Galicia (today Jalisco); some old buildings of pure colonial style are still standing. At that time, the city had the honor of being awarded the title of "Very Noble and Loyal Town" by the Spanish throne. Throughout this region, the traveler goes by many crossings of creeks. Their clean waters form very small cascades of white foam, set against the colors of thousands of flowers. Even though this region is more than fifty kilometers from the Pacific coast, its wonderful vegetation preserves the characteristics of the tropics. Ernie had an excellent chance to record a surprising vision of the land of Nayarit with his camera.

Just after we arrived in Ixtlán del Río, Nayarit, and being at the table after our meal, I received a courteous call from General Pablo Rodríguez S., chief of military operations in the state and who had presently come from the south. I met him at the home of General José Lacarra, military commander of the Ixtlán garrison. General Rodríguez gave me a big hug and introduced me to Colonel Filiberto Gómez, governor of the state of Mexico and president of the Mexico–Los Angeles Highway Commission. He has been coping with the construction of the road at the state limits of Nayarit and Jalisco, in the wild area of Plan de Barrancas. They had just arrived from Barrancas, their uniforms covered by dust after a horse ride.

The introduction was made with the formal mutual phrases of courtesy. General Rodríguez invited me to explain to Colonel Gómez the cinematographic project that I have undertaken. While giving this explanation, I emphasized that my plan had been to present a film that could provide the best depiction of the highway, the building of which has been done with so much enthusiasm. The film would show the lifestyle and customs of the regions that it crosses, together with relevant aspects of the economic and natural resources of the West Coast and other parts of the country's interior. [I added] that this [film], no doubt, would generate new waves of tourism, awakening the interest of businessmen who want to contribute to the economic progress of Mexico, a nation struggling to occupy its deserved position in the world. Above all, this effort, although a small one, will help thousands of viewers who ignore us or have a false opinion of us, to make a better appraisal of the invaluable wealth of the country and of the culture of the Mexican people.

After he had patiently listened to my account, Colonel Gómez openly exclaimed: "¡Caramba! Every so often our minds and souls get tired, but when someone speaks to us with the enthusiasm and faith as you have done, the spirit reacts and gives energy to our body once again. Believe me, Calles, I am working tirelessly in order to finish as soon as possible a highway that would connect Los Angeles with Mexico, so that thousands of automobiles can travel with maximum security and comfort between both places. Collaborating with me and doing their best are the Generals Rodríguez, Espinosa, and Lacarra, who are providing me with troops who work without a rest. Right now we have three thousand men opening up the terrain that is located in Plan de Barrancas. I invite you tomorrow to come with us and see the magnitude of the works needed for this International Highway." Our conversation went on freely as we sipped a comforting punch.

The governor of the state of Mexico, Colonel Filiberto Gómez, is one of the most notable rulers of the moment. He has efficiently dealt with each of the problems that have emerged. Colonel Gómez is representative of the practical man, trying hard to learn and prepare his mind for great deeds. He is one of the closest collaborators of General Plutarco Elías Calles and is engaged in modeling the future of Mexico by creating a highway net in all directions of the country. He is a tourism fanatic and has provided many incentives to new industries in the state that he governs. This translates into an influx of capital that creates more jobs in paper, clothing and tobacco factories. Colonel Gómez has contributed to the success of the nationalist campaign that is currently in progress, not because of his labor of propaganda but more effectively because he is industrializing the country.

Appendix 3

The next morning, Angelita, Ernie, and my pet Águila accompanied me, together with all the movie equipment. Governor Gómez and Generals Rodríguez and Lacarra, in addition to several officers and assistants, were ready to leave. After a short ride, we arrived at the edge of the Plan de Barrancas and we gasped at the magnificence of nature in this spot, which by comparison makes the Grand Canyon of Arizona look small. The depth of this precipice is greater than the one in Arizona, with the uniqueness that affords a view dotted with vegetation. Although the narrow mountain passes are plentiful, the plan of the highway is simply admirable. The wavy design and the simplicity with which traffic in both directions will flow are also commendable. The three thousand workers here represent the dignified but anonymous "Juanes" of the Army; they could be seen scattered throughout the road, providing a lively element to the indescribable sight. Observed from an elevation where we stood, they gave me the impression of a trickle of hard-working ants. We had barely recovered from this astonishment when Ernie was already activating his camera, capturing scenes and details that will give a better idea of the place and the work in process.

We returned to Ixtlán where the next day a spirited polo match took place. The players were military men and they showed off their expertise as riders and amateurs of this sport. It was time to continue our journey heading south. Yet we were forced to ship our automobile by train from Ixtlán to La Quemada, in the state of Jalisco, thus bridging the expanse of the precipices of Plan de Barrancas. The soldiers took care of the shipping of the car, carried out amidst an unexpected rain shower. Colonel Gómez was with us on the train ride to La Quemada, where we said goodbye to him. He gave orders so that the authorities along the road would assist us in our mission.

Continuation published on April 18, 1932:

We made a stop in Magdalena, a pleasant and scenic town on our way to Tequila. The next morning, a group of gentlemen driving luxury cars met us just outside Tequila. The city mayor, Eduardo G. González, a state representative, Señor Gutiérrez, and other persons welcomed us and we rode with them to an advantage point where we could see the panorama. From an altitude of 3,000 meters above sea level, we contemplated the town of Tequila and surrounding area, which looked like a chessboard of symmetrical squares of green scattered among the white-colored buildings. The church towers stood out and the vapor coming out of the chimneys of the liquor factories seemed to be enveloping the temple. At exactly that moment, the sunrays bathed the town, producing a marvelous effect of light that did not go unnoticed by Ernie Smith. He focused the lens of his camera and photographed a beautiful sight of the city, which is jealously guarded by the silhouette of the abyss.

Once in town, we shot many details typical of Tequila and yet reminiscent of some European villages. A young man, sent by Señor Guillermo Freytag, approached us. He invited us to come to the mezcal factories of Don José Cuervo and heirs, of which Señor Freytag is the official representative. This gentleman showed us around each section of the factory, also called "Taberna." Inside there are numerous pots with thousands of gallons in each one, a sufficient amount to make drunk the whole city of Los Angeles. We tasted the delicious drink called tequila. At first, Ernie drank with certain reserve; once he had gotten used to it, he exclaimed approvingly: "Whoopee!" From this place we were taken to Quinta El Retiro, residence of the widow of Señor Cuervo. We entered the spacious and elegant dining room and were treated to a "botana" consisting of high-quality mezcal, in addition to olives, peeled oranges and Spanish cheese.

I cannot resist informing that the Quinta El Retiro is something unexpected: a regal mansion provided with exquisite tapestries and furniture of very good taste. Led by Señor Freytag, we toured the rooms of the house and saw a large garden, with plenty of rose bushes and plants of all kinds, sculptures and fountains in the manner of Versailles. On behalf of the family, Señor Freytag treated us as guests of honor, assigning our rooms with that proverbial politeness that says "You are in your own home." This is a sincere phrase, not just a formality, as every Mexican family observes it. We thanked him and let him know that the honor was ours. If the Cuervo family reads these words, they should be aware once again of our deep gratitude.

A servant announced that dinner was ready. So were we, as the tequila we drank stimulated our appetite. If the tequila was superb, the food was plentiful, varied and exquisite. There were times when I felt I was dreaming a fairy tale, thinking that the entire splendor around us was the effect of tequila. But I got back to reality and had to acknowledge that if Quinta El Retiro resembled the Eden, this paradise was made more pleasant by the hospitality and courtesy of its inhabitants.

On February the 24th we arrived in Guadalajara and we paid our first visit to the governor, meeting him at his office in the Palacio. This is a nice and massive edifice built of skillfully carved stone, located across from the main square. Wide cement walkways, cast iron benches and buttressed lamps form the Plaza Principal. At the center of it, surrounded by flowerbeds and plants, there is a kiosk with ornate columns topped by bronze caryatids. In this historical palace, there is a marble plaque at the foot of the monumental stair with an inscription remembering the imprisonment of Don Benito Juárez, who was saved precisely here by Don Guillermo Prieto's beaming rhetoric.

Governor Juan de Dios Robledo dedicated a few minutes to our visit. He is a very affable person who knew about my work through Colonel Gómez. The governor sincerely congratulated me and offered his firm support to my project.

It took two days to film the most important aspects of the so-called Perla de Occidente, which is not only famous for its legendary history and its pottery shops in Tlaquepaque and Tonalá but also for the beauty of its women who have inspired many works of art in music and literature. Today, there is a new governor in the state of Jalisco, the young and cultivated attorney Don Sebastián Allende.

Leaving Guadalajara and driving on an excellent highway, we passed by Ocotlán. It is an attractive little town on the Lake of Chapala, with abundant commercial traffic. The majestic lake produces a kind of fish that is larger than the best Spanish sardine but of silver color and delicious meat. Passing through Ixtlán, Jalisco, we arrived in Zamora, in the state of Michoacán. This city has been blessed by nature, being rightfully called the Mexican Paradise. Only one day we stayed in Zamora, continuing to Morelia, which is the capital of the state and has many wonderful boulevards and superb edifices. It is here that the tasty fruit jellies called "Ates" are made. The garments of local Indians are exquisitely embroidered, as if they were the work of magic hands threading countless filaments.

Michoacán, birthplace of the current president of Mexico, Engineer Pascual Ortiz Rubio, is one of the states with larger Indian population. This is due to the steep and mountainous topography that has isolated groups of people and prevented them from mixing their blood with foreigners. Among the ethnic groups of the region, the Tarascans are dominant. We sighted some of them carrying "huacales," or wooden crates, on their backs. These measure one meter and a half long and eighty centimeters wide. They use the crates to transport pottery and other wares that they sell at distant places. To avoid being robbed, the Indians always march in groups of two and three, but sometimes you see twenty-five individuals walking together. They don't seem to care carrying such a weight, but it is the sheer size of the "huacales" that attracts the attention. When they pass by a ranch that has a scale, curious people try to calculate the weight of their load; it is about 70 kilos (152 pounds), which shows that they are lifting a burden similar to that of their own bodies. Believe it or not, in spite of the bulk, a "huacalero" usually walks twenty or thirty miles in a day; this is double the distance that a beast of burden is made to travel. From sunrise to sunset the "huacaleros" do not rest, and they only make a stop to eat. They also carry with them a long cane with a metal tip that they use in rough terrain and as a support when they get up.

Continuation published on April 19, 1932:

Morelia's asphalt streets make the automobile ride so pleasurable. This place has a rich historical past and we started by visiting the old Colegio de San Nicolás, a school founded by the Bishop and missionary Vasco de Quiroga in 1541. Getting their education in this institution were men of the caliber of Don Miguel Hidalgo y Costilla, father of Mexican Independence, and Don José María Morelos y Pavón, of whom Napoleon once said with admiration that he could dominate the world if given five men like Morelos.

Lake Páztcuaro, with its island of Janitzio at the center, offers the tourist a new and attractive view. The red tile of the houses that are scattered in random arrangement, the fishing boats tied to their docks, and the huge nets that the fishermen spread out to dry by the sun rays; all these things make up an enchanted landscape. Páztcuaro is an unmatched sight at dusk.

It is true that the traditions of the Tarascans are disappearing. But in spite of all the foreign influences, deep inside the Indians keep their old beliefs and many of their habitual customs. Regarding matters of love and marriage, there are many who still observe the rituals of their ancestors. Flirting usually takes place at or near the town's fountain, where the young women gather around to fill up their jugs. The suitor begins by asking the girl for water and she lets him drink from her jug. Some candidates try hard to please the women and help them fill up their containers. But generally they approach the girls along the way, where one can see the couples flirting. The woman appears timid and embarrassed, ripping the leaves of a plant with one hand and with the other balancing the heavy jug on her shoulder. Every day a man can see his sweetheart in this manner, but addressing the subject of marriage might take one or two years.

When a young man is sure that his love is corresponded, he goes to the fountain and grabs the girl by her shawl; he does not let her go until she says "yes" to his plea. Then, with a stick that he carries concealed in his blanket, he breaks her jug, getting her soaked with water. The young woman's girl friends come hurriedly and offer her a change of clothes and a new pitcher. She returns home with the borrowed dress and pitcher. The suitor keeps her wet clothes; to recover them, the girl's father has to pay him six cents for each garment. The next day, the youngster deposits a load of firewood at the door of the girl's home. He does not return until after three days; if he notices that the firewood has been accepted, the marriage is assured. The local priest finally takes charge of the wedding ceremony.

Señor Adrián Legaspi, representative of the state of Mexico, welcomed us in Zitácuaro. He invited us to a private dinner and showed us a telegram he had just received from Colonel Filiberto Gómez. The governor wanted to meet us at the mining town of El Oro, where a reception in his honor was going to take place. Señor Legaspi accompanied us to that prosperous settlement. When we arrived, we became aware of the widespread joy of the people. Later, Colonel Gómez came to greet us with a warm hug. We stayed there for three days, enjoying the banquets, dances and picnics, after which we left for Toluca. I must acknowledge the fact that during our expedition from Nayarit to the south, everything became easier for us thanks to the official help and support of Colonel Gómez, for whom I only have expressions of deep respect.

Before entering Toluca, the capital of the state of Mexico, we caught a glimpse of the Nevado de Toluca, an extinct volcano that rises 4,578 meters above sea level and which is the third greatest elevation in the country. The natives called it "Xinantécatl," meaning Naked Lord. It is situated 22 kilometers south of Toluca. At the bottom of its crater, there are two beautiful large lakes that are nourished by melted ice and snow. By a special invitation from the governor, we were taken to his charming Quinta El Carmen, where we had lunch. He introduced us to his gracious wife and daughters, who were very kind. We stayed in the Hotel San Carlos. Two days later, we joined Governor Filiberto Gómez, the generals Agustín Mora and Raúl Garate, and other government officers. In eight automobiles, we ascended on a splendid road to the crater of the volcano. We stopped very frequently and the governor pointed out to the imposing landscape, explaining his plans to make this route a tourist attraction. The clouds crowning the volcano started to dampen the automobiles, which went up the road effortlessly. From the surface of the lakes to the edge of the crater, there is an approximate altitude of one thousand meters. The setting is harsh and imposing. There is a marvelous view of the villages of this beautiful Valley of Toluca, and beyond one can see the winding course of the Lerma River. Its waters pass through various states and finally meet the Pacific near Santiago Ixcuintla, Nayarit. Intriguingly, the water of the volcano's lakes changes colors within seconds constantly. Thanks to the magnificent road that the dynamic Colonel Gómez has built, the tourist can enjoy the view of the lakes and the panorama of the Valley. We have recorded all these aspects for our movie. In addition, I am pleased to inform you that a nice hotel will open soon in the crater of the volcano, near one of the lakes.

During our visit to Toluca, where we shot many interesting scenes, I took a moment to ask the governor how to get an interview with the president of México, to whom I wanted to convey a letter from the Los Angeles mayor, Mr. Porter. The colonel showed a lot of enthusiasm in taking me to see the president. The next morning, a fresh sunny day, we rode comfortably on the highway to Mexico that traverses beautiful places like the city of Lerma and the wooded area of Desierto de los Leones. We passed the Monte de las Cruces, a historical site....

Before entering the capital of the Republic, near the edge of the Fábrica Nacional de Pólvora in Santa Fe, there is a view of the Chapultepec Hill, on which the famous and historic castle rises. Moctezuma had long ago occupied the hill, and Netzahualcóyotl planted the millenary trees or Ahuehuetes that surround it. Chapultepec became the residence of the Aztec rulers. One of the things that still survive is a well, excavated on solid rock and measuring almost 28 meters deep. Today, there is an elevator inside this tunnel. After numerous phases of construction and other adaptations, the Castle of Chapultepec became again the official residence of Mexican rulers. The building adjacent to it, which is made of beautiful stonework, used to be the headquarters of the celebrated Colegio Militar, or military academy...

Overlooking the Valley, a terrace surrounded by pergolas on the north and south sides serves as a deck and has recently built access ramps... At the foot of one of the ramps, resembling Indian culture, there are two serpent heads of Teotihuacan style, which were sculpted by

Appendix 3

Miguel Ángel Fernández... McGregor's new monument honoring the young cadets killed during the United States invasion in 1847 has been erected on this terrace. One of the brave military students was Juan Escutia, born in Tepic and whose relatives are still living. Surrounding Chapultepec is one of the prettiest wooded areas in America, with a large lake, the old Jockey Club edifice, the grotto, the Fountain of Don Quijote, the Automobile Club and the Fountain of Frogs, which is an exact replica of the one in Seville, Spain.

Without making a stop, we went up to the castle to meet Mexico's president. Colonel Gómez introduced us to him. Señor Pascual Ortiz Rubio, who has been guiding the destiny of our country in a laudable manner, is a simple, tranquil man. He greeted me at one of the drawing rooms of the castle; with his friendly ways he gave me courage to express the object of our visit. I informed him of my plans and the untiring perseverance with which I have been working for the benefit of my country. Finally I told him about this film, begging him to participate in it by acknowledging the message I was bringing... from the mayor, Señor Porter... The president showed interest in receiving this letter in front of the camera. I must confess that our esteemed president performed with striking spontaneity, as if he were accustomed to the chores of the film studios.

During our conversation, Señor Presidente demonstrated his ample culture, which is made more noticeable by his affability and modesty. He had phrases of encouragement for my humble efforts and listening to them was a great reassurance. The interview lasted more than half an hour and took place in an atmosphere of familiarity, which helped me very much to control the emotion produced by the fact of being materially and spiritually close to the man who, with great modesty, occupies the highest office of the land. He allowed us to film with cohesion, making use of different close-ups and locations; these were scenes related to the completion of the mission that led me to his presence. Appearing also in the scenes were his general staff, some acquaintances of the president, and Señor Domínguez, who was the first person that greeted us at Chapultepec.

The president seemed to be quite interested in knowing the condition of the roads; the guarantee of security for travelers; the kind of services offered to tourists, in particular those that were furnished to us; the state of my car upon arrival, and the attractiveness of the places we visited. I answered to all questions in the same manner that I explained in my letters. Before Señor Presidente showed any signs of fatigue, we said goodbye to him. He assured me that he would answer Mr. Porter's letter as soon as possible. What a pleasant and long-lasting impression it was! I will always remember the fine treatment that the president of the Mexican United States conferred upon us!

A little later, we were absorbed by the whirl of the most beautiful, romantic, exceptionally stately capital of Latin America. We picked up here and there surprising scenes of the City of Palaces. It would be necessary to write books and more books to describe these beautiful sights, being beyond the reach of my modest undertaking. Still, in the film that I enthusiastically began to make will be included: Xochimilco and its canoes, San Ángel and its flowery orchards; Teotihuacán and its majestic archaeological zone; Mexico and its multicolored collection of avenues with old and new constructions; Texcoco, Coyoacán and Tepeyac, which is the sanctuary of the miraculous canvas that has borne for centuries the image of the gracious Dark-skinned Virgin of Guadalupe, venerated by generations of Bronze Races...

I went to the studios of the Nacional Productora de Películas to visit Antonio Moreno, who kindly showed us the trailer of *Santa*. It seems that they have been able to make a film that will be as famous as the novel written by Federico Gamboa.

Pro-Patria

To end my letter, let me express my deepest gratitude to the persons who contributed to make a film of which I am satisfied. Among them, Señor Enrique Ferreira, our consul in San Diego, California, takes a special place. I am preparing my return to Los Angeles and look forward to shake hands with you again.

Your friend and loyal servant,
Guillermo Calles.

Permission to reproduce these letters courtesy of *La Opinión* (Los Angeles, California).

Appendix 4: Recovering a Film Script of *El indio yaqui*

Just when this book was being readied for production in January 2010, a script of *El indio yaqui* surfaced. Richard "Dick" Domínguez found it in his home in Whittier, California, inside a keepsake box left by his father, the actor José Domínguez. This script belonged to Guillermo Calles, as shown by his handwritten notes on almost every page. It is in Spanish and consists of thirty-one typewritten legal size pages bound by three metal clamps at the top. The story's title is *El Yaqui*. Although the author's name and other film credits are absent, the cast members are introduced in the titles that accompany the narration.

The manuscript's information is organized in three columns. First comes the number of the scene or take (starting at 1 and ending at 407), followed by a second column establishing a scene's location or introducing a title. The third column explains the nature of the shot (close-up, full shot, etc.), and provides a brief description of the action. If a title is announced, this column presents the dialogue or gives background information about a character. It also includes the name of the actor playing the part. In addition, the script's third column sometimes recommends special optical effects, like fades, use of iris and superimpositions. The narration is concise and its style unpretentious; the dialogues are realistic, using ordinary language.

It is obvious that this particular script was utilized during the editing of the film, as there are many inscriptions altering the original text. Some notes modify the dialogue or introduce a new shot; a few times the word "color" is written next to the description of a shot. The numbering of scenes is often affected by this reorganization. Another indication that this was a blueprint for editing are certain remarks about a scene that had been shot twice and another scene that did not come out satisfactorily. The handwritten marks on this script turn it into a priced item; it is like entering the cutting room and watching director Calles assemble his film.

Autobiographical references are noticeable since the beginning of the screenplay. One of the first titles introduces the character of Dorotea Tollos (Agustina López), an elderly Indian woman "of pure Yaqui extraction who has resided in the United States for over 25 years." This portrayal bears a resemblance to Calles's mother, Anatolia Guerrero, a Tarahumara Indian who immigrated to Arizona in 1901. The same title adds that Dorotea "is looking for the Cinematographic Studios in order to sell a story written by her son." Although the sentence was later changed to read "a story about her son's life," the parallel between some aspects of Calles's own experiences and this fictional account is made plain.

The script sheds light on Joe Ryan, Roy Stewart and Neal Hart, well-known screen personalities making cameo appearances in the movie. Neal Hart's popularity as a "friend of Mexicans" is emphasized in a title. In addition, the manuscript brings up the names of other performers who were not mentioned by reviewers at the time of the film's release. Some little-known actors doing bit parts in *El indio yaqui* are Tex, Roux, and Valenzuela. Tex might be the most difficult to identify, as there were so many performers with that nickname. The second one is probably Antonio Roux, who was the brother of actress Carmen La Roux. Pedro Valenzuela may well be the full name of the third actor. Valenzuela appeared in several silent movies including one where he interpreted Pancho Villa. Last but not least, the dogs that come out in the film merit the script's attention. "Eagle" or "Águila" is the Yaqui Indian's companion, while "Lady" is the German Shepherd of Roy Anderson (Juan V. Calles). The pets are described as very loyal and smart, demonstrating their skills on several occasions. A little dog that is guarded by Lulu (José M. Duarte) also appears in the story.

Even though Calles was not a professional writer, his handling of the story is particularly lucid. There is a balanced outline that combines elements of action, comedy and tragedy. The appropriate use of shots, their continuity and the inclusion of plain dialogues enhance the efficacy of the cinematographic work. An example of a carefully built sequence is the one describing the Yaqui Indian's tribulations and violent death. In a romantic fashion, the Indian avenges the death of the beautiful Betty Anderson (Betty Brown) and then says to her brother Roy: "So long, my good friend. It is time for me to follow your little sister. Now you take care of my mother."

The recovery of the script of *El indio yaqui* brings us closer to deciphering a "lost" film that generated so much enthusiasm in its time. Following its release in 1926, a number of reviews detailed several aspects of the story. The commentaries of critics Homero Lizama Escoffie, Gabriel Navarro, Gonzalo Becerra, and Armando Vargas de la Maza offer the irreplaceable perspective of people who actually saw the movie. These opinions are made more relevant after examining the original screenplay, heightening our sense not only of a film but also of the culture that produced it. Perhaps now we can answer why *El indio yaqui* aroused the sentiments of Mexican audiences in a way very few films did.

Chapter Notes

Preface

1. *Ilustrado* (Mexico City), September 26, 1929.
2. *Hispano-América* (San Francisco, CA), September 25 and October 9, 1920.
3. *San Antonio Express* (San Antonio, TX), May 23, 1926, p. 17.
4. *Ilustrado*, September 26, 1929.

Chapter 1

1. *La Opinión* (Los Angeles, CA), October 29, 1933.
2. *Revista de Revistas* (Mexico City), October 1, 1933.
3. Confirming his racial roots, Frank Morriss, a film critic who knew him well, said in 1953: "Willie Calles, a Tarahumara Indian who is now 64 and lives in Mexico City, came to Hollywood more than 40 years ago and worked on his first picture in 1912." *Winnipeg Free Press* (Manitoba, Winnipeg, Canada), October 22, 1953.
4. Although a few questions remain unsolved, the essential facts of Calles's life are now in place. Biographical information on his early years comes from the Mexican Civil Registry, U.S. population censuses and immigration records, as well as from conversations with members of his family. Two personal chronicles appearing in *La Opinión* and *Revista de Revistas* in 1933, in addition to an article published by *Cine Mundial* when Calles died in 1958, give support to the following narrative.
5. Joseph F. Park, "The 1903 'Mexican Affair' at Clifton," *Journal of Arizona History* (Summer 1977), 119–48.
6. Linda Gordon, *The Great Arizona Orphan Abduction* (Cambridge: Harvard University Press, 1999), pp. 90–91.
7. *The Bisbee Daily Review*, June 5, 1903, as quoted by Joseph F. Park.
8. Gordon, *The Great Arizona Orphan Abduction*, pp. 239, 241.
9. *Ibid.*, p. 241.
10. Margaret Regan, *The Irish Orphan Abduction: A Tale of Race, Religion and Lawlessness in Turn-of-the-Century Southern Arizona*. Entry posted on March 15, 2007, http://www.tucsonweekly.com/gbase/Currents/Content?oid=93635 (accessed June 28, 2007).
11. *Ibid.*
12. William Curry Holden, *Teresita* (Owings Mills, MD: Stemmer House, 1978), pp. 218–19.
13. *Ibid.*, p. 196. Regarding the practice of "curanderismo," it is interesting to note that Calles quite often characterized "faith healers." Due to his physical type, he was chosen to personify witch doctors in many Mexican movies.
14. History of Silverbell Complex, Vignettes in Time Exhibit, BLM, http://www.statemuseum.arizona.edu/exhibits/blm_vignettes/silverbell_history.shtml (accessed May 21, 2005).

Chapter 2

1. *La Opinión* (Los Angeles, CA), October 29, 1933, p. 3.
2. Anthony Slide, *The Big V: A History of the Vitagraph Company* (Metuchen, NJ: Scarecrow Press, 1987), pp. 3 and 56.
3. Diana Serra Cary, *The Hollywood Posse: The History of a Gallant Band of Horsemen Who Made Movie History* (Norman: University of Oklahoma Press, 1996), p. 45.
4. *The State* (South Carolina), August 10, 1913.
5. *The Ogden Standard* (Ogden City, UT), April 10, 1913.
6. *The Lima Daily News* (Lima, OH), September 27, 1913.
7. *La Opinión*, October 29, 1933, p. 3.
8. *Fort Wayne Journal-Gazette* (Fort Wayne, IN), April 19, 1914.
9. Slide, *The Big V: A History of the Vitagraph Company*, p. 116.
10. *La Opinión*, October 29, 1933, p. 3.
11. *The Ogden Standard*, September 28, 1917.
12. *The Ogden Standard*, October 3, 1917.
13. *Manitoba Free Press* (Winnipeg, Manitoba, Canada), July 20, 1918.
14. *The Ogden Examiner* (Ogden, UT), September 15, 1918.

15. *Manitoba Morning Free Press* (Winnipeg, Manitoba, Canada), August 7, 1918, p. 11.
16. *El Informador* (Guadalajara, Jalisco, México), May 23, 1920.
17. *Olean Evening Herald* (Olean, NY), April 24, 1919. Another source suggests a rather interesting scene: The film's promotion by the Grand Theater in Newark, Ohio, mentioned that in the twelfth episode of *The Man of Might*, "the Aztec Indians play a prominent part." *The Newark Advocate* (Newark, OH), June 13, 1919.
18. Buck Rainey, *The Strong, Silent Type: Over 100 Screen Cowboys, 1903–1930* (Jefferson, NC: McFarland, 2003), p. 221.
19. *La Novela Film*, "De cara a la muerte" (Barcelona, Spain: Cinematográfica Miró, No. 23).
20. Slide, *The Big V: A History of the Vitagraph Company*, p. 56.
21. *The Coshocton Tribune* (Coshocton, OH), July 11, 1920.
22. *The Boys' Herald* (London, England), July 9 and 23, 1921; *Boys' Cinema Weekly* (London, England), June 12, 1920.
23. Slide, *The Big V*, p. 88.
24. *Excélsior* (Mexico City), July 31, 1921, 3rd section, p. 3. To understand the meaning of a change of citizenship, it is useful to look at the Declaration of Intention of the U.S. Naturalization Service in the 1920s. It reads: "I will before being admitted to citizenship, renounce forever all allegiance and fidelity to any foreign prince, potentate, state, or sovereignty, and particularly to [that State] of which I may be at the time of admission a citizen or subject."
25. Francisco E. Balderrama, *In Defense of La Raza: The Los Angeles Mexican Consulate and the Mexican Community, 1929 to 1936* (Tucson: University of Arizona, 1982), p. 8.
26. Douglas Monroy, *Rebirth: Mexican Los Angeles from the Great Migration to the Great Depression* (Berkeley: University of California Press, 1999), pp. 38–40.
27. World War I Draft Registration Card, A-, June 5, 1917; and United States Population Census, Los Angeles, CA, 1920.

Chapter 3

1. *La Opinión* (Los Angeles, CA), October 29, 1933, p. 3.
2. Gabriel Ramírez, *Miguel Contreras Torres* (Guadalajara: Universidad de Guadalajara, 1994), p. 118.
3. *Ibid.*, p. 119.
4. *Ibid.*, p. 22.
5. *La Patria* (El Paso, TX), May 23, 1922, p. 4.
6. *La Patria*, April 2, 1922.
7. *La Patria*, May 17, 1922, p. 1.
8. *La Patria*, May 31 and June 9, 1922.
9. *Amigo del Hogar* (Indiana Harbor, IN), September 1, 1929.
10. *La Patria*, July 9, 1922.
11. *Ibid.*
12. *La República* (El Paso, TX), October 15, 1921, p. 1. David Dorado Romo, *Ringside Seat to a Revolution: An Underground Cultural History of El Paso and Juárez, 1893–1923* (El Paso, TX: Cinco Puntos Press, 2005), p. 183.
13. *La Prensa* (San Antonio, TX), February 11, 1921.
14. *Olean Evening Times* (Olean, NY), August 22, 1922. *The Davenport Democrat* (Davenport, IA), May 18, 1922.
15. *El Heraldo de México* (Los Angeles, CA), June 17, 1924.
16. *The Galveston Daily News* (Galveston, TX), September 28, 1924.
17. *Nebraska State Journal* (Lincoln, NE), April 15, 1924.
18. *Behind Two Guns* is available on DVD through Grapevine Video.
19. *The Veredict of the Desert*— Movies —*New York Times*, http://movies2.nytimes.com/gst/movies/movie.html?v_id=115511 (accessed March 12, 2007). Also *The Port Arthur News* (Port Arthur, TX), November 2, 1924.
20. Ángel Miquel, *Por las pantallas de la ciudad de México: periodistas del cine mudo* (Guadalajara: Universidad de Guadalajara, 1995), p. 108.
21. *El Heraldo de México*, November 7, 1922.
22. *La Opinión*, June 6, 1936, pp. 4, 5.
23. *La Opinión*, November 8 and 29, 1926.

Chapter 4

1. *La Prensa* (San Antonio, TX), January 17, 1926.
2. *La Prensa*, July 11, 1926, p. 12.
3. Eduardo de la Vega, "Guillermo el Indio Calles," *Dicine* (Mexico City), No. 49, January 1993, p. 18.
4. *Ibid.*, p. 19.
5. Homero Lizama Escoffie, "El Indio Yaqui," *Púrpura y Oro, Revista mensual ilustrada de Literatura y Ciencias* (Mérida, Yucatán, México), August 1927.
6. *The Yaqui*, http://movies.nytimes.com/movie/117863/Yaqui/overview (accessed March 7, 2007).
7. Joanna Hearne, "The Cross-Heart People: Race and Inheritance in the Silent Western," *Journal of Popular Film and Television* 30 (Winter 2003), 181–96.
8. *El Heraldo de México* (Los Angeles, CA), September 4, 1924.

9. *El Heraldo de México*, September 5, 7 and 12, 1924; January 24, 1925.

10. Another interesting piece was Gabriel Navarro's *Alma yaqui*, which described the courage and dignity of the Indians who joined the Mexican Revolution, siding either with the Federal army or with the rebel militias. A performance of *Alma yaqui* took place at the Teatro Hidalgo on June 27, 1932, on the occasion of a benefit show dedicated to Calles.

11. *La Prensa*, July 11, 1926, p.12.

12. *Ibid*.

13. *Ibid*. Salvador Gonzalo Becerra's article "La gesta de una raza" was published by *El Heraldo de México* (Los Angeles, CA) on May 23, 1926.

14. *El Heraldo de México*, June 6, 1926.

15. *Ibid*.

16. *The Albuquerque Journal* (Albuquerque, NM), February 28, 1930.

17. de la Vega, "Guillermo el Indio Calles," *Dicine* (Mexico City), No. 49, January 1993, p. 18. See also *El Dictamen* (Veracruz, México), June 3, 1927.

18. Gabriel Trujillo Muñoz, *Baja California: ritos y mitos cinematográficos*, p. 17.

19. Celso Aguirre Bernal, *Compendio histórico biográfico de Mexicali, 1539–1966* (México, author's second edition), p. 298.

20. Federico Dávalos and Esperanza Vázquez Bernal, *Filmografía general del cine mexicano: 1906–1931* (México: Universidad Autónoma de Puebla, 1985), p. 109.

21. Gabriel Trujillo Muñoz, "Baja California cinematográfica," *Microhistorias del cine en México* (Guadalajara: Universidad de Guadalajara, 2000), p. 44.

22. *La Prensa*, May 2, 1922, p. 7.

23. *La Prensa*, May 10, 1922, p. 4.

24. *La Prensa*, May 23, 1922, p. 4.

25. Aguirre Bernal, pp. 217–307.

26. *Los Angeles Times* (Los Angeles, CA), March 26, 1926.

27. *El Heraldo de México*, November 9 and 14, 1926; December 8, 1926. On November 8, 1926, *La Prensa* of San Antonio, Texas, said that Calles intended to establish a school for acting in Mexicali, Baja California, his goal being to find local talent for the *Raza de bronce* cast.

28. Trujillo Muñoz, *ibid*., p. 45.

29. *El Heraldo de México*, December 8, 1926.

30. Trujillo Muñoz, *ibid*., p. 47.

31. *Los Angeles Times*, February 27, 1927.

32. *El Heraldo de México*, April 2, 1927.

33. *The Oakland Tribune* (Oakland, CA), July 26, 1927; *The Hayward Review* (Hayward, CA), August 23, 1927.

34. Trujillo Muñoz, *ibid*., pp. 46–47.

Chapter 5

1. *La Opinión* (Los Angeles, CA), March 18 and 21, 1928.

2. *El Heraldo de México* (Los Angeles, CA), March 8, 1928.

3. *El Heraldo de México*, March 25, 1928.

4. *La Opinión*, March 23, 1928, p. 4.

5. *La Opinión*, April 14, 1928, p. 4.

6. *La Opinión*, March 31, 1928, p. 4.

7. *La Opinión*, June 1, 1928, p. 4; also May 12, 1929, p. 8.

8. *La Opinión*, February 8, 1928.

9. *La Opinión*, June 1, 1928.

10. *La Opinión*, November 11, 1928.

11. *La Prensa* (San Antonio, TX), January 13 and 20, 1929.

12. *La Prensa*, February 10, 11 and March 1, 1929.

13. *La Opinión*, May 14, 1929, p. 4.

14. *La Opinión*, June 23, 1929, p. 15.

15. "Loreley," "Dios y ley. Cartones de Hollywood por correo aéreo," *Ilustrado* (Mexico City), September 26, 1929.

16. *La Opinión*, August 4, 1929, p. 14.

17. *La Opinión*, December 8, 1929, p. 14.

18. *Ibid*.

19. *La Opinión*, January 28, 1930, p. 4.

20. *Las Noticias* (Guadalajara, Jalisco, México), February 2, 1930.

21. *El Informador* (Guadalajara, Jalisco, México), February 5, 1930, p. 4.

22. *La Prensa*, March 22 and October 5, 1930.

23. *La Opinión*, August 13, 1930.

24. *La Opinión*, October 16 and December 28, 1930.

25. *Regeneración* dialogue transcript deposited in the archives of the Cultural Education Center, New York State Archives, Albany, NY.

26. *La Opinión*, June 3, 1932, p. 6. *The Brownsville Herald* (Brownsville, TX), January 5, 1940.

Chapter 6

1. George J. Sánchez, *Becoming Mexican American: Ethnicity, Culture and Identity in Chicano Los Angeles, 1900–1945* (New York: Oxford University Press, 1993), p. 211.

2. *La Opinión* (Los Angeles, CA), December 29, 1931, Section 2, p. 4.

3. *Ibid*.

4. *Cinema Reporter* (Mexico City), May 8, 1957, pp. 36–37. The author of this article is recounting events that happened in the early 1930s.

5. Gabriel Ramírez, *Lupe Vélez, la mexicana que escupía fuego* (México: Cineteca Nacional, 1986), p. 76.

6. See, for example, Juan B. Heinink and Robert G. Dickson's *Cita en Hollywood, antología de las películas norteamericanas habladas en español* (Bilbao: Ed. Mensajero, 1990).
7. Francisco E. Balderrama, *In Defense of La Raza: The Los Angeles Mexican Consulate and the Mexican Community, 1929 to 1936* (Tucson: University of Arizona Press, 1982), p. 60.
8. *La Opinión*, January 16, 1932, p. 6.
9. *La Opinión*, April 15, 1932, p. 6.
10. *La Opinión*, August 2, 1930.
11. Eduardo de la Vega, *Fernando Méndez* (Guadalajara: Universidad de Guadalajara, 1995), pp. 31–32.
12. *La Opinión*, April 15, 1932, p. 6.
13. *La Opinión*, April 24, 1932, p. 5.
14. Tzvi Medin, *El minimato presidencial: historia política del maximato, 1928–1935* (México: Ediciones Era, 1982), p. 117.
15 *La Opinión*, June 26 and 29 and July 1, 1932.
16. *La Opinión*, July 20, 1932, p. 4.
17. *La Opinión*, July 7, 1932, pp. 4, 8.
18. *La Opinión*, July 10, 1932, p. 5.
19. *La Opinión*, July 24, 1932, p. 7.
20. Ibid.
21. *El Informador* (Guadalajara, Jalisco, México), October 12, 13, 14 and 15, 1932.
22. Esperanza Vázquez Bernal recently found this petition in Mexico City's Archivo General de la Nación. The document's full title is "Carta dirigida por los Productores de Películas Nacionales al C. Diputado y General don Rafael E. Melgar, Presidente del Comité Pro-Campaña Nacionalista de la Cámara de Diputados." November 1932. Archivo General de la Nación, México, D.F.
23. *La Opinión*, October 29, 1933, p. 3.

Chapter 7

1. Santini, *Primera guía cinematográfica mexicana, 1934* (México: Ed Santini).
2. *Filmográfico* (México City), May 1933. *México al día* (México City), May 15, 1933, p. 48.
3. *Filmográfico*, September 1933.
4. *Revista de Revistas* (México City), October 1, 1933.
5. *Filmográfico*, November 1933.
6. *Ilustrado* (México City), May 1934.
7. *La Opinión*, February 4, 1934, p. 8.
8. *Filmográfico*, July 1934.
9. *Revista de Revistas*, October 1, 1933.
10. *Revista de Revistas*, June 17, 1934.
11. *Todo* (México City), February 25, 1936.
12. Federico Dávalos and Esperanza Vázquez Bernal, *Carlos Villatoro: Pasajes en la vida de un hombre de cine* (México: UNAM, 1999), pp. 48–57.

13. Villatoro assembled an impressive collection of film stills from this era. Historians Federico Dávalos and Esperanza Vázquez Bernal recovered this collection from Villatoro's granddaughter and published a volume dedicated to the pioneer actor. Thanks to their investigation, a number of rare scene and production stills from movies directed by Calles have emerged. Part of the Carlos Villatoro photographic collection is now kept in the Agrasánchez Film Archive.
14. *La Opinión*, June 25, 1936, p. 2.
15. *Revista de Revistas*, June 28, 1936.
16. *La Opinión*, February 19, 1932, p. 6.
17. María Eugenia Bonifaz de Novelo, "The Hotel Riviera del Pacífico: Social, Civic and Cultural Center of Ensenada," *Journal of San Diego History*, http://www.sandiegohistory.org/journal/83spring/riviera.htm (accessed July 27, 2006).
18. *The Hollywood Reporter* (Hollywood, CA), October 27, 1936.
19. Gabriel Trujillo, *Baja California: ritos y mitos cinematográficos* (Mexicali: Universidad Autónoma de Baja California, 1999), p. 20.
20. Esperanza Vázquez Bernal, *Los estudios cinematográficos mexicanos, 1930–1940* (unpublished manuscript, 2004), pp. 47–52.
21. Ibid. See also *The Hollywood Reporter*, December 11, 1936, p. 7.

Chapter 8

1. *Revista de Revistas* (México City), January 23, 1938.
2. *La virgen de la sierra* dialogue transcript deposited in the archives of the Cultural Education Center, New York State Archives, Albany, NY.
3. Rogelio Agrasánchez, Jr., *Mexican Movies in the United States: A History of the Films, Theaters and Audiences, 1920–1960* (Jefferson, NC: McFarland, 2006), pp. 27–31.
4. *La Prensa* (San Antonio, TX), April 24, 1938, Section 2, p. 3.
5. Cited by Emilio García Riera, *Historia documental del cine mexicano*, first edition (México: Era, 1969–1978), vol. 1, p. 184.
6. *The New York Times Film Reviews*, March 6, 1939.
7. *La Prensa*, August 7, 1938, Section 2, p. 2.
8. García Riera, *Historia documental del cine mexicano*, second edition (Guadalajara: Universidad de Guadalajara, 1997), vol. 2, p. 91.
9. Juan Andreu Almazán, *Memorias del General Juan Andreu Almazán: informe y documento sobre la campaña política* (México: Senado de la República, 2003), p. 228.

Chapter 9

1. Rogelio Agrasánchez, Jr., *Mexican Movies in the United States: A History of the Films, Theaters and Audiences, 1920–1960* (Jefferson, NC: McFarland, 2006).
2. Julianne Burton-Carvajal, *Matilde Landeta, hija de la Revolución* (México: IMCINE, 2002), pp. 75–84.
3. Juan Bustillo Oro, *Vida cinematográfica* (México: Cineteca Nacional, 1984), pp. 297–301.
4. *Cinema Reporter* (México City), October 6, 1954, p. 22.
5. *México Cinema* (México City), November 22, 1954.
6. *Cinema Reporter*, November 24, 1954, p. 20.
7. *Cine Mundial* (México City), March 1, 1958.
8. *The Bismarck Tribune* (Bismarck, ND), August 20, 1954.
9. *Excélsior* (México City), March 2, 1958, section A, p. 33.
10. *Cine Mundial*, March 1, 1958, p. 15.

Bibliography

Archives and Collections

Archivo General de la Nación (México). Fondos Pascual Ortiz Rubio, Lázaro Cárdenas.
Carlos Villatoro Collection. Agrasánchez Film Archive. Harlingen, Texas.
Ernest Domínguez Photographic Collection. Whittier, California.
New York State Archives. Motion Picture Division. Censorship of Mexican Movies.
Richard J. Domínguez Photographic Collection. Whittier, California.
Rudy Calles Photographic Collection. Agrasánchez Film Archive. Harlingen, Texas.

Mexican Civil Registry Records

Births. Chihuahua, Chihuahua, 1891.
Deaths. Chihuahua, Chihuahua, 1893.

Catholic Church Records

Births. Ciudad Guerrero, Chihuahua, 1853.
Marriages. Ciudad Guerrero, Chihuahua, 1869.

U.S. Population Censuses

Graham County, Arizona. 1900.
Greenlee County, Arizona. 1920.
Los Angeles County, California, 1920, 1930.
Maricopa County, Arizona, 1910.
Pima County, Arizona, 1910.

U.S. Military Documents

World War I Draft Registration Cards. 1917, 1918.

U.S. Immigration Service

Manifests of Alien Passengers Sailing from Mexico, 1937.
Manifests of Entry from Mexico. Border Crossings, 1908–1935.

Interviews

Beatriz Calles de Roiz, interview by author (August 2007).
Richard "Dick" Domínguez, interview by author (March 2008).
Gloria Ortega, interview by author (July 2007).

Film Dialogue Transcripts

Regeneración (1930). New York State Archives.
La virgen de la sierra (1938). New York State Archives.
El vuelo de la muerte (1933). New York State Archives.

Documentaries

The Bronze Screen: 100 Years of Latino Images in Hollywood Films.
Los Mineros. Héctor Galán Productions, 1992.

Newspapers and Magazines

The Albuquerque Journal, Albuquerque, New Mexico, 1930.
Amigo del Hogar, Indiana Harbor, Indiana, 1929.
The Bismarck Tribune, Bismarck, North Dakota, 1954.
Boys' Cinema Weekly, London, England, 1920.
The Boys' Herald, London, England, 1921.
Cine, México, D.F., 1978.
Cine Mundial, México, D.F., 1958.
Cinema Reporter, México, D.F., 1954, 1958.
Cleveland Plain-Dealer, Cleveland, Ohio, 1934.
The Columbus Ledger, ?, 1922.
The Daily Courier, Connellsville, Pennsylvania, 1922, 1924.
The Davenport Democrat, Davenport, Iowa, 1922.
El Defensor, Edinburg, Texas, 1930.
Dicine, México, D.F., January 1993.
El Dictamen, Veracruz, México, 1927.
Excélsior, México, D.F., 1921, 1933, 1958.
The Hayward Review, Hayward, California, 1927.

El Heraldo de México, Los Angeles, California, 1920–1923.
Hispanic News, San Bernardino, California, 2008.
Hispano América, San Francisco, California, 1920.
Ilustrado, México, D.F., 1929.
El Informador, Guadalajara, México, 1919, 1930.
The Lima Daily News, Lima, Ohio, 1913.
Magazine Fílmico, México, D.F., 1928.
Manitoba Free Press, Winnipeg, Canada, 1918.
Marshfield Times, Marshfield, Wisconsin, 1918.
México al Día, México, D.F., 1933.
México Cinema, México, D.F., 1942, 1954, 1958.
Modesto Evening News, Modesto, California, 1924.
Nebraska State Journal, Lincoln, Nebraska, 1924.
The New York Times Film Reviews, 1933–1939.
The Newark Advocate, Newark, Ohio, 1919.
La Novela Film, No. 23, Barcelona, Spain, ca. 1919.
Novelas de la Pantalla, México, D.F., 1940–1943.
The Oakland Tribune, Oakland, California, 1927.
The Ogden Examiner, Ogden, Utah, 1918.
The Ogden Standard, Ogden City, Utah, 1913.
Olean Evening Herald, Olean, New York, 1919.
La Opinión, Los Ángeles, California, 1926–1940.
La Patria, El Paso, Texas, 1922.
The Port Arthur News, Port Arthur, Texas, 1924.
La Prensa, San Antonio, Texas, 1926–1940.
Púrpura y Oro, revista mensual ilustrada... Mérida, Yucatán, August 1927.
La República, El Paso, Texas, 1922.
Republican Press, Salamanca, New York, 1919.
Revista de Revistas, México, D.F., 1933–1939.
Rotográfico, México, D.F., 1928.
The State, South Carolina, 1913.
Stevens Point Daily Journal, Stevens Point, Wisconsin, 1928.
Todo, México, D.F., 1936.
Winnipeg Free Press, Manitoba, Canada, 1953.

Official and Trade Publications

Cine Sonoro Mexicano, 40 Aniversario. Comisión Organizadora de los Actos Conmemorativos del 40 Aniversario del Cine Sonoro Mexicano. México, D.F., 1971.
Godoy, Alberto L. *Directorio cinematográfico internacional de México, 1938–1939.* México, D.F. Ed. Jack Starr-Hunt, 1939.
Filmográfico. México, D.F., 1932–1937.
The Hollywood Reporter. Hollywood, California, 1936.
Mundo Cinematográfico. México, 1931–1937.
Santini. *Primera guía cinematográfica mexicana, 1934.* México: Ed. Santini, 1934.

Secondary Sources

Agrasánchez, Rogelio, Jr. *Mexican Movies in the United States: A History of the Films, Theaters and Audiences, 1920–1960.* Jefferson, NC: McFarland, 2006.
_____. *Miguel Zacarías, creador de estrellas.* Guadalajara: Universidad de Guadalajara-Archivo Fílmico Agrasánchez, 2000.
Aguirre Bernal, Celso. *Compendio histórico biográfico de Mexicali, 1539–1966.* México, author's second edition, 1968.
Almazán, Juan Andreu. *Memorias: Informe y documentos sobre la campaña política de 1940.* México: Senado de la República, 2003.
Anna, Timothy, et al. *Historia de México.* Barcelona: Crítica, 2001.
Ayala Blanco, Jorge y María Luisa Amador. *Cartelera cinematográfica, 1920–1929.* México: UNAM-Centro Universitario de Estudios Cinematográficos, 1999.
Azuela, Mariano. *Los de abajo*, in *La novela de la revolución mexicana* edited by Antonio Castro Leal, Vol. I. México: Aguilar, 1964.
Balderrama, Francisco E. *In Defense of La Raza: The Los Angeles Mexican Consulate and the Mexican Community, 1929 to 1936.* Tucson: University of Arizona Press, 1982.
Bonifaz de Novela, María Eugenia. "The Hotel Riviera del Pacífico: Social, Civic and Cultural Center of Ensenada." *Journal of San Diego History.* http://www.sandiegohistory.org/journal/83spring/riviera.htm (accessed July 27, 2006).
Burton-Carvajal, Julianne. *Matilde Landeta, hija de la Revolución.* México: IMCINE, 2002.
Bustillo Oro, Juan. *Vida cinematográfica.* México: Cineteca Nacional, 1984.
Calles, Pascual. *Memorias de Pascual Calles, Sr.* Unpublished manuscript, no date.
Cary, Diana Serra. *The Hollywood Posse: The Story of a Gallant Band of Horsemen Who Made Movie History.* Norman: University of Oklahoma Press, 1996.
Casasola, Gustavo. *Historia gráfica de la Revolución Mexicana, 1900–1960*, Vol. 4. México: Trillas, 1970.
Cien años del cine mexicano. CD-ROM. México: IMCINE-Universidad de Colima-CONACULTA, 1999.
Cineteca Nacional. *Filmografía mexicana de medio y largometraje.* México: Cineteca Nacional, 1985.
Ciuk, Perla. *Diccionario de directores del cine mexicano.* México: Consejo Nacional para la Cul-

tura y las Artes (CONACULTA) y Cineteca Nacional, 2001.

Cuadernos de la Cineteca Nacional, Testimonios para la historia del cine mexicano. Eugenia Meyer, coordinadora. Vols. 1–7. México, Cineteca Nacional, 1975 y 1976.

Dávalos Orozco, Federico. *Albores del cine mexicano.* México: Clío, 1996.

_____, and Esperanza Vázquez Bernal. *Carlos Villatoro, pasajes en la vida de un hombre de cine.* México: UNAM, 1999.

_____ and _____. *Filmografía general del cine mexicano, 1906–1931.* México: Universidad Autónoma de Puebla, 1985.

Diccionario Porrúa de historia, biografía y geografía de México. 4ª edición. México: Porrúa, 1976.

Domínguez, Richard J. *Movie Industry Early Pioneers.* Unpublished manuscript, no date.

Espinosa, Emil C., Jr. *The Genealogy of the Calles Family Beginning with Mariano Calles.* Unpublished manuscript, no date.

Fetrow, Alan G. *Sound Films, 1927–1939: A United States Filmography.* Jefferson, NC: McFarland, 1992.

García Riera, Emilio. *Historia documental del cine mexicano.* First edition. México: Era, 1969–1978.

_____. *Historia documental del cine mexicano.* Second edition. Guadalajara: Universidad de Guadalajara, 1997.

_____. *México visto por el cine extranjero.* México: Era-Universidad de Guadalajara, 1987.

Gonzales, Manuel G. *Mexicanos: A History of Mexicans in the United States.* Bloomington, Indiana: Indiana University Press, 2000.

González Casanova, Manuel. *Las vistas: una época del cine en México.* México: Instituto Nacional de Estudios Históricos de la Revolución Mexicana-Secretaría de Gobernación-Museo Casa de Carranza, 1992.

Gordon, Linda. *The Great Arizona Orphan Abduction.* Cambridge: Harvard University Press, 1999.

Hearne, Joanna. "The Cross-Heart People: Race and Inheritance in the Silent Western." *Journal of Popular Film and Television* 30 (Winter 2003): 181–196.

Heinink, Juan B., and Robert G. Dickson. *Cita en Hollywood, antología de las películas norteamericanas habladas en castellano.* Bilbao: Ed. Mensajero, 1990.

Héroe de Nacozari, El. Los emplayados, Primaria "Francisco Zarco y Lealtad," http://redescolar.ilce.edu.mx/redescolar/publicaciones/publi_que paso/jesus-garcia-corona.htm (accessed June 30, 2007).

Hershfield, Joanne, and David R. Maciel. *Mexico's Cinema: A Century of Films and Filmmakers.* Wilmington, DE: Scholarly Resources, 1999.

Holden, William Curry. *Teresita.* Owings Mills, MD: Stemmer House Publishers, 1978.

Kanellos, Nicolás. *Hispanic Firsts: 500 Years of Extraordinary Achievement.* Detroit: Visible Ink Press, 1997.

_____. *A History of Hispanic Theatre in the United States: Origins to 1940.* Austin: University of Texas Press, 1990.

Katchmer, George A. *A Bibliographical Dictionary of Silent Film Western Actors and Actresses.* Jefferson, NC: McFarland, 2002.

Keller, Gary D. *A Biographical Handbook of Hispanics and United States Film.* Tempe, AZ: Bilingual Press, 1997.

Kobal, John. *Hollywood: The Years of Innocence.* New York: Abbeville Press, 1985.

Lahue, Kalton C. *Bound and Gagged: The Story of the Silent Serials.* New York: Castle Books, 1968.

Márquez, Alicia. "Breve historia del documental sobre el mundo indígena en México" in *Los mundos del Nuevo Mundo.* Various authors. México: Cineteca Nacional-IMCINE, 1994.

Medin, Tzvi. *El minimato presidencial: historia política del maximato, 1928–1935.* México: Ediciones Era, 1982.

Meyer, Michael C., and William L. Sherman. *The Course of Mexican History.* New York: Oxford University Press, 1979.

Miquel, Ángel. *Mimí Derba.* México: Filmoteca de la UNAM-Archivo Fílmico Agrasánchez, 2000.

_____. *Por las pantallas de la ciudad de México: periodistas del cine mudo.* Guadalajara: Universidad de Guadalajara, 1995.

Moisés, Rosalío, Jane Holden Kelley and William Curry Holden. *A Yaqui Life: The Personal Chronicle of a Yaqui Indian.* Lincoln: University of Nebraska, 1977.

Monroy, Douglas. *Rebirth: Mexican Los Angeles from the Great Migration to the Great Depression.* Berkeley: University of California Press, 1999.

Mora, Carl J. *Mexican Cinema: Reflections of a Society, 1896–2004.* Jefferson, NC: McFarland, 2005.

Muñoz, Fernando. *Sara García.* México: Clío, 1998.

Orellana, Margarita de. *La mirada circular: el cine*

norteamericano de la Revolución mexicana, 1911–1917. México: Ed. Joaquín Mortiz, 1991.

Park, Joseph F. "The 1903 'Mexican Affair' at Clifton." *Journal of Arizona History*, 18 (Summer 1977): 119–48.

Pérez Monfort, Ricardo. *Estampas de nacionalismo popular mexicano*. Colección Historias. México: CIESAS, 2003.

Pérez Turrent, Tomás. *La fábrica de los sueños: Estudios Churubusco, 1945–1985*. México: IMCINE, 1985.

Portas, Rafael E. y Ricardo Rangel. *Enciclopedia cinematográfica mexicana. 1897–1955*. México: Publicaciones Cinematográficas, S. de R. L., 1955.

Ragan, David. *Who's Who in Hollywood: The Largest Cast of Film Personalities Ever Assembled*. New York: Facts on File, 1992.

Rainey, Buck. *Serial Film Stars: A Biographical Dictionary, 1912–1956*. Jefferson, NC: McFarland, 2005.

———. *The Strong, Silent Type: Over 100 Screen Cowboys, 1903–30*. Jefferson, NC: McFarland, 2003.

Ramírez, Gabriel. *Crónica del cine mudo mexicano*. México: Cineteca Nacional, 1989.

———. *Lupe Vélez, la mexicana que escupía fuego*. México: Cineteca Nacional, 1986.

———. *Miguel Contreras Torres*. Guadalajara: Universidad de Guadalajara-CIEC, 1994.

Regan, Margaret. *The Irish Orphan Abduction: A Tale of Race, Religion and Lawlessness in Southern Arizona*, http://www.tucsonweekly.com/gbase/Currents/Content?oid=93635 (accessed March 15, 2007).

Reyes, Aurelio de los. *Cine y sociedad en México, 1896–1930. Vivir de sueños*. Vol. I (1986–1920). México: UNAM, 1983.

———. *Medio siglo de cine mexicano, 1896–1947*. México: Ed. Trillas, 1988.

Reyes, Luis, and Peter Rubie. *Los hispanos en Hollywood: celebrando 100 años en el cine y la televisión*. New York: Random House Español, 2002.

Romo, David Dorado. *Ringside Seat to a Revolution: An Underground Cultural History of El Paso and Juárez, 1893–1923*. El Paso, TX: Cinco Puntos Press, 2005.

Sánchez, George J. *Becoming Mexican American: Ethnicity, Culture and Identity in Chicano Los Angeles, 1900–1945*. New York: Oxford University Press, 1993.

Slide, Anthony. *The Big V: A History of the Vitagraph Company*. Metuchen, NJ: Scarecrow, 1987.

Smith, Albert E. *Two Reels and a Crank*. Garden City, NY: Doubleday, 1952.

Thomas, Tony. *The Great Adventure Films*. Secaucus, NJ: Citadel Press, 1976.

Torres San Martín, Patricia. *Crónicas tapatías del cine mexicano*. Guadalajara: Universidad de Guadalajara, 1993.

Trujillo Muñoz, Gabriel. "Baja California cinematográfica" in *Microhistorias del cine en México*. Eduardo de la Vega, coordinador. Guadalajara: Universidad de Guadalajara, 2000.

———. *Baja California: ritos y mitos cinematográficos*. Mexicali: Universidad Autónoma de Baja California, 1999.

Vaidovits, Guillermo. *El cine mudo en Guadalajara*. Guadalajara: Universidad de Guadalajara, 1989.

Vázquez Bernal, Esperanza. *Los estudios cinematográficos mexicanos, 1930–1940*. Unpublished manuscript, 2004.

Vega Alfaro, Eduardo de la. *Fernando Méndez*. Guadalajara: Universidad de Guadalajara, 1995.

———. *Gabriel Soria*. Guadalajara: Universidad de Gadalajara-CONACULTA-IMCINE, 1992.

———. *Raphael J. Sevilla*. Guadalajara: Universidad de Guadalajara-CUCSH-CONACULTA, 2003.

———. *Raúl de Anda*. Guadalajara: Universidad de Guadalajara, 1989.

Viñas, Moisés. *Índice cronológico del cine mexicano, 1896–1992*. México: UNAM, 1992.

Wilt, David E. *The Mexican Filmography, 1916 through 2001*. Jefferson, NC: McFarland, 2004.

Index

A la orilla de un palmar 117
A lo macho 129
A través de Sonora 56, 89
Acosta, Dionisio 71
Acosta, Enrique 48
Acosta, Rodolfo 136
Adams, Ann Newhardt 72
Adams, Oriel Lester 72
Agua Caliente hotel-resort (Baja California, México) 114
Águila (dog) 48, 80–81, 89, 92, 111, 116, 149
Águila, Guz *see* Guzmán Aguilera, Antonio
El águila y el nopal 81
Aguilar, Antonio 143
Águilas doradas (Hills of Gold) 115
Aguirre, Inés 115
Ahí viene Martín Corona 133
Alarcón, Juan de la C. 34
Alas abiertas 33
Alazraki, Benito 140
Alba, Luz 106
Alfonso XIII (King of Spain) 65
Alma insurgente 34
Alma yaqui (play) 96
Almaraz, Francisca 32, 149, 152
Almas rebeldes 117–119
Alonso, Luis *see* Roland, Gilbert
Álvarez, Luis 129
Álvarez, Miguel Ángel 46
Amable, José 3
Amador, Carlos E. 124
Anáhuac Film Corporation 44
ANDA (Asociación Nacional de Actores) 138, 141, 143
Anda, Raúl de 111, 117–119, 124, 128, 139
Andreu Almazán, Juan 130
The Arab (1915) 21
Aragón, Alejandro 100
Araiza, Elisa 59
Aranda, Benjamín 65, 69, 72
Areu, Enrique 82, 84
Areu, José 82–83
Areu, Roberto 83
Argota, Victoria 124
Arizona Copper Company 11
Arizona Rangers 11
Armendáriz, Pedro 111
Arozamena, Amparo 129
Arozamena, Eduardo 117

Así es México 89
Así es mi tierra 117
El automóvil gris 33, 120
Aymond Film Corporation 39
Aztec Theater (San Antonio, Texas) 3
Azteca Film Company 33
Azteca Theater (Belvedere, California) 3
Azuela, Mariano 130

Baja California 56–58, 89
Bajo el cielo de Sonora 135
Balderrama, Francisco 30
La banda del automóvil 33
Banuet, Conchita 103
Barberán, Joaquín 107
Bard Theater (Los Angeles, California) 53
La barranca de la muerte 139
Barret, Carolina 124
Battle of Saipan (WWII) 149
The Beast of Hollow Mountain 136
Becerra, Salvador Gonzalo 53–54
Bedoya, Alfonso 117, 119–120
Behind Two Guns 43–44
Beirute, Yerye 143
Bell, Jorge 106
La bella vaquera 29
Biederman, David 62
Bird of Paradise 96
Black Beauty (1921) 29
Blackton, J. Stuart 18
Blanco, Victoria 111, 120, 122
Blaze O'Glory 77
Bohr, José 77, 81
Bom, Franz 2
The Boudoir Diplomat 87
Boys' Cinema Weekly (magazine) 4, 28
The Boys' Herald (magazine) 28
Boytler, Arcady 111
Bradbury, Robert N. 43, 47
Branded a Thief 41–42
Bravo, Carlos "Carl-hillos" 139–140
The Bronze Race 62
Brown, Betty 47, 50
Browne, Betty *see* Brown, Betty
Bruckner, Sidney T. 143
Buchelli, Efrén 120
Burrola, Pablo 57, 60
Bussón, Alfonso 69
Bustillo Oro, Juan 138

El caballero misterioso 72
Cabello, Carlos 107
Calderón, Guillermo 120
Calderón, Rafael 100
Calderón, Virgilio 120
Calhoun, Rory 136
California Theater (Los Angeles, California) 86
Calleia, Joseph 136
Calles, Anatolia Guerrero de 7, 14–15, 75, 111, 134–135, 146, 150, 154
Calles, María Ángela Salcedo de *see* Salcedo, Angelita
Calles, Belén 10, 32, 65, 148
Calles, Juan *see* Calles Guerrero, Juan N.
Calles, Juan Nepomuceno 7, 8, 146, 148, 153, 154
Calles, Juan V. 48, 50, 148
Calles, Justina Hernández de 148, 153
Calles, Margarita 48, 82
Calles, Rodolfo *see* Calles, Rudy
Calles, Rudy 5, 146–148
Calles family 5, 13, 16
Calles González, Mariano 7, 34
Calles Guerrero, José de la Luz 7, 14–15, 48
Calles Guerrero, Juan N. 7, 66
Calles Guerrero, María de Jesús 7, 15, 65–66, 75, 146–148, 150–151
Calles Guerrero, Pascual 7, 16, 32, 146–148, 153
Calles Guerrero, Rosendo 7, 14–15
Calvillo, José María 146, 151
Calvillo, Juan 15
Calvillo, María de Jesús Calles de *see* Calles Guerrero, María de Jesús
Camarillo de Frausto, Dolores *see* Fraustita
Las campanas de Capistrano 84
Campillo, Anita 124, 127–128
Camus, Germán 33, 62
Canciones y recuerdos 144
Cantinflas 117
Cantú Robert, Roberto 87
El caporal 34, 39
Captain David Grief 143
The Captain of the Grey Horse Troop (1917) 21
Cárdenas, Lázaro 113, 116; administration 114

Index

Cardona, René 77, 107
Carewe, Edwin 71
Carleton, Lloyd B. 52
Carrasco, Esequiel 102
Casanova, Fernando 139
Castillo, Carmen 73, 76
El cementerio de las águilas 114
Century Film Corporation 115
Ceprano, Dorita 82–85
Chagoya, Captain 107
Chaplin, Lita Grey 67
Chapultepec 33
Chapultepec Castle 94, 150
Charity events 81
El charro 5, 82
El chasis 29
Chávez, César 148
A Cheyenne Brave 52
La Chillona 102
Churubusco studios 132
Cine Regis (Mexico City) 107
Cinelandia Theater (Mexico City) 102–103
The Circus 71
Ciudad Guerrero (Chihuahua, México) 7–8
Clemente, Steve 150
Clifton-Morenci (Arizona) 8, 10–14
Colima Volcano 135
Colina, Rafael de la 89
Collar, Esteban 107
Compañía Cinematográfica Cuautla 46
Compendio Histórico Biográfico de Mexicali (book) 56
Confesión trágica 3
La conquista de México see *Alma insurgente*
Contreras, T. 73
Contreras Torres, Miguel 34, 36–39, 81, 88, 110
Coolidge, Dane 52
Corazón bandolero 109
Corella, Francisco M. 62
Corella Beltrán, Rafael 56–58, 60–62, 72, 89
Cornejo, Pancho 3
El Cristo de Oro 71
El Crucifijo de piedra 139
Cruz, Joe de la *see* Cruz, José de la
Cruz, José de la Cruz 19, 21, 46
Cruz de Palenque (Chiapas, Mexico) 3
Cuauhtémoc 33
Cuervo, José 93
Cueto González, C. 111
Cugat, Xavier 76
Curiel, Federico 143
Curry Holden, William 14

Dada, Jorge M. 127
La dama enlutada see *La banda del automóvil*
Daniel Boone through the Wilderness 44, 47
D'Arcy, Roy 67

Dávalos, Federico 124
Davy Crockett at the Fall of the Alamo 47
Delirio tropical 143
DeMille, Cecil B. 21, 52
Derba, Mimí 33
The Desert Trail 65
Devaluation of Mexican currency 136, 138
The Devil's Island 111
Día de la Raza 71, 81
Díaz, Antonio 124
Díaz, Lucha 103
Díaz, Porfirio 8, 12, 16
Diestro, Alfredo del 88, 129
Dietrich, Marlene 87
Dios y ley 72–77, 79–81, 96, 121, 135, 145, 151
Directors' Guild 139–144
Directors Union 119
The Dirty Little Half-Breed 42–43
Domínguez, Beatrice 19
Domínguez, David 153
Domínguez, Dick 5, 151, 153
Domínguez, Ernest 5
Domínguez, Eugenio 149
Domínguez, Joe *see* Domínguez, José
Domínguez, José 15, 32, 48, 65–66, 68, 70, 75–76, 121, 146, 148–152, 154
Domínguez, Pepe *see* Domínguez, José
Domínguez, Phillip 153
Domínguez, Richard *see* Domínguez, Dick
Domínguez, Richard, Jr. 153
Domínguez family 5
Don Catarino 81
Don Juan diplomático 87
Don Q, Son of Zorro 48
Duarte, José M. 47–48, 50–51, 54, 56, 102
Ducrow, H. 22, 52
Duncan, William 22, 26, 30, 37–38, 41, 67, 121
Durán y Casahonda, Juan M. 127

Echeverría Álvarez, Rodolfo *see* Landa, Rodolfo
Egan, Richard 136
Eisenstein, Sergei 129
Elías, Arturo 11
Elías, José 65, 69
Ellis, Paul 77–88
Elías Calles, Plutarco 88
Elías González, Adalberto 52–53
En defensa propia 33
En la hacienda 33
El enamorado 133
Enciclopedia Cinematográfica Mexicana 142
Escalante, Esteban V. 7, 97, 100, 108, 114, 127
Escalona, Beatriz *see* Noloesca, Chata

Espaldas mojadas 136
Espinosa, Belén *see* Calles, Belén
Espinosa, Emil C., Jr. 146, 148
Espinosa, José Ángel "Ferrusquilla" 143
Espinoza de los Monteros, Laura 72
Estévez, Carlos 21
Estudios América 143
Evans, Nelson H. 22
The Examiner (newspaper) 57
El Excéntrico (magazine) 148

Fábregas, Virginia 16
El fanfarrón 129
El fantasma se enamora 141
Farfán, Roberto 116, 117
The Fast Express 48
Faust Rocha, Miguel 87
Un feliz vagabundo 45
Fernández, Antonio 104
Fernández, Emilio 109–111, 117, 119, 141, 143
Fernández, Indio *see* Fernández, Emilio
Ferreira, Enrique 67, 88
A Fight for Millions 23–24
Fighting Fate 28
The Fighting Strain 41, 47
The Fighting Trail 22, 52
Film exhibition monopoly in Mexico 100
Film exhibition union strikes 138
Filmográfico (magazine) 103, 105, 107
Filmoteca of UNAM 55
Films denigrating Mexicans 38–39, 57
Flores Magón, Ricardo 12
A Fool's Paradise 38–39
Un fotógrafo distraído 75
The Four Horsemen of the Apocalypse 21
Fraustita 116
Frausto, Antonio R. 103, 111, 116
Fuentes, Manuel 132

Galindo, Alejandro 117, 139
Galindo, Pedro 117
Gamboa, Federico 33, 95
Gamio, Manuel 2
García, Esther 59, 60, 62
García, Eufrosina 120
García, Fidencio 116
García, Sara 120
García Corona, Jesús 13, 103
García Moreno, Gabriel 55
García Riera, Emilio 130
Garza, María Luisa "Loreley" 2, 76
Gastini, Eduardo 60–61
El gaucho Múgica see *La justicia de Pancho Villa*
Gavira, Gabriel 115
Gazcón, Edgardo 138
Gil, Felipe 117, 123, 127
Gilland, Gladys 41
The Girl of the Golden West (1914) 21

192

Index

Girón, Adolfo 72, 111
The Golden Gift 39
Gómez, Filiberto 93, 94
Gómez Landero, Humberto 139
Gómez Muriel, Emilio 124
González, Francisca 7, 146
González, Rogelio A. 141
González Alfonso, Antonio 99
González Jiménez, Ernesto 70, 77, 85
Gordon, Linda 5, 10, 12
Graña, Jesús 102
Las grandes fiestas del Centenario (1921) 33
The Great Depression 86, 88, 90, 96, 102
El Grito (magazine) 148
Grovas, Jesús 138
Guadalajara (Jalisco, Mexico) 93, 99
La guarida del buitre 136, 139, 142
Guerrero, Anatolia *see* Calles, Anatolia Guerrero de
Guerrero, Carmen 73, 75–76
Guerrero G., Praxedis 12
Guillermo, Oliverio 73
Guzmán Aguilera, Antonio 107, 129

Hart, Neal 41, 47, 53, 65, 69, 121
Hearst, William Randolph 57
Hell's Oasis 47
Hermanos 29
Hernández, Justina *see* Calles, Justina Hernández de
El héroe de Nacozari 103–106
Herrera, Víctor 41
Hidalgo Theater (Los Angeles, California) 81, 86
Hoffberg, J. H. 84
Hollywood Spanish-language talkies 87
El hombre sin patria 38
Hondo 136
La huella del chacal 139, 142
Hughes, Charles Evans 90
Hughes, Roy 41

Imperial Copper Company 14–15
Imperio Azteca studios 116
Ince, Thomas H. 57
Inda, Stella 129
Indians, war against 8
Indigenismo 2, 3, 4
El indio (film) 114
El indio (novel) 3
El indio yaqui 7, 47, 51–56, 64, 71, 73–74, 81, 121, 148
Infante, Pedro 133, 141
Inflation and its influence on the Mexican film industry 138
Ingraham, Lloyd 69
Iris Theater (Mexicali, B.C., Mexico) 56, 61
Irish orphans in Arizona 12
Izaguirre, Lauro 53

Janitzio 114
La jaula de los leones 81, 84
Jíbaro tribe 132
Jiménez, Serafín 116
Joan the Woman (1917) 21
Johnson, Edith 26, 41, 67
Juárez Compañía Cinematográfica Mexicana 41
Judas 111, 113
Junco, Víctor 136
Just a Little Bull 41
La justicia de Pancho Villa 129–131

Kalfer, Frederick E. 72
King, Henry 19
Konga roja 130

Lamar, Adriana 107
The Lamb 52
Landa, Rodolfo 141–144
Landeros, Elena 81
Landeta, Matilde 133, 139
Landres, Morris 115
La Roux, Carmen 59, 65, 67–68, 70, 73–74, 114–115, 121
Lasky Studios 32
Latin Motion Pictures Extras Association 149
Lederer, Otto 26, 43
The Left Hand Brand 41, 47
El León de la Sierra Morena 81
Licking the Greasers 57
Liga Protectora Latina (Pasadena, California) 148
Lizama Escoffie, Homero 49
Llamas, María Eugenia "Tucita" 133
Llamas de rebelión 39
Llata, Carmina de la 102
La Llorona (1933) 102
Logan, Jacqueline 77
Logia Masónica Minerva 148
Lola Casanova 134
López, Agustina 48–49, 51
López Moctezuma, Carlos 134
López y Fuentes, Gregorio 3
"Loreley" *see* Garza, María Luisa
Los de abajo 119, 130
Lubin Manufacturing Company 18, 21, 145
Lucenay, Martín de 129

Machado (Mexican artist) 95
Magaña, Delia 76
The Man of Courage 39
The Man of Might 25–26, 28, 47
Mano a mano 102
María Elena 111, 116
La Marie 21
Martí, Alberto 117
Martin, Chris Pin 45
Martín Garatuza 111
Martínez, Flora 102
Martínez, Juan 75–76
Martínez, Pepe 124
Martínez Casado, Juan José 111, 115
Máximo Theater (Mexico City) 108

Mayan Theater (Los Angeles, California) 3
Mayo Indians 14
Medel, Manuel 117
Medina, José I. 99
Melford, George 87
Méndez Bernal, Alberto 90
Mendoza, Víctor Manuel 120, 123, 135
Metcalf (Arizona) 8, 14
Mexicali (Baja California, México) 56–57
Mexican Air Force 107
Mexican anarchist movement 12
Mexican immigrants in the United States 8
Mexican Revolution 8, 16, 19, 113, 134
A Mexican Tragedy 18–19, 145
Mexican War Pictures (1913) 19
México antiguo y moderno 3
México auténtico 89
México Film studios 106
México, país de romance 89
México Theater (Los Angeles, California) 81
México Theater (Mexicali, B.C., Mexico) 56, 86, 99
El milagro de la Guadalupana see La Virgen del Tepeyac
Mitla (Oaxaca, Mexico) 3
Mojica, José 99
Molina, Carlos 65–66, 68–69, 73, 121
Molina, Charlotte 41
Montalván, Celia 71, 87
Montiel Sarita 133
Moral, Jorge del 107
Morenci (Arizona) 8, 10–14, 144
Moreno, Antono 21, 69, 95
Moreno, Mario *see* Cantinflas
Moreno, Rita 136
Morlett, Fausto 60
Morrison, James 18, 28, 29
Movarry, Medea de 88
La mujer que supo amar see Regeneración
La mujer que yo perdí 133
Murillo, Fidel 75, 97
Múzquiz, Carlos 136

Nacional Productora de Películas 88, 102, 104–106
National Film Corportation of America 42
Navarro, Gabriel 22, 48, 53, 69, 76, 90, 96–97
Navarro, Jesús 124
La Negra Angustias 134
Negrete, Jorge 129
Nevado de Toluca 94
New York State Archives 4, 124
New York State film censorship 126–127
El Niño Fidencio 65
Nobleza ranchera 129

193

Index

La noche de los mayas 114
Noloesca, Chata 81
Noriega, Eduardo 136
North of the Rio Grande 57
Norton, Barry 67
Novara, Medea de *see* Movarry, Medea de
La novela film (magazine) 4, 26

Oasis 29
Obreros Libres 12
Ojeda, Manuel R. 21, 45, 113
Olivo, Valerio 21
Orange Grove Theater 86
Oro mexicano 114, 116
Oroná, Vicente 117, 134–135
Ortega, Gloria 5, 147, 153
Ortiz, Lilia 53
Ortiz Rubio, Pascual 81, 94, 99–100, 150
Oxide Copper Company 14

Padula, Vicente 129
Page, Geraldine 136
Paige, Jean 29
Paramount Sound News 81
Parra, Apolonia 7
Partido Liberal Mexicano 12
Patiño Gómez, Alfonso 120
Pavón, Blanca Estela 133
PECIME (Periodistas Cinematográficos de México, A. C.) 144
Peón Ramón 143
Pereda, Ramón 87, 103, 106–107, 114
Peredo, Luis 33
Pérez, José Eduardo 124, 128
Perucho, Arturo 140
Pescadores de perlas 65–66, 120–123
Pesqueira, Alfonso 57
Placer y venganza 111
PNR (Partido Nacional Revolucionario) 113
Por la Patria 34
Portas, Rafael E. 142–143
Porter, John 88
Portillo, Rafael 141
Princess Red Wing 52
El Príncipe rojo 29
Producciones Cinematográficas Baja California, S. A. 114, 116
Producciones Seyffert 127
Prohibition era 114, 116
Propaganda against Mexico 56–57
Pro-Patria 3, 6, 89–90, 96–97, 99–101
La propiedad única 29
El pulpo humano 106
El puño de hierro 55
La Purísima Barrio 151–152
La Purísima Catholic Church 152

El que a hierro mata 46
Queen, William 41
Quinn, Anthony 136
Quintana, Elvira 143

Railway tragedy at Nacozari (Sonora, Mexico) 13
Rainey, Buck 26
Ramírez, Antonio M. 46
Ramírez, Gabriel 49
Ramona 71
Rangel, Ricardo 142–143
De raza azteca 34, 36–39, 52, 81, 110, 121
Raza de bronce 55, 58–59, 61–64, 71–72, 81, 151
Red Wing and the Child 52
Red Wing's Gratitude 52
Reed, Maxwell 143
Regan, Margaret 13
Regeneración 82–85
Regenerado 41
Remex Cooperative 113
Rendón, César 124
Rennie, Michael 136
Resurrección (1931) 88
Resurrection 88
La Revolución Mexicana (film) 65
Rey, Roberto 87
Rickson, Joe 69
Rico, Mona 77
Río, Dolores del 32, 70–71, 96, 114–115
Rio Grande Film Production Company 39
Rivas, Gabry 45
Rivas Cacho, Carmen 124
Rivero, Fernando A. 129, 144
Robert, Paird 90
El Robin Hood Mexicano 73
Rodríguez, Abelardo L. 56–58, 61–62
Rodríguez, Ana M. 46
Rodríguez, Joselito 88
Rodríguez, Manuel F. 48–49
Rodríguez, Roberto 88
Rodríguez brothers 88, 105
Rodríguez Granada, José 141
Rogers, Walter 26
Roiz, Beatrice Calles de 5, 148, 150, 153
Roiz, Marianne 5, 150, 153
Roland, Gilbert 88, 136
La rosa de Xochimilco 129
La rosa del desierto 45
Rosas, Enrique 33, 139
Rosas Priego, Alfonso 139
Rosas Priego, Rodolfo 139, 142
Royal Cross of Honor 14
Ruben Goes West 75
Ryan, Joe 25–26, 47

Sáenz, Juan A. 53
Sáenz de Sicilia, Gustavo 89, 103–104
Sais, Marin 43
Sala, Ángel T. 120, 122
Salcedo, Angelita 82–83, 89, 94, 97, 149–150
Salcido, Abram 11
Salvador, Jaime 142

San Ángel Inn studios 143
Sánchez, George J. 86
Sánchez García, José María 36, 96–97
Sánchez Hernández, Ramón 133
Sánchez Molgoza 46
Sánchez Valtierra, Manuel 44
Sangre yaqui (play) 52–53
Santa (1918) 33
Santa (1931) 34, 88, 95
Santa Ana, Daniel M. 146
Santuggini, Carlota 34
The Scarlet Brand 65
Sección de Directores 141, 142
Selander, R. Leslie 41
Sentencia 135
Serenata mexicana 81
Seri Indians 134
Seven Cities of Gold 136
Sevilla, Raphael J. 117
Seyffert, Alejandro 124, 129
Shorty's Trip to Mexico 57
Shumway, Walter 47, 50, 54
Sid Grauman's Chinese Theater 70, 87
The Silent Avenger 28
The Silent Vow 41
Silverbell (Arizona) 14–16
Sindicato de Autores y Adaptadores 138
Siqueiros, Plácido 75–76
Sisters of Charity 12
Sitting Bull 143
Smashing Barriers 25, 28
Smith, Albert E. 29
Smith, David 29
Smith, Ernie 89, 93–94, 97
Smith, Harry T. 127
Sol de gloria 65–66, 69–74, 114, 120–123, 151
Solano, Gustavo, "El Conde Gris" 67
Solís, Enrique 129
La Sombra Vengadora 138
La Sombra Vengadora contra la Mano Negra 138
Sombras de gloria 77, 81
Sombras habaneras 77
La Soñadora 33
Soñadores de la gloria 88
Sono-Art Company 77
Soto, Fernando "Mantequilla" 133
Soto la Marina, Armando "Chicote" 124
sound, transition to, films in Spanish language 77, 80–84, 88–89
Spanish Air Force 108
The Squaw Man (1913) 21, 52
Stewart, Roy 47
STIC (Sindicato de Trabajadores de la Industria Cinematográfica) 140
STPC (Sindicato de Trabajadores de la Producción Cinematográfica) 139–143
Strike of Mexican miners 10, 12, 145
El sueño del caporal 39

Index

Tabaré (1919) 33–34
Talán, Raúl 5, 143
Talmadge, Norma 88
Tamayo, Marina 117
Tarahumara Indians 7, 146
Tarascan Indians 93–94, 134
Teatro Colón (El Paso, Texas) 37, 100
Teatro de Bellas Artes (Mexico City) 141
Tena, Dolores 7, 146
Tepee Love 45
Tepeyac 34
Tepic (Nayarit, Mexico) 93
Tequila (Jalisco, Mexico) 93
El Tesoro de Pancho Villa 111, 116
The Texan 48
La tierra del mariachi 128
Tierra muerta 134–135
La tigresa (1917) 33
Tijuana (Baja California, Mexico) 57, 114–116
Tirado, Romualdo 53, 68, 70, 77, 81, 86
Tomochic (Chihuahua, México) 8
Torá, Lía 87–88
Torena, Juan 77
Torres, Irma 135
Torres, Nancy 117
Torres Pirrín, Eusebio *see* Don Catarino
Toussaint, Carlos 139
Tovar, Alfonso 58–60

The Treasure of Pancho Villa 136
Los tres huastecos 133
Treviño, Jorge 117
Tribu 109, 110
Trillo, Loló 129
Trovadores Tamaulipecos 107
Trujillo Muñoz, Gabriel 59–60

Urrea, Teresita *see* Santa de Cabora, la
UTECM (Unión de Trabajadores de los Estudios Cinematográficos de México) 119, 129

La Valentina 129
Valentino, Rudolph 21, 116, 148–149
Vargas de la Maza, Armando 54
Vázquez Bernal, Esperanza 116, 124
Vega, Eduardo de la 49, 90
Véjar, Carlos 128
Vélez, Lupe 88
Vélez, Reina 81
Venegas, Emma 46
La venganza del indio 84
The Verdict of the Desert 41, 44, 47
Viajes de Bernal a México 90
Villa, Francisco 56, 129–130
Villaseñor, Alfonso 60
Villatoro, Carlos 113, 117, 120, 123–124, 128
La virgen de la sierra 119, 123–124, 126–129
La Virgen del Tepeyac 71

The Virginian (1914) 21
Vitagraph Company 4, 21–24, 26, 32, 39, 89, 148
Vitagraph Studios 28
El vuelo de la muerte 106, 108

Warner, J.B. 43
Warner Bros. 4
Wayne, John 136
Webb, Robert D. 136
White, Justina 153
Wilson, Bert 41
Winters, Shelley 136
World War I 21
World War II 148

Xydias, Anthony J. 43–44

El Yaqui 52
The Yaqui Cur 52
The Yaqui Girl 52
The Yaqui Indian 54
Yaqui Indians 8, 14, 92, 135
Yo, el aventurero 143
Young Deer, James 52

Zambrano, Adela 39, 41, 44
Zapotec language 110
El Zarco 34